THE RELATIONSHIP FIELD SERIES • PART I

PARTNERS
in PASSION

Positively transform your intimate relationships
by understanding the mystery of energy exchange

David Price Francis

Partners in Passion
Copyright © 2010 David Price Francis

The information contained in this book is intended for educational purposes only. The author is not rendering professional advice or services to the individual reader.

ISBN: 978-0-9815509-0-9

To order additional copies, please visit:
www.dpfrancis.com
or
www.EnergyWorlds.com

Printed in the United States of America

KORA
PRESS

Dedication

This book is dedicated to those who seek to understand,
transform and bring energetic evolution to all their relationships.

Acknowledgements

I want to thank the many people who have helped in the production of this work, beginning with Liz Wild who has patiently and persistently seen through every draft from the time of its inception and has helped me in so many lectures and workshops. Thank you to Alison Goudreault for the cover artwork, design assistance and creative input and to Ursula Flurer for her unwavering belief in this project. Thanks also to Karina Edwards for the interior diagrams, Peter Šobr-Sosnowski for his assistance in layout and design and Tania Šobr-Sosnowski for her contribution. I also wish to thank Suzanne Cook and Tammy Michalek for their valuable input and help.

I also wish to make a special mark of thanks to Joanna Infeld, my partner for over thirty years, for her creative and practical contributions in so many ways. I look forward to working with you on the next two volumes of *The Relationship Field* series.

Contents

Introduction
The Relationship Field

All our personal relationships begin in the worlds of energy. As human beings we are spirit and soul entities living inside a mortal, physical body and are not, as science sometimes informs us, bio-chemical beings with consciousness as a by-product. As energy beings we have ultimate control over what we generate within and radiate out from our personal energy field. This in turn determines what signals we attract and repel from the energy fields of others.

A relationship field is formed when we bring our personal energy field, also known as "the aura" and "our personal space" into contact and communication with the energy field of another person. The moment two energy fields meet, a third field starts to form which is neither wholly of one person or the other but is a unique combination and transmutation of the two. This third field is the true seat of love, attraction, passion and repulsion. It is not that we come to love or hate another person, but that we love, hate or are possibly indifferent to the third field which forms between us. This third field is unique and will never exist in exactly this configuration between any two other people on Earth. The power it contains determines the quality, charisma and longevity of a relationship.

Just as there has never been another human being exactly the same as you, with your unique fingerprints, genetic structure, soul and spiritual qualities and the unique expression that comes from your eyes, so there has never been another energy field exactly like yours, or like that which is caused between you and the unique energy field of another person. These mutual relationship fields contain the entire range of the qualities of human emotional and energetic expression. They can be strong or weak, heating or cooling, they can bring us peace and also cause us great aggravation and pain.

Some relationship fields can be mild, while others have such power and intensity they make us "go weak at the knees" and "knock us off our feet." We all know those moments when our eyes meet those of a stranger only to find that by some kind of energetic alchemy, some unseen magic, power leaps across the space between us and a highly charged and very potent third field quickly starts to manifest. How we cultivate this third field, the powers and forces that cause it to form and the energetic laws that govern it, are the subject matter of this book. Once you begin to view your relationships and interactions from the perspective of "field first," your life will be enhanced immeasurably and you will enter new realms of possibility. As Marcel Proust once said, in order to see a new world you either have to change the world or change the way you perceive it.

The understandings and perceptions contained in *Partners in Passion* will change the world as you know it by offering you new ways to perceive your relationships and interactions, from the most mundane to the most sacred. It includes vital and practical understandings about the different natures of energetic force that live in men and women and how to understand and enhance the flow of energies between the genders.

The Balance of Power

Energies are the driving powers behind all human behavior and endeavors. It is the properties, qualities and natures of different energies that have inspired the human spirit, soul and mind throughout history. Energies have driven us to build empires; they have divinely inspired us and sometimes they have driven us insane. There has been no greater power and influence in the energetic worlds than the relationships between men and women. When a balance of energies can be attained in the relationships between women and men, the passion between them is magnified enormously. In *Partners in Passion* we look at exactly why this is the case, how it works and how we can achieve this multiplication of passion in our own lives and in our mutual relationships.

Partners in Passion is an energetic guide to all man/woman relationships and how to enhance them. It introduces the idea of energy dating and explores practical techniques to enhance your energy dating experiences, whether in a new relationship or with a partner of many years. It also offers help in understanding the nature of energies at play in other types of relationships, such as the mutual relationship fields between same-sex couples and offers explanations and practical techniques to help in the formation of constructive relationship fields in all aspects of human life and endeavor.

Conscious enhancement of the energies at play in our personal and global relationships is absolutely possible and certainly can be achieved. It starts by understanding that the underlying dynamics which give birth to the material worlds are the energy worlds of unseen forces and powers. Therefore, any movement for real change must originate from these worlds. Everything on Earth begins in the realms of energy and then condenses into matter. Think about where you were a hundred years ago and where your consciousness will be in a hundred years' time. All human beings clearly condensed here from the realms of spirit, soul and energy. It is into these realms we will return.

Just as our spirit, soul and consciousness come from the realms of energy, so too does our gender. The two great masculine and feminine powers of Creation are designed to work together in equality, harmony and partnership. Though men and women are clearly different by design, we are complementary to each other and together are able to achieve energetic processes and results that are impossible for each gender to achieve alone.

Through the trace of thousands of years, the masculine energy has taken dominance and subdued the feminine. We are all suffering from the results of this subjection—men and women alike.

In *Partners in Passion* we explore how this energy imbalance can be remedied and how the differences that can keep men and women apart also offer the very strengths we need to move forward together.

Call to Action

The swiftest way to bring about world change in our lifetime is to rectify the imbalance in the power of our gender relationships. Victor Hugo once said that there is nothing more powerful than an idea whose time has come. In our time women's empowerment is more than an idea; it is a force of nature whose time has come.

For years now we have seen the cracks beginning to appear in the iron dam that men have erected to keep this wave of power under control. The dam is now breaking and the masculine construction and constriction of our worldly ways and institutions is about to change forever. There is no greater issue that we face together than how to balance the power and multiply the passion between men and women, who are like the left and right hands of Creation here on Earth. We live in a time in which the chronic imbalance between the freedom and expression of these twin powers is adversely affecting all life.

Through the last ten thousand years the masculine power has run amok and has taken over the institutions, religions and societies of the world. All around us we see the results of this process, from the endless wars between nations to the devastation of the planet's natural resources and the destruction of her eco-systems. Almost anywhere we look we can see the detrimental and corrosive effects of the masculine domination of life on Earth.

Partners in Passion addresses fundamental inter-gender issues and explains why these are the most crucial matters to take up in our time. It follows these issues through the fields of personal and global relationships, revealing how simple, practical changes can reap huge rewards both personally and globally.

When we make these vital changes in our lives we cause a surge of energetic enhancement throughout all our relationships. These changes are guaranteed to be effective because they work in accordance with the underlying energy exchange processes of Creation. The first important step we can take is by increasing our understanding of these processes, what causes them and how they work. It is here we shall begin our journey as we explore together what it truly means to be partners in passion.

Chapter One
Men, Women and Passion

Unexpectedly, a man and woman meet. Looks are exchanged. Energies leap across the space between them. Both feel it. The level of its power stops them in their tracks. Their breathing deepens as a flood of energy surges through them. They go weak in the knees. The loop of power between them increases in strength. A gasp escapes their lips. Right then and there in the now of the moment the rest of the world fades away. Their world has irrevocably changed. Their destinies are now linked. A stream of energy so strong it is almost tangible flows between them. The thunderbolt has struck and they will never be the same again...

In large measure or small, once or many times, we all share this experience of Cupid's energetic arrows; the unexpected transmission and reception of a stream of energy so powerful we cannot mistake or deny it. This intangible energy, moving at the speed of light, can flash across a room to find one mark out of a thousand people. It can leap from one life to another while on a plane, a crowded street, or across the room at a party. We never know when and where it is going to strike next. It is as if we have a weather system in our energy field that surrounds and travels with us. Somehow, in that place and time, the meeting of our weather system with another's causes streaks of passionate lightning to flash across the intervening space, joining us energetically and creating a highly charged relationship field between us. It is a moment that reaches inside and simultaneously touches both our souls.

Whenever women and men share the same space and time, this energy is at play in some fashion. It offers a sense of sharing, encouragement and inter-gender support in the high quality realms of fresh, clear energy and helps things to move along with a zing, zip and sparkle. When the thunderbolt of passionate energy appears in our lives, we may or may not follow through and approach the other person. We may never learn their name or hear them speak but we both know that something has been exchanged in the realms of energy and power, causing a shared moment and experience.

Whether or not we choose to act on this exchange depends upon many things, ranging from our upbringing, our ability to be spontaneous, how inhibited we are, or if we are already engaged in a committed relationship. Some will act and discover where the thunderbolt leads them, while others will dream about it for a few days. Some may wonder "What if?" on an occasional basis for the rest of their life.

Interaction Guaranteed

This story of the thunderbolt represents a great energetic truth. The great masculine power, to which half the world's population is attached, is strongly attracted to the great feminine power, to which the other half of the world's population is attached. These two great universal powers continuously pulse throughout our planet in such a way as to guarantee interaction between men and women every moment of every day. Cupid's energetic arrows are flying ceaselessly all around the world, connecting the great masculine power of the universe to the great feminine power of the universe through the medium of its twin human agencies here on Earth: women and men.

The scale of this energy exchange is staggering. Through the dynamics of man/woman interaction and procreation, approximately four new lives enter this world every second. In any twenty-four hour period over three hundred and forty-thousand new babies are born. This means the equivalent of the entire population of Manhattan appears, newborn on the planet, approximately every four days. This demonstrates just how powerful the attraction between these two great energies must be to result in such a magnitude of physical interaction here on Earth.

Complementary Creations, Different by Design

Women and men are complementary creations designed to process different flavors of universal power and soul energy, which interact powerfully and continually with each other and are built into our differing design features from the time of our formation in the womb.

The prime force for the procreation and continuance of human life on Earth is the energy exchange between these twin powers. Our gender is decided at the time of our conception according to the DNA blueprint that formed in our beginning. We are ordained at conception to appear in a physical body with either a masculine or feminine inclination, expressed in modern genetics by the terms XX (feminine) or XY (masculine).

The ancient mystery schools of Egypt and Babylon used different symbols to express the same universal truth. They referred to these two powers as the masculine power of the rod, which they linked to the numerical symbol 1, and the feminine power of the cup, which they linked to the numerical symbol 2. They recorded some of their knowledge and understandings about these masculine and feminine powers in a system of knowledge that we know today as the tarot. Card 1, the Juggler or Magician, depicts aspects of the masculine power while card 2, the Priestess, expresses features of the feminine power. The original tarot cards were not designed for divination or fortune-telling but were a system of knowledge and understanding that could be used to open up any question on Earth, as well as being used for helping and counseling others. There is much to be understood about the natures of masculine and feminine from this system of knowledge and understanding that has been passed on to us from ancient times.

If, as some organized religions suggest, the exchange of energies between men and women is the root of original sin, then whoever and whatever designed the system would have to be the biggest sinner of them all. The power of this mutual exchange is built into us at such a depth that it is perpetual and inescapable. Far from being in any way sinful, the exchange of energies between women and men was designed from the beginning to help us know the joy of sharing and joining in processes and forces bigger than ourselves. It is a vital part of our living experience on Earth. Whatever causes us to appear on this blue planet far on the eastern edge of the Milky Way, also determines that we appear here representing two different and yet complementary powers, born into two different design structures, both of which are embodiments of the human being.

Women and men, seen from this perspective, are terminals for two complementary kinds of power, energy and force. We occupy twin polarities and, as the anode and the cathode of the human race, there is a guaranteed process of interaction between us. We are like the left and right hands of the human tribe, designed to be twin expressions of the human appearance here on Earth. If the energies of one expression spin clockwise, the energies of the other spin counter-clockwise and the two are designed to work together in a dance of mutual respect and equality of opportunity. We contain complementary powers that are naturally equal but natured differently. The power that passes through one terminal is in no way superior to that which passes through the other.

The concept that men are from Mars and women are from Venus, which John Gray popularized in his books on relationships, is rooted in ancient understandings that men and women are twin expressions of perpetually regenerating human soul power. Ancient sages also understood that males and females are connected to energies that are complementary but not the same. They understood that the masculine energy field tends to be more red inclined in its energetic nature and runs hotter, while the feminine energy field tends to be more blue inclined in its energetic nature and runs cooler. "Sugar and spice and all things nice, that's what little girls are made of," the nursery rhyme tells us and, by contrast, "Frogs and snails and puppy dogs tails, that's what little boys are made of." According to ancient astrology, frogs and snails are both divinated to the hotter, red, arterial nature of Mars, together with vinegar and other sour things, while sugar and spice are connected to the venal, cool, blue sweetness of Venus. It is worth remembering that the so-called Ancients spent thousands of years exploring not only the physical but the energetic properties of the planet and universe in which they lived and we would be wise not to disregard the knowledge they passed on to us too glibly.

Ancient Secrets

The great masculine and feminine powers to which we are all connected organize and express themselves differently. This is what the Ancients meant by astrologically representing these forces as the god Mars and the goddess Venus respectively, symbolized by a rod of iron and a chalice of copper. They knew that both men and women are powered by human soul energy but the energy is flavored and aligned in a different way. This suggests that men will get one part of the picture and women will get another part. Together, if they learn to listen to each other and appreciate the other person's view, they have a chance of appreciating the whole.

There are many energy secrets encoded within the alphabets of the world, including English. The letters "M" and "W" demonstrate a core feature of how and why passion passes between men and women.

In certain esoteric understandings of the alphabet "M" stands for the energy of the man and "W" stands for the energy of the woman. They are the same symbol but a mirror image of each other. This illustrates that both men and women contain complementary powers within design features which can cause them to think they are the opposite of each other, when they are in actuality two halves of one design. The "M" and "W" symbols when joined together become two complete diamond formations. The inter-relation of these two symbols demonstrates how these two energies can complete each other.

Wherever There's a Yin, There's a Yang

The ancient mystery schools of Egypt and Babylon and the sages of ancient China studied in depth the workings of the energies that power human beings, including the exchange of forces between men and women. An emblem for this exchange of energies that has been passed on to us today is now known as the yin/yang symbol. This symbol contains the mystery of why and how passionate interaction is guaranteed between men and women at its most fundamental levels. It also demonstrates how this primary energy exchange is built into our very design. It shows how, even if we decide to go to the most hidden monasteries or nunneries in the world, this energy exchange will continue whether we wish it or not, even if it occurs over long distances. It also demonstrates that whatever one's sexual orientation, the fundamental laws of this great energy exchange still apply.

The yin/yang symbol demonstrates that man is not made entirely of masculine power and that woman is not made exclusively of feminine power. In reality, man and woman contain and are connected to both energies, but the proportions are different. It is this deliberate design feature in the energy worlds that guarantees there will always be perpetual interaction between the two genders and the ongoing creation of mutual relationship fields. Creation designed it to be so and planted the powers that cause the great laws of attraction and passion within us. There is no escaping these dynamics and the laws that govern them, even if we want to.

In this diagram, the masculine energy or "yang," often represented by the colors black or red, is represented by the shaded areas. Set within the yang energy symbol is a smaller circle of feminine or yin energy, often expressed by the colors white or blue. The yang energy wants to "get its own back," as part of its core is trapped within the yin or feminine power. Likewise, the feminine yin energy, represented by the unshaded areas of the diagram, wants to win back that part of its core that is trapped within the masculine yang. Thus, the two powers perpetually chase their missing part, seeking to complete themselves.

If we were able to see the yin/yang symbol in action, it would not be stationary but would be spinning at great speed, as both the yin and the yang chase that part of themselves that is held within the other. If this yin/yang symbol could be represented by a moving hologram rather than a two dimensional flat image, we could appreciate more easily that it represents a core expression of how all life on Earth, including man and woman, is energized and generates energy by its interactions.

The spinning yin/yang symbol would generate a force field of considerable power. It is the fact of this force field, present to a greater or lesser extent in all man-woman interaction, that is fundamental to the mutual relationship fields formed between men and women. This prime force field is weaker or stronger according to the genetic make-up, hereditary and astrological influences of the individuals involved and this in turn causes a strong or weak attraction between them. This is what I term "passion automatic" while "passion voluntary" is determined by factors more within our personal control such as our attitude and address to life, our career, religious beliefs, hobbies and the like.

The yin/yang symbol represents the generating power of the human and planetary soul that is made up of these twin energies perpetually working together in combination. The symbol represents a natural equality, as it takes both energies working together to keep it spinning, generation after generation. Things that spin draw in power and energy as well as creating a force field around them and, as the yin/yang symbol spins, it draws new power and energy into the human race, by which we are able to live, develop and progress. Each new generation is different from the one before, both in its energies and in the physical expression of these energies.

What This Means for You

If you are born into the body and soul of a woman for this incarnation, you contain two parts feminine energy and hold the higher part of the masculine energy within you. If you are born into the body and soul of a man for this incarnation, you contain two parts masculine energy and hold the higher part of the feminine energy within you. We each contain both powers. Our gender is an expression of the power that is within us by majority but we also contain a smaller, higher part of the opposite gender. This is the deeper meaning of the yin/yang symbol when applied to human life.

The yin/yang symbol also demonstrates the energy dynamics of attraction in same-sex relationships. In a homosexual relationship the man seeks his missing core energy not within the concentrated power held by the woman, but within the masculine energy of another man. The same is true for the woman in a lesbian relationship. Rather than seeking the concentrated feminine power held within the core of the man, she finds it in the feminine power of another woman. The system of energy exchange is designed to work primarily through the exchange of powers and forces between men and women, which allows for maximum energy exchange, procreation and the reproduction of the species, but other variations are clearly permissible and possible.

The yin/yang symbol expresses fundamental laws of how energy and matter work together and represents a natural energy engine that is in perpetual motion. You and I are part of that energy generator and every day there are new energies generated within us and in co-relationship with others. Whether we like it or not, we are part of the bigger picture of energy exchange that is taking place within the human race as a whole. There is no way to escape it. What we can do is try our best to understand it so we may bring ourselves into better harmony with how these complementary energies are designed to work together.

Our personal experience of the energy exchange between men and women, including our first love, lost love and last love, are all contained within the energy dynamics represented by the yin/yang symbol. Without the existence of the great masculine and feminine powers and the guaranteed interaction they are designed to cause, none of our personal experiences of this great exchange of energies would be possible.

The yin/yang symbol represents not only the interplay between the souls of men and women but also the interplay between the great masculine and feminine powers, wherever they appear in the universe. The cover of this book shows the yin/yang symbol in blue and yellow, which represents the interplay between the blue of the planet and the yellow of the sun. These two colors also represent a higher expression of the relationship field between men and women, a theme which is developed throughout the three volumes of *The Relationship Field* series.

Energy Dating

When a man invites a woman out on a date, he is inviting out the higher masculine energy that she contains within herself. He wishes to complete and energize himself through her. If she accepts his invitation or invites him out, she is seeking to bring to herself the higher feminine energy that he contains within his masculine wrapper.

When the mystery of exchange works well, both become more complete and energized by the experience and at higher levels can even know the satisfaction of energetic completion for a moment. This most often comes through the medium of sexual exchange but it can happen simply by them both being in the relationship field caused between them. It explains why lovers often seek to stay together so they can prolong this sensation of greater energy connection and completion. It also explains why, when people find what they feel is their energy match or soul mate, they wish to settle down, stay together and develop the power and quality of their mutual relationship field over time. They feel that their energy levels are at optimum when they are together and decide to embark upon the next part of their life's journey as energy partners. This feeling is often connected also with the idea that this is the man or woman with whom they choose to raise a family, meaning that the energetic and material ecology of the relationship field the two people can create between them will be good for raising children, while they pursue their life's purpose within it.

The Nature of Passion

As passion plays such a vital part in all that follows, it is worthwhile to pause a moment to clarify exactly what I mean by the word passion. A closer examination of this word gives us a profound indication of what passion actually is. The word "passion" says to "pass-ion." It is to have something pass through us of an energetic or ionic nature. An "ion" is defined in *Webster's Collegiate Dictionary* as "an atom or group of atoms that carries a positive or negative electric charge." Therefore, to have a passion for someone is to transmit a stream of ions towards them that they may feel and reciprocate, or not.

The passions that we feel can be of many different natures but they are all based in the energy worlds of power and force. A passion of any kind is always an energetic process and begins first in these realms. We humans are energetic beings that generate and produce negatively and positively charged particles or ions, just as Webster's dictionary suggests. These particles, aggregating together, form waves of energy. These energy transmissions can be of such power that they can travel over distance and pass from our energy field into the energy field of others and vice-versa, creating mutual relationship fields. The nature of the relationship field that forms between people entirely depends upon the qualities, power and level of the ions that pass between them over the course of time.

Passions can be high or low, refined or coarse. They can be pleasant to receive and give us enjoyable energy sensations throughout our being or can be very unpleasant to receive. They can produce waves of such intensity that they can almost "knock you over." Passions even have colors that become visible when one has the eyes to see them and they range through the full spectrum of red to violet. Expressions such as "red with rage," "green with envy" and "having a yellow streak" suggest the colors of different kinds of passion that appear in a person's energy field.

There are many kinds of passion: dark passion, illumined passion, the passion of joy, the passion of grief. In Christianity there is what is described as The Passion, a process of such energetic power and of such an extraordinary nature that to a Christian it stands above all others.

The passions we transmit and receive are as real as the material world that is also made of charged particles, although moving much more slowly. Although the energy waves that make up our passions are intangible their results are long-lasting, as every passion that passes through us is printed in the record of our energy field, also known as the human aura, and in the greater energy field of the planet's aura, also known as the astral light, the astral field and the astral plane. Rather than using these more ancient terms I use the contemporary terms "human energy field" and "planetary energy field" and refer to the different contents and levels to be found therein under the term "energy worlds."

Human history is, indeed, a story of the powers and forces, hopes and desires living in the energy worlds of the human and the planet shaping the material world, rather than the other way around.

Love Is the Third Field

The most powerful of all passions in human relationships is the power of love. The power of love in man/woman relationships is neither a property of the man nor the woman. It is a third power created between them in their mutual energy exchange and transference. If both man and woman have personal and individual energy fields, which they certainly do, then the power of love resides in this third mutually created field. It is this third field, which I refer to as "the relationship field," that contains all the processes ever to take place between any two partners in passion. Thus the power of love can aggregate between any two people through the passage of time, as can any other property that exists in the energy worlds of the human, such as hope, fear, depression and inspiration.

In this sense a man does not love a woman or a woman love a man. They both love those special energies that are created in their mutual field when they are together. This is why they can pine and long for each other in all the ways that the great love poets of the world have given expression to. The passion they feel can be of such intensity that all else in life pales by comparison. The lovers want only to be together inside the special magic created when they are with each other and their energy fields meet and merge.

Once two such people decide to commit to each other for the long term, however, then the work really begins. The honeymoon of mutual attraction and passion lasts only so long, unless a mutual decision is made to move with it in a purposeful direction.

There are definite, practical ways to build the power and sustain the passion in every relationship field. These practical techniques work at many levels, from the physical to the emotional, the sexual to the mental. The next step in this journey of understanding the nature of passion and how to build the relationship fields we want is to look deeper into the exchange of energies between women and men and how we are fundamentally "wired for passion."

Chapter Two
Wired for Passion

The powerful relationship field between men and women is made possible due to the difference in our energetic and physical design. In ancient times this difference was symbolized by the key symbols of the rod and the cup—also known as the wand and the cleft.

Rods and Cups

The rod, obelisk, straight line and number 1 are ancient symbols of masculine power. The cup, chalice, circle and number 2 represent feminine power in many ancient systems of knowledge. Examples of such symbols can be found in the crook and flail carried by the Egyptian pharaohs and the scepter and globe held by the royalty of Britain. In architecture the spires of Christian churches symbolize the masculine power as Christians reach for "Our Father, who art in heaven," while the circular stone and wooden henges and labyrinths of early Europe represent the symbology of those seeking to connect to the healing power and well-being of our Great Mother, planet Earth.

Each of us is born with the physical emblem of the rod or the cup, which is connected to the great yang or yin power that flows through us. Where the yang and the yin are present, the potential for the power, glory and passion of energy exchange is also. The passion we feel for the energies and presence of the other gender manifests in many different ways, such as gift-giving, producing poetry and song, dressing up for a date, sexual consummation, committed relationships and marriage.

As symbols, the rod and cup are found throughout the ancient learning system of the tarot including the symbols of wands and cups in the fifty-six cards of the minor arcanum. They can also be found in religious buildings in the shapes of the masculine spire and the feminine dome. The rod symbolizes transmission and is often used to represent solar energies, while the cup symbolizes reception and is associated with planetary energies. In addition to being associated with the powers of Mars and Venus, in ancient days the masculine power was associated with the sun and the feminine power with the planet, moon and Milky Way.

The cup and rod are the two fundamental shapes in nature that symbolize the two great powers represented in the yin/yang system, necessary for the production of new energy and new life. When the two powers meet and energy is exchanged, a new third power is caused to exist. We often call this power "love" and this is why we often refer to the sexual act as "making love."

Love is not only made when rod physically meets cup but when the energy field of the woman interacts with the energy field of the man. When the two differently charged energy fields meet, there is a natural exchange of energy that has a greater or lesser degree of passion and power according to the strength and nature of the charges in the energy fields of the two individuals and their mutual compatibility. This power of energetic love can manifest at many levels within the mutual relationship field. We will take a much closer look at these levels of potential energetic love in Chapter 9, The Seven Levels of Love and Sex.

Clues in Spells and Spelling

Within their construction, the written languages of the world contain clues to the workings of energies. One of the ways to reveal these clues is through the art of anagramming, which is done by shapeshifting one word or phrase into another to find new insights and unsuspected meanings. It is quite magical how in English and many other languages, this shapeshifting can reveal a great deal about the content and nature of the word we are seeking to understand.

Having studied the energy patterns of language for many years, I believe this is no accident but is caused by a co-incidence of specific energy patterns. It is not a random effect at all. Language is one of the most crucial media for the transmission, reception and exchange of energies and each specific letter in every language in the world contains its own energetic character. The letters in any word spell out a particular energetic power combination and no other, thus the almost magical connection between how we spell something and the power of casting a spell.

When shapeshifting the word production we discover it contains both the words "rod" and "cup" and spells out the phrase "rod into cup." This shapeshifting of the word production tells us that when the power symbolized by the rod meets the power symbolized by the cup, a third power is always produced. The nature of the passion produced can be high or low, refined or coarse, but a passion of some kind is always produced and present.

The Power of Puberty

Children are born with the emblem of the cup or the rod. In girls and boys the physical equipment is present, but the power to use it for the purpose of energy exchange is latent.

We have all experienced the power of puberty and know that it comes unbidden, in its own time. We do not wake up one morning and decide "Today is a good day for puberty." Like many of the great events of our life, it happens upon us and is outside our control. The great masculine and feminine forces are bigger than we are and cannot be dictated to.

As with all our experiences, puberty begins in the worlds of energy. It represents one of the most profound energy shifts of our life. Puberty commences with the onset of the great masculine and feminine powers which start to flood through the body, soul and mind of a growing youth. This is followed by changes in chemistry and biology that manifest physically. The onset of puberty brings with it new perceptions of the world and often commences with dreams in which the opposite sex take on new and powerful roles. This is the brain and mental faculties starting to work with these new energies during the hours of sleep. The unconscious and semiconscious levels of our mind and being are preparing for the change before the conscious mind even realizes it is coming. It is the time for moving on from the energies of childhood into the energies of becoming a young woman or man. The boy becomes powerfully connected to the red/yang energy of the male and the girl becomes connected to the blue/yin energy of the female.

Often this rite of passage is confirmed by a special ceremony in which the young person is recognized as having graduated from childhood into adulthood. A ceremony in which other graduates offer confirmation and advice is a most natural response.

It takes time for the electrical circuitry in our bodies to build the capacity to handle the high amperage power that comes with full connection to the masculine and feminine forces. This is why the full connection is not there right from the start—it would be more than a youthful system could handle. When the boy becomes a man and the girl becomes a woman, a new level of power and passion is able to happen and the nature of the possible relationship field between them changes dramatically.

The sheer power of these new currents that are released through the emotions and race through the nerves cause enormous changes in a very short period of time. The so-called opposite sex starts to become a major point of focus. Suddenly we move from being children into becoming young men and women. Part of this change manifests physically, but the greater change happens energetically.

The Great Energy Exchange

As men and women we are wired for passion and energy exchange. The great masculine and feminine energies cause not only physical differences between us, but differences in how energy flows through our human systems. These energy differences are wired into our human energy blueprint from the time of our formation in the womb.

Women and men are designed to receive, transmit and process forces differently in both our body and soul. Regarding the power that flows through our hands, for example, men transmit soul energy primarily through the right hand and receive this energy primarily through the left. Conversely, women transmit soul energy primarily through the left hand and receive soul energy primarily through the right. This does not mean that one hand is entirely transmissive and the other entirely receptive. As with the yin and yang powers in men and women, the hands are transmissive and receptive by preponderance. The two hands contain both energies, but in different proportions.

One way you can check this for yourself is through the simple practice of energy dowsing. If you hold a pendulum over your right hand, it will usually circle in the opposite direction than when you hold it over your left hand. This is part of the energetic wiring of the yin/yang symbol within us. Our hands contain two different polarities of soul power.

As we investigate further, we find that the polarity of our soul energy reverses at several points as the energy moves through our body.

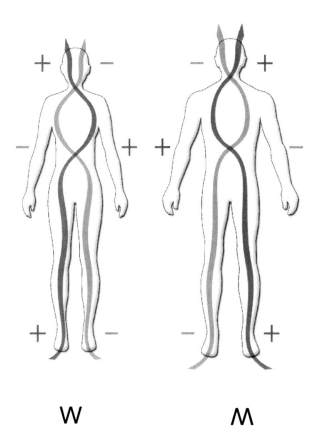

W   M

The energy crisscrosses at the solar plexus and again at the neck. In part, this means that men tend to work more with the left brain and transmit energy through the left eye. Conversely, women tend to work more with the right brain and transmit energy through the right eye. This helps to explain why women tend to be more intuitive and men tend to be more analytic.

As men tend to be more energetically based in the left hemisphere of their brain and women tend to be more energetically based in their right, this explains why they can have such very different perceptions about the same thing. Neither is right or wrong; they both see part of the picture. When these two different perceptions are brought together they offer a more profound and textured understanding of any given subject.

When a man and woman stand opposite each other, face to face, they are able to transmit and receive a full circuit of mutual energy. This position maximizes the power passing between them. Standing next to each other produces a different effect in the energy fields, depending on which side of each other they stand. When their hands are positive to positive, which means that the man is on the woman's left side, the transference of energies between a couple is amplified, but when they stand negative hand to negative hand, the flow of energy is diminished. Just knowing and applying this simple fact of energy exchange makes a difference in the power present in their mutual energy field at any time and is of significant help when energy dating.

The same is also true when a man and woman sleep together. Even as they sleep, the energy exchange continues and whichever side of their partner they sleep on makes a difference. When a couple tosses and turns during the night this is not only caused by the body seeking its best physical comfort but by the soul drawing more or less energy from the partner's energy field.

By understanding the energy wiring diagram of the man and woman we can work more consciously and effectively to boost the exchange of soul power that passes between us.

Venus and Mars

The symbols for Venus and Mars, passed on to us from ancient times, are a representation of the two natures of masculine and feminine energy.

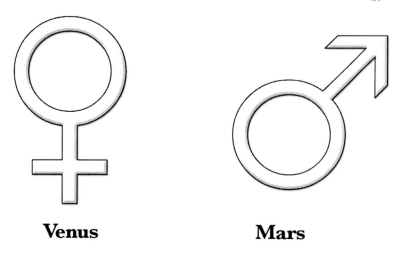

Venus   **Mars**

The symbol for Venus represents both an ability to receive, as indicated by the circle, and being well-grounded and connected to planetary energy, as indicated by the symbol of the cross, itself an ancient symbol for the feminine energy of Mother Earth.

The symbol for Mars demonstrates how masculine energy is always ready to charge off in a new direction and is far less balanced. Masculine power, as represented here, has a sense of being incomplete and having something missing. It, therefore, seeks completion outside of itself. The feminine principle, as shown in the Venus symbol, is more complete unto itself. It was because of this ancient understanding of the masculine and feminine natures that the poet Robert Graves entitled a volume of his poetry *Man Does, Woman Is*. This reflects how the masculine energy tends to look to complete itself by doing and, therefore, a man's focus is often more outside of himself. By energetic design, a woman is often more able to be present in the moment and appreciate life more as it is happening. It is not by chance that when we shapeshift the word "woman" we find the words "am now."

Men who become contemplatives, such as Saint Francis of Assisi, often focus upon the yin within to find their way and cultivate their feminine, creative power. Women who become world leaders in a masculine-dominated world often do so by cultivating their inner, masculine power. In this context, Margaret Thatcher, the prime minister of Britain from 1979 - 90 became known as the "Iron Lady." Iron, in astrology, is the metal divinated to Mars and indicates a masculine force. In contrast, the police are commonly known as "cops" or in Britain as "coppers" which is the metal divinated to Venus, and are referred to as "the thin blue line" that keep society from descending into violence and disorder. Indeed, the United Nations peacekeepers can be identified, in part, by the distinctive blue helmets or berets they wear. This association with blue is because at a deep, instinctive level we know that blue is a cooling color, while red brings heat into a situation. We even see this reflected in our daily life in the colors indicating hot and cold on kitchen and bathroom taps.

In the realms of the rod and the cup, man seeks to find relief from the red force that drives him forward every day. Woman is able to take this energy into herself and cool it which is why, in the energy worlds, the sexual act tends to cool the man and warm the woman. The woman passes her energy to the man and she naturally seeks to transmit her power to a man who will work with it constructively and bring good results on her behalf.

In the days of courtly chivalry, the lady would give her knight a token that he would wear as he went on his quest, symbolizing that he was her representative and she supplied him the power with which to act. Venus and Mars, the powers of feminine blue and masculine red, represented in the bio-chemical worlds by the steroid hormones testosterone and estrogen, are most effective when they are working together in a mutually agreed direction and in a mutually empowering relationship field.

Male and Female Numbers

Although the Ancients ascribed the rod-like nature of the number 1 to the masculine energy which is always seeking to initiate and to transmit, and the cup-like nature of the number 2 to the feminine power which is better able to receive, contemplate and give birth, this does not mean that a woman cannot initiate or a man cannot receive. Both genders are capable of working with both energies, but the Ancients understood that there are certain natures built into the energies themselves. They symbolized these characteristics by the prime numbers and natures of odd and even: the symbols 1 and 2.

The system of nine numbers that we inherit, like the alphabets of the world, contains many inner mysteries. There are secrets that exist within the mental tools we rely upon and use the most every day of our lives, being letters and numbers. The odd numbers 1,3,5,7,9, for example, were known to the school of Pythagorus as being symbols of a masculine inclination, while the even numbers 2,4,6,8 represented symbols of a feminine inclination. Surviving into our language today is the idea that the nature of something "odd" is that it stands out while to "even" something out is to bring it to smoothness. Again we see the juxtaposition of the natures of these two prime forces and how any real system depends upon both of them working together at full and in harmony for maximum effectiveness.

The Ancients also gave us further clues to the masculine nature of the number 1 and the feminine nature of the number 2 in the first two cards of the tarot. As mentioned earlier, card 1 of the tarot is called the Magician or the Juggler and represents the masculine principle, while card 2 is the Priestess and represents the feminine principle. The rest of the tarot is born from these first two principals, just as all other numbers are born out of the combinations of the original odd and even numbers, 1 and 2.

When the power represented by the number 1 meets the power represented by the number 2, a third power is immediately produced. This third power is more than the power of 1 being added to the power of 2. It represents a unique new property that has never been created before. In our human affairs, after the rod and cup have come together and there has been transference of energies between them, the new life of a child that is produced is utterly unique and new. It is more than the properties of the mother being added to those of the father. The mother and father provide the gateway through which a new spiritual possibility is born that has traits of them both, but is a unique individual unto itself.

When two energy fields come together in the process of energy dating, the energy field of the man (1) meets the energy field of the woman (2) and a unique new relationship field is born (3). The level and quality of energetic love that is produced by the interaction of these two energy fields causes the two people to be more or less attracted to each other. This is why the number 3 is the first number that expresses the power of mutual love and opens the possibility of a mutually fulfilling journey.

Short and Long Term Cycles

The energy system of the woman is designed to work over longer periods of time and has a longer cycle and rhythm than that of the man. Again, this fits with the difference in nature between red and blue because the red/yang principle works on a hotter, short term frequency, while the frequency of the blue/yin principle works on a cooler, long term frequency.

Whereas the man, like the Juggler, needs to remake and juggle his energies afresh every day, the woman, like the Priestess, naturally works on a longer time and energy cycle. In the material worlds this is confirmed by the natures of the sperm and the egg. The man produces millions of fresh sperm on a daily basis that have a shelf life of only three days. If they are not used promptly they are disposed of. The eggs of the woman, by contrast, are produced while she is forming in the womb and last for the duration of her life. They are usually released at the rate of one per lunar month over approximately four-hundred lunar cycles or thirty-six years. Whereas the sperm of the man are made new every day, the eggs of the woman can last for eighteen-thousand days! This difference in the physical design of men and women also reflects real differences in the energy worlds.

Menstrual Energies

The ability in the woman to naturally engage with a longer energetic rhythm is demonstrated powerfully in her ability to bear children and in the menstrual cycle itself. The fundamental rhythm of the menstrual cycle is twenty-eight days. This twenty-eight day rhythm coincides with the twenty-eight day cycle of the moon and also an energetic cycle of the sun, in which the solar magnetic field reverses every twenty-eight days. The combined processes of these two twenty-eight day cycles produce fifty-six influences, the exact number of cards in the minor arcanum of the tarot, giving rise to our modern pack of playing cards which contains four suits of thirteen cards plus four jokers (which were knaves in the original tarot system), making fifty-six cards in all.

The woman's menstrual cycle is much more than a physical process. It is an energetic process that manifests physically. Whereas the man's energy processes work on a daily basis, the energy field of the woman is energetically open to exchange for approximately twenty-four days of her monthly cycle and changes into a more closed energy state for four days. Inbuilt into her design is a rhythm of six cycles active and one at rest, each cycle being four days in length.

This cycle of six cycles active and one at rest we find often recurs in natural law and lore. It appears in the measurement of the cycles of the tides about which it is said, "Every seventh wave is a big one." In South Africa there is a recorded practice among tuberculosis sufferers of going to the ocean at dawn and trying to leap into the seventh wave as this is believed to have healing properties according to local folklore. It also appears in the Hebrew creation story as told in the Book of Genesis, in which God labors for six days and rests on the seventh. The seven fold nature of the feminine cycle also indicates that this Creation story has, like most of the religious teachings in the world, been given a masculine bias. It is not the masculine aspect of God that labors for six days to give birth but the feminine aspect, which we know of as Creation, that must give birth. Upon study, the laws of the universe show us clearly that the supreme originating cause cannot be a solely masculine power but must contain both the masculine and feminine. The most active power in giving birth to the universe in the Creation story was not the masculine vector of God, but the feminine aspect and the description of six days active and one at rest is a clue left for those who have not yet succumbed to masculine-dominated prejudices and programming.

During the time of menstruation the energy field of the woman becomes more closed to new impressions because her system is cleaning and clearing out the residual energies of the previous six four-day cycles. While this process happens she becomes much less receptive to energy transference from others, including her chosen partner in passion.

The closing off to her partner in the energy worlds usually begins a day or two before the physical onset of menstruation. This is the energetic root of premenstrual syndrome (PMS). She often may become what appears to her partner as distant at this time and rejects his energetic advances. Because he does not understand what is happening, he often becomes more insistent, causing her to reject him more fiercely. Many quarrels between couples take place at this point in the energy cycle of the woman. The good use of a calendar and the plotting of when her period is likely to begin can save a couple from many fights and misunderstandings. This is so well known that I recently read of a subscription service on the Internet that provides its subscribers with a computer alert when PMS is due to begin.

It is most important to realize that the fact of menstruation is the physical confirmation of a process taking place in the energetic worlds first. Even the descriptive word "period" can help us understand what is happening energetically in the process of menstruation. Grammatically, a period marks a stop before the continuation of the next sentence. In a woman's energy flow, the time of menstruation marks a period of pause in the energy intake processes of her life during which certain processes are brought to a stop. It is an excellent time for contemplation of what has happened during the previous twenty-four days and preparing for the next twenty-four. There is far more to menstruation than a physical act or biological function. The physical is accompanied by a definite energetic charge and change.

It is because men and women work with complementary forces and, therefore, experience life differently that leads to the source of much interpersonal frictions between the genders. Once we understand we are fundamentally different and start to appreciate what these energy differences are, then we can work together to maximize our mutual strengths. This is a vital first step in balancing the power and multiplying the passion between us. We need to understand first that we are wired differently, not only physically, but first and foremost, energetically.

It does not work for the man to try and make the woman "more like me" as Professor Higgins in *My Fair Lady* exclaims. Within the differences in our design lie our greatest passion potentials and our greatest strengths. If, however, our differences are not understood, welcomed and encouraged, we can find ourselves energetically at odds, which leads to conflict and friction. We can see the results of exactly this imbalance all around us in the cultures of the world.

The Ability to Be Long

Part of the design of the energy exchange between men and women is that feminine energy cools men down and restrains their aggressive tendencies. This naturally regulating energy system is thrown out of balance if men subjugate women and prevent them from exerting their influence in the realms of, for example, political power.

The fact that feminine energy cycles naturally work on a longer term basis means that women should naturally be closely involved in the long range planning of all social, economic and political projects. Whereas the masculine energy tends to focus on getting a result today, the nature of the feminine energy is naturally more conservative. She is designed to have the ability to think not only for herself but also for the future of her children and even her children's children's children. Men naturally work for results in the short term with less consideration for tomorrow. Again, we can see how the detrimental results of masculine domination turn up in the short term thinking of many modern societies. It is future generations who will ultimately pay the price for our high level of wastage today. For the future of all it is crucial that the energies of masculine and feminine work together and create a balanced and harmonious relationship field between them not only at the personal level, but also on a global scale.

Passion Automatic

When man and woman meet, the feminine yin power in the woman seeks out and attracts the feminine power that the man contains. The masculine yang power in the man reaches for the masculine power that the woman contains. Both parties do this simultaneously. It has come to be referred to as "checking each other out." This is not a conscious action. It is attraction automatic. It is why you automatically look in the eyes of the opposite sex unless you are trained not to. Something passes in the energy worlds between you. It is also why possessive, fearful men have trained "their" women to look away and never have eye contact with another man. This is because some men understood how this process of energy exchange works and wanted to keep the energies reserved only for themselves. What they did not understand is that when a man tries to imprison the feminine power and keep it only for himself, everybody ultimately loses, including him.

As this automatic energy transference happens between a woman and a man something extra travels with it. This something extra is part of the inner nature of the person themselves and the character of what they have built in their energy field during their lifetime. This is why the look from one man may give a woman a sense of well-being and carry with it an energizing essence, even though she has never met him or spoken to him before, while the look from another man can "give her the creeps" or "gross her out."

There is a whole spectrum of looks, each having a different mix of energies and powers traveling with them in accordance with what the person has going on in their aura, mind and emotions. When we look at someone, we not only receive impressions from them, but we also direct energy at them through our eyes.

Passion Voluntary

We can choose to develop our understanding and consciousness of the great masculine and feminine energies, and come into greater harmony with them to live fuller, more enjoyable and rewarding lives. If we so choose, one of the first steps in enhancing the power and quality of all our relationships is in the realization that we are energy beings in physical bodies and that the great masculine and feminine essences that we are attached to are not, in fact, "ours." They are on loan to us for this lifetime and are part of our learning and development experience here on Earth.

According to how we choose to think, use our feelings and bio-energetically generate, we can enhance these original energies, making for an increase in the passion and power in our lives. There are a multitude of practical steps we can take to enhance the level of energetic love and increase the quality of our relationship fields. Many such practical techniques and suggestions are offered in the chapters that follow. Working with only a few of these techniques can make a tremendous difference in the level of power, passion and energetic love in your life.

Chapter Three
The Power of Three

The term "energetic love" appears throughout *Partners in Passion* and progressively deepens our understanding of the many possible natures and levels of love and how these are absolutely dependent upon the level and quality of the forces and powers in the energy worlds a person connects to and brings into themselves. The level of energetic love we are able to create within our own energy field and then transmit into the energy worlds of the planet is determined by how we think, feel and act. When we connect to the higher powers and forces of the planet's energy worlds, we generate much more powerful and potent signals of energetic love than when we connect to low level energies. Throughout the chapters that follow there are practical exercises and techniques to help you connect to these higher energies, to change and charge your personal energy field and the relationship fields you share with others.

The Passion Multiplier

What now follows are three energetic shifts that can be applied to improve all your relationships and make a powerful and immediate difference in your personal energy field and your mutual relationship fields. They also represent a fast and effective way to make a real difference in the world today. You do not need to become perfect at achieving them because perfection is not the goal here, you simply need to implement them in your daily going on. I group these three energetic shifts together under the name "The Passion Multiplier" because, practiced together this is exactly what they accomplish.

The Passion Multiplier is based on the laws of energy transference between people. It is not a theory but is rooted in the reality of human energy exchange and the mathematics of the transmission, reception and magnification of energies and forces in human behavior and between energy fields.

The laws of human energy exchange dictate that the passion between any two people is a direct resultant of the energetic love independently produced by each individual, multiplied together and appearing in their mutual energy field. When the energetic love of each person can be enhanced and the energy pathways between them made clear, there is an enormous increase in the passion and love that both are able to generate and feel. This third power appears, grows and glows in their energy field causing others to say, "Look at them. They must be in love." or "What a great relationship they have. I always feel good when I am with the two of them together." This charisma is caused neither by one field nor the other but by the third force that is generated when they meet, the power of three.

A fascinating example was presented to me at a seminar I was leading in Toronto where a couple I had first met five years before came up and spoke to me. They had with them a very large dog. "Do you remember him? He was only a puppy when we last met." I did, indeed, remember and he was a most happy and friendly-looking fellow. "Let us tell you something about this dog," they continued. "Whenever we hug, it doesn't matter where he is in the house—we can be upstairs and he can be in the basement—the moment we hug, he comes bounding up to join in. It is like he has a sixth sense and comes to find us."

Even when the dog could not see the couple hug, he was attracted by the increase in charge in their relationship field and could feel this over distance. I have noted often that dogs and cats seem more directly responsive to changes in energy fields than many human beings!

The Passion Multiplier will charge your energy field and, particularly when undertaken with your partner, help to balance the power and multiply the passion in your mutual relationship field. The three essential shifts that make up The Passion Multiplier are:

Shift 1. To raise the level and improve the quality of the powers and forces of the energy worlds working through you, thereby increasing the level of energetic love in your personal energy field.

Shift 2. To help the people you are in relationship with raise the level and improve the quality of the powers and forces of the energy worlds working through them, thereby helping them increase the level of energetic love in their energy field.

Shift 3. To improve the balance of power in the energy exchange between the genders both personally and globally and to help create natural equality between the feminine and masculine powers thereby.

These three shifts work naturally together. They offer the possibility of powerful and transformative change for you as an individual and for all your relationships, together with making a significant difference in the global gender field.

The Passion Multiplier in Action

When we mathematically model how energetic love grows in our relationship fields, we swiftly see how The Passion Multiplier can be caused to either work for us or limit the passion in all our relationships, both at a personal and global level.

The Personal Sphere

Every person has the possibility of living a life that generates a greater or lesser quantity and quality of energetic love, according to the levels of their energetic processes and connections. On a scale of 1 to 50, let's say that each partner in a couple can connect to and process 1 unit of energetic love at the minimum level, all the way up to 50 units at the maximum level of energetic possibility. When two people come together in a relationship, they power each other's energies, for better or for worse. In a man/woman relationship the total passion they experience in their mutual relationship field, according to The Passion Multiplier, is a product of the energetic love generated by the man multiplied by the energetic love generated by the woman.

In a relationship where both the man and the woman have the highest generation of energetic love, the level of passion in their mutual relationship field, using our scale, can be as great as 50 units (man) multiplied by 50 units (woman), producing 2,500 units of passion passing between them and generating out into the world. At this level both partners are highly spiritually developed and know themselves to be free to act according to their own will within their mutual agreements.

Now, let's use a more attainable example of 20 units of energetic love generated by the woman multiplied by 20 units of energetic love generated by the man, totaling 400 units of mutual passion. Such a relationship field is still at the high end of the scale of passion generated between two people and involves a great deal of personal development, freedom and mutually agreed purpose.

By contrast, however, when a man holds his partner in suppression, although he may generate 8 units of energetic love (he is unlikely to reach any higher as he is so dominant upon another life) the woman may be prevented from being at more than 5 units of power in the fulfillment of her possibility. This is not to say that she is not capable of a great deal more but she is held there by the oppression of the man. The level of passion in their mutual relationship field now becomes 8 units of power (man) multiplied by 5 units of power (woman) producing 40 units of passion. The difference between the last two examples—400 to 40—is ten times the power and the passion in their relationship field. In percentage terms this is a 1,000 percent difference!

This last example demonstrates how a massive change in the production and exchange of power in a relationship can occur by the liberation of the feminine from masculine suppression. When this occurs, the relationship can climb into realms of passion and energetic love that would be inconceivable without taking this crucial step.

Although in the above examples we used positive numbers for ease of explanation, in the real world there can be negatively as well as positively charged energy fields. What this means is that one partner can have a positively charged field at, say, 20 units, but the other partner can be a processor and container of so much toxic energy that they produce a destructive energy field around them which may qualify as below zero. When a positive is multiplied by a negative what is the result?

As an ancient Chinese sage once said, "What happens if you take a fine vase and bring it down upon a rock?" Answering his own question he then said, "The vase breaks." After a pause he continued with another question, "What happens when you take a rock and bring it down upon a fine vase?" Again he paused and then answered, "The vase breaks."

The person who suffers in this process is the person who has the positively charged field, because the toxic field caused by their partner gradually destroys the energetic love they originally had in their own field, except in very special circumstances where both partners agree to set out together on a road of self-improvement and development and are truly able to hold to it.

It is wise to realize that when you link your energy field with that of another person, you can bring a great increase of energetic love into your life, but also you can bring toxicity and depression into your life as well. The Passion Multiplier works to multiply both enhancing and toxic energies in the mutual relationship field. Always remember, both happiness and depression are contagious in the energy worlds.

The Global Picture

The Passion Multiplier demonstrates how balancing the power between the genders is a highly significant step in bringing peaceful change to the planet. Not only will the level of power expressed through people increase but, due to the effect of The Passion Multiplier, this increase will be magnified and expressed through all aspects of human affairs.

The Passion Multiplier demonstrates the importance of men and women being free to be themselves, to discover their own uniqueness and personal power and not be hampered by cultural taboos that insist upon keeping them at lesser than they are. These taboos are mostly based in fear and insecurity and hamper our gender interactions both personally and globally.

If, in a relationship, either party puts restrictions upon the other that are not come to by free and clear mutual agreement, then The Passion Multiplier will be inhibited and a lesser result will be produced. The severe limitations placed worldwide on the opportunities of women in the workplace, in politics and in law are examples of restrictions that greatly diminish the power of The Passion Multiplier. It is also true that wherever there are emotional, mental and sexual restrictions placed upon either gender by the other the effectiveness of The Passion Multiplier is held back enormously. These restrictions are often further enforced by male-dominated religions and the myth of a masculine God.

A painful example of the suppression of the feminine is seen in cultures where men have been so afraid of feminine power that they set in place the custom of female circumcision to prevent women from enjoying their natural sexual power. This custom passed on from one generation to the next is often enforced by the older women who, having been forced into submission by men, insist that the practice they experienced is also visited upon their daughters. Men who insist upon the sexual castration of their wives can only expect a man/woman relationship in which The Passion Multiplier produces a very low result.

Men, too fearful of the feminine energy to allow its empowerment, have also produced outrageous laws that permit so-called "honor killings." These have nothing to do with any real codes of honor but are tied to the determination of some men to retain dominance in what God and Creation designed to be a man/woman partnership of equality and mutual empowerment.

On a global scale a significant change that we can cause to happen through our own actions is to free the power and passion of women in all realms, including social, educational, emotional and sexual. This will not be at the expense of men, who will also benefit from the greater passion available to all by the freeing of the enormous energy potential that the women of the world represent.

Balance the Power

You do not need to be in a sexual relationship for The Passion Multiplier to work for you. The laws of the exchange of forces between all women and men are in process regardless of whether a sexual relationship exists. The exchange does, however, become more intense and specific when two people decide to link their lives and energy fields together as partners in passion.

In any dynamic where men and women discuss and decide on, for example, political, business, economic or social issues, if the men are dominant, then the energies available to the group as a whole are strictly curtailed, as is the level of potential process between them and the quality of the result they can come to. You may not be able to change the balance of power at governmental level, but balancing the power in your personal man/woman relationships is a vital step towards real change on a global scale.

Government bodies and institutions of fifty percent women would reflect the energy dynamic between the genders and produce a more naturally balanced decision-making process. This would represent a great step forward in the forum of world governments and the energies that world leadership could call upon in its decision-making processes.

When the energies of women are subjugated, men cannot energetically develop and move on. This means that the human race as a whole is held back from its development possibility. It is like a twin engine plane that is only working on one of its engines. It can go around in circles but cannot lift off the ground! It is like this in global terms and also in personal relationships. If either partner is over-dominant within the relationship, the level of energetic love that can actually be exchanged is minimal.

This explains why cultures that are based in male-dominated hierarchies will become increasingly anachronistic, as they are left behind while the rest of the human race moves on. Unfortunately, millions of women are trapped in societies that insist on carrying forward masculine-dominated religions that have no place in the future. These women will continue to be trapped until the rising tide of feminine energy becomes so unstoppable that these social structures are swept away.

Righting the Balance

Imagine if the first qualification for a leadership gathering would be that it is energetically balanced between the energies of the male and female, as each gender naturally makes up half of the human team. The Passion Multiplier would thus be caused to work for the whole human race, even in the realms of government, to help enhance all our futures.

The greater presence of the feminine influence in all decision-making processes would bring the most rapid positive change to our human condition. If women made up fifty percent of the government structures and institutions of the world would the level of warfare we experience be as high as it is now? Would world hunger still be at its current levels? Would governments be able to get away with the continuing practice of loading huge debt onto future generations?

It is known in medicine that diseases of the human system are born out of an imbalance of one kind or another. Research into the formation of cancer indicates that this disease forms most readily in an acidic ecology and if we take actions to bring our systems back into balance by making them more alkaline then cancer does not form as easily. Similarly, when an imbalance occurs between the HDL and LDL cholesterol, then heart attacks and strokes become more likely. All disease is based in imbalance of one kind or another.

As it is in the human system, so it is in human affairs. The human race is designed to have a natural balance between yang and yin, the masculine and feminine energies, in all its endeavors. Too much masculine dominance produces an acidic ecology that is cancer-forming in the affairs of the human race. When the system is out of balance, the basis for decision taking and forward projection is warped and wrong attitudes prevail. Rather than thinking long-term about the future, the pressure is on how to get by today. So, for example, tomorrow's resources are used up leaving a worsening legacy for the next generation who will have to deal with the toxic residues left by the decisions of masculine-dominated governments today. The worsening planetary situation is a direct result of the imbalance between the masculine and feminine energies among the leaders of the world.

Opportunity is clearly biased toward the masculine gender in almost all societies today. It is, therefore, a charge upon those men who wish to work with The Passion Multiplier in full strength to go out of their way to help women toward a greater equality of power and opportunity. How many offices in which a man is the boss are actually organized by women, for example? Why are women valued less in the workplace when men would not be able to function successfully without them? Why do women often earn less than men for doing work of equal value? Somehow, in the trace of world history, society has come to be dominated by the red, masculine power of the male. From this dominant position men have rigged the rules so the contribution of the male is almost always more highly valued in wealth and status than the contribution of the female. In the power exchange between Mars and Venus, Mars has used its red energy to become dominant to the detriment of all. On the walls of human history we find "Testosterone Rules!" writ large.

The proof of a man's strength is expressed as much in what he does not do as in what he does. It is often easier in the workplace for men to dominate women than it is for them to dominate other men. The man who chooses to push women around is both a bully and a coward and most often picks upon the so-called "weaker sex" because he does not dare try to push the men around. The truth in this is also that the women are not the weaker sex. How much strength and fortitude does it take to raise children, keep a household running, while simultaneously caring for a husband and juggling a career as many women do? Women are not weaker; they are simply not configured or designed to be like men. We are built differently and we process energies differently. We are both weaker without each other.

Maximize the Personal Passion

To maximize the passion in your personal relationships it is vital to find ways to right the balance and to overcome the effects of historical bias. For men, this means actively seeking ways to sponsor the opportunity of the women in your life. For women, it means insisting on being your own person, self-determined and capable of standing up against the psychology of being dependent on the male that has been developed throughout history. Both are naturally of equal power and importance within the laws of Creation and the purposes of God.

In personal relationships where two people come together as free individuals, strong in stature in their own right, the level of passion is much higher than a relationship in which one is the bully and the other is cowed.

The Fruits of Possession

At a personal level, if one partner is dominant and holds the other back from their spiritual potential, then The Passion Multiplier determines that both will lose. When you put possession on your partner and restrict their freedom mentally, emotionally, sexually or in any other way, you reduce the passion potential because you put the power structure between you out of balance.

This does not mean you can do what you want any time you feel like it. It means that you would naturally discuss your relationship with your partner to discover what rules or laws you choose to be mutually bound by. Then the power balance that you cause between you is chosen consciously according to what you mutually decide you want.

Build the Power, Magnify the Passion

As discussed in Chapter 1, both men and women are connected to enormous universal energies. There is a natural equality in these charges. They are designed to work together as twin frequencies of God and Creation through the human team.

In the same way that the planet's binary power ensures that there are always an approximately equal number of women as there are men here on Earth, so the great masculine and feminine powers are meant to operate in equality of action and opportunity through the left and right hands of the human race: men and women. This does not mean that they become the same, far from it. Both need the permission to give their individual uniqueness every opportunity to expand and grow. The more they are able to fulfill their unique natures, the greater the conductivity and power that will pass between them.

The way to build the power between both parties is not to emasculate the male but to have both female and male powers running as close to maximum as possible. In this respect the task for the male is easier than the female, because the female has to overcome the effects of thousands of years of repression.

History has mostly been written by men, biased towards men, and even the religions of the world focus on a masculine God. In the Judeo-Christian tradition, for example, women are reduced to the status of being secondary, created from an original rib of man. Men, therefore, have the task of overcoming the effects of thousands of years of wrong programming and assumed superiority, which is no easy task in itself.

By building the power of the feminine to its rightful level of influence and by encouraging the masculine to be true to its own power, we can go forward in fuller passion together.

Chapter Four
Fields of Experience

W hen we realize we are spiritual beings in a physical body, it inverts our world view and we begin to perceive the world and everything in it energy worlds first. We start to appreciate that our physical bodies formed inside a unique energy field and we are the material manifestation of the energies we process and the energetic field that surrounds us. It is our energy field and what lives inside it that causes us to have the posture we have, choose the clothes we wear and adopt the mannerisms that are part of our particular personality. In viewing the world this way we begin to understand that personality is a compound of energies in our field and it is this compound which causes our unique charisma, which can be of high or low quality, depending upon the energies we accumulate and connect to. Everything we do and say provides clues as to the natures of force that live inside our energy field. It is this field that intrigues and attracts us to another and which we engage with when we begin building a mutual relationship field during the process of dating.

As our perception shifts into seeing people energy worlds first, we begin to recognize that people are conduits or terminals for essences, entities, forces and powers of multiple kinds. We understand more clearly that when we engage with people we engage firstly with the energies they are connected to and carry with them. These energies can make us feel many different sensations, such as the enhancement of well-being or tired and drained. It depends entirely upon the forces and powers we have collected in our energy field throughout our life, the energies another has collected in theirs and the interplay between the two.

When we meet another human being we meet the energy record of everywhere they have ever been and everything they have ever done. It is this energy record that psychics and clairvoyants connect to when they give a reading. We carry the energetic record of our parents, teachers, friends, lovers and enemies in our energy record and it is all there to be accessed and read, like an open book, for those who have the ability to read it. With training we can teach ourselves to be more open and receptive to these signals and so develop our own sixth sense of the energies that live within both ourselves and another person.

Just as our own energetic record is full of the signals of our past and present processes, so too is the energetic record of the planet as a whole. This great astral field, which has also been known as the akashic record, holds the history of all peoples and their actions. This history is not inert like print on a page but is energetically alive. It is a living history and when we call the signals, energies and powers that live therein unto ourselves, we give them the theater of our mind, body and soul in which to enact.

We are terminals for energy processes of many different kinds which, aggregated together, make us who and what we are at any particular moment in our lives. When we enter into a relationship with another person, we not only join them physically but also energetically, as all the powers, signals, forces and essences which live in our energy field begin to interact with the powers, essences, signals and forces that live in theirs.

If this interaction is shallow, we may meet someone in the afternoon and forget about them by the evening. But then there are those meetings which, once having happened, our lives are never the same again. It may be the look of powerful energetic attraction from a man or woman whom we unexpectedly meet on the street. It may be the look of a spiritual teacher that takes our perception of the world and turns it upside down.

We never know what is around the next corner, in the next room or within the next energy exchange. These interactions are part of the great adventure of life in this place of meeting, exchanging, merging, blending, marrying and parting. One thing that is certain is that none of us will leave this theatre of appearances the same as when we came into it. We are marked by the experience of life on planet Earth, a great part of which is the experience of sharing passions, processes and relationship fields with others.

We are born alone and we will die alone, but along the way there are many relationships we will know. Some will enhance us and some will diminish us and certainly, in aggregate, they will all be a major factor in causing us to become what we eventually turn out to be.

Also, as the therapist says, you may be here to recover from a hurt that has been caused to you, but realize that on the other side of the city, country or world someone else is in a therapist's office, seeking to recover from the hurt that you have caused in them.

We Are Energy Conductors

As human beings we are both generators and conductors of energy. We generate passions within our energy field according to how we think, feel and act. We then project these passions outside of us and attract more of the same kind of energy from the energy field of the planet, which contains all the energies released by all people for thousands of years. It is this simple fact that is at the root of the so-called "Law of Attraction" which has garnered so much attention in recent years.

The word "conduct" itself gives us direct clues as to how this process works by the multiple meanings it contains. It is our unique combination of behaviors, our "conduct," which determines what essences, powers, forces and energies we actually conduct through our energy field and attract from the energy worlds of the universe. We are like the conductor of an orchestra: according to the directions we give, the different sections of the orchestra are called upon and play particular melodies. The conductor in this analogy is our consciousness, the orchestra is the many inner energies which make up our life and the audience are those energies which are attracted by the Law of Attraction from the energy worlds of the planet to listen to and augment the piece of music we compose and play. When we play music that is soothing, calm and peaceful we attract like energies from the astral light of the planet. When we play music that is hot, martial and war-like, we attract these very energies from where they wait in the planet's energy worlds.

Within the realms of everyday speech there are many clues how the energy worlds of the planet work in relation to the human energy field. When we approach a group of people and ask, "Who is in charge here?" the expression "in charge" means exactly that: whose energy field contains the energetic charge of leadership? When a leader is "dis-charged" from their station, the opposite case applies and the charge of leadership leaves them.

There are thousands of different energies we can conduct through ourselves from the energy worlds of the planet. We only have to look at world history to see the range of possible human behaviors, all of which produce energy transmissions of different natures. From the lowest act in human history to the highest, each life has left an energetic impression within the energy worlds of the planet, although some impressions are more powerful than others. These energies are available to us every day of our lives.

To conduct low levels of energy, force and power, we have to develop a low character and become an energetic low-life. To conduct higher energies we need to spiritually develop and make a spiritual shift in our life. This is because very high energies can only be conducted through someone who has built a level of spiritual development that allows for the anchorage of more refined kinds of power. These higher levels are often shown in spiritual art around the world by the depiction of bright illumination around the head in the form of halos, crowns and fire and through the symbolism of bright gems placed in the area of the third eye.

An expression of a relationship working with high level power and passion is held in the concept of a king and queen. A true king or queen is not made so by material wealth or lineage, but by the energetic power and passion in their life. Crowns and coronets were not originally made of physical metal but were energetic patterns that could be seen around the heads of spiritually developed people. The way to be a king or queen of spiritual development is still open to us today. It all depends upon the energies we process and the quality of the relationship fields we build.

The Energy Worlds

As members of the human tribe we are spiritual beings in mortal, planetary bodies. We are conductors of energy from the unseen worlds of the planet and the universe into the seen worlds of material reality. Every time we conceive an idea and then give it form, we give birth to the originating energy that we conduct through our human faculties.

There are many kinds and levels of energy we can bring into ourselves. As human beings, we have access to every energetic signal that any person on Earth has ever released into the energy worlds of the planet. The range of energetic signals include the enlightenment of Buddha, the Passion of Christ and those that were released by Adolf Hitler and the Nazis. The energy record of every relationship between man and woman has been recorded in the astral record of the planet and is available to us. Whether we know it or not, we are energetically influenced by the relationships of all those that have gone before us through the great revolving door of planet Earth. Clearly, those relationships that influence us the most are those we have been under the greatest influence of, beginning with our parents, teachers and the relationships we witnessed every day while growing up. We are, however, also affected by the powers and signals of history and all those energies that have been recorded in the energy field of planet Earth.

According to the energies, powers and forces we build in our personal energy field, so our field becomes more or less attractive to the energies, powers and forces that other people build in theirs. Our energy field is like the résumé of all we have ever thought, felt and done in the material and energetic worlds. It is like the shop window in which we display the energetic contents that are to be found within our personal store. Every energy signal we conduct through our faculties in the trace of our life leaves a residual imprint in our energy field. These traces combine to produce patterns and colors that can be seen by people who have trained themselves how to read these signals. I will be explaining exactly how to do this in the next chapter.

Similar energies are attracted to each other because they are on the same wavelength. This is why certain people seem destined to meet and why the power of synchronicity is such an acknowledged part of human affairs. Goethe, the German philosopher, believed that men and women could build such powerful energetic fields around themselves that they became energetically drawn to each other as if by destiny. He called this idea "elective affinities" and wrote a novel based upon it with *Elective Affinities* as its title. Today we speak of soul mates, twinned souls, the Law of Attraction and even explore the idea that two people are destined to be together because of interactions between them in past lives.

Energetic charges that are alike attract each other. I read an account by the actress Jamie Lee Curtis in which she described flipping through a magazine and seeing a photograph of three men. "I looked at the man on the right, wearing a plaid shirt and a waggish smirk. I'd never seen him before, but I pointed at him. 'I'm going to marry that man,' I said to my friend." She then continued to tell the story of how they met and said, "This winter will be our 20th anniversary. I'll never know why I thought we'd understand each other when I saw his photograph. Hidden in that smirk, I think, was a little secret that only I knew." (*O Magazine*, November 2004, p. 72)

A photograph is a radio set to the energetic frequency of a person and is a direct link into their energy field. Through a photograph you can receive the energetic nature of everything a person is. This is why people who are very sensitive to the energy worlds can be resistant to having their picture "taken." They feel it takes something from them and also offers energetic access to people they might not know. Both these ideas are true. However, a photograph may also offer an energetic doorway for another person to find and connect with you that will change your life for the better. It is mostly with this hope that people post their photographs on dating websites. Love works in mysterious ways.

The Field of Relationships

As human beings we have the power to choose what energies we plant in our own energy field, in the energy fields of others, in the energy field of the planet, the universe and ultimately, even the energy field of God.

The farmer plants seeds with the expectation of receiving back abundance. So it is with the field of our lives, the energy field in which we plant our energetic seeds. In this field, just as in the field of the farmer, we do, indeed, reap what we sow. One of the most powerful ways this appears is in the field of our relationships, which I call the relationship field. When we plant seeds of love and care this is what we will grow, magnified a hundredfold. Small, apparently insignificant actions can cause real differences in ourselves, in our relationships and in the world.

All relationships begin in the unseen worlds of energy and power. When we transmit a signal, we transmit it not only into our own energy field, but also into the fields of the people around us. When we think the best of another person, we power the higher part of their energy field. When we think the worst of them, we power the lower energetic frequencies that live within their aura. We are all a mix of the high and the low, the good and the bad, the bold and the bashful, the ugly and the beautiful. We should not be too surprised, therefore, when the people we are in relationship with repetitively act out the very energies that we are powering in them by how we think about them and the energies we transmit to them.

A great key to assisting another is to deliberately call over their best features and qualities so these qualities can be encouraged to grow stronger. Our thoughts and feelings are an energetic food we supply to ourselves and to the people around us. Just as we use plant food for our plants, we can use the food of our energies to support and nurture what is near and dear to us. We express what we hold sacred above all through the power of our choices. Suspicion breeds more suspicion, while unselfish love helps grow the power of love in others and in ourselves.

Standards and Conduct

Standards of conduct play a vital part in our development as human beings and also in the development of our relationship fields. The saying, "Think the best and know the worst" is not an open ticket to an "anything-goes" attitude. It describes a deliberate position in which we try to lend power to the qualities we want to help grow and offer denial to those we do not want. In offering this denial, however, we should not pretend these destructive signals do not exist, as this would be naïve and potentially leave us exposed to their detrimental effects. To feign ignorance of something does not offer a shield against it.

Standards of conduct define the conduct that is acceptable from us and also from others. Sometimes, although you hold great love for someone, it may be necessary to let them go because the energies they bring into your life are too destructive for you to abide.

The more we come to understand the nature of the energy worlds and the different qualities of signals that live therein, the more crucial we realize it is to have definite standards we will not go below. We are able to choose the nature of energies we process and it is these energies which ultimately determine the kind of person we become. This is no casual matter and so, for example, the friends we choose to have close by are a powerful influence into our lives and the contents of our relationship fields.

When we choose to change our friends, we are not so much changing our friends as changing the energy signals we decide to process and attract to ourselves. It is the energy signals we generate when together that cause our friends to want to associate with us in the first place. Imagine that you hang out with a group of friends whose interest focuses upon the latest in music. When you meet, you talk music, think music, and exchange ideas about music. But then you decide you want to focus upon and talk about the mysteries of life after death and no longer consider music as a priority. You start to not fit in with the group signal and unless you find a way to talk about life after death through music, it will not be long before you no longer feel like part of the group.

When we look at our life in this way we can look back through the journey of our days and see how many friendships we had that were based on the shared energy experiences of the time. How many people do you still know with whom you attended kindergarten, elementary school or college? Most likely there are a few and those who you still know are probably people with whom you shared many energetic bonds at many levels, so your lives maintain dynamics in common that you can still share in the present.

Fields of Possibility

We live our lives within many overlapping energy fields. Our personal energy field or aura is contained within the energy field of the planet. Planet Earth revolves and evolves within the aura of the sun, which itself is contained within the energy field of the great spiral galaxy, the Milky Way. The Milky Way is held within the aura of the universe, which is contained within the energy field of Creation. All of these energy fields are connected to and infused with the essence, power and spirit of the Cause of Creation or God. Our personal energy field is, therefore, connected to the energy fields of the Great Creation and every moment of our lives—sleeping and waking—we breathe in and out the cosmic energies of the universe. These cosmic energies are in the food we eat, the water we drink, the air we breathe and the energy impressions we draw in through our five senses every moment of our lives. We can also connect to the energy fields of others through our two higher senses: clairvoyance and telepathy. Indeed, the more we become tuned in to the range of frequencies of another person, the easier it is to pick up clairvoyant (meaning clear-sighted) and telepathic messages.

The main difference between clairvoyance and telepathy is that by clairvoyance we pick up what is happening in the energy field of another without their awareness. Telepathy is the conscious and deliberate transmission of an energetic message from one person to another and is, therefore, a more advanced skill.

When two people's energy fields are on the same frequency, content transfers more easily between them. At higher levels this happens consciously, as in the example of telepathy, but it is also going on all the time in the realms of the semiconscious and unconscious mind. An easy to see example of this process can be found in the mystery of infectious yawning. When two friends are together throughout the day, there is ample opportunity for their energy fields to balance out and come onto a shared frequency. Let us say they sit up talking late into the evening. As the hour draws late and their soul energy is becoming depleted, one of them yawns.

When a person yawns, they suck in extra energy from the nearest available source that is on their wavelength. When two people are sitting together and are in energetic empathy, the nearest available energy source is the energy field of the person they are sitting with. There is now a rush of power from one person's energy field to the other. The person who experiences the energy loss now feels suddenly at less and their energy intake systems are triggered so they also yawn. Within minutes a curious scene takes place as first one person and then the other yawns as a kind of energetic tug of war ensues with the extra energy that both need being claimed by first one person, then the other. It is no surprise that soon after such a yawning match both parties often retire to bed where they may move into the cycle of energy recharge we call sleep.

In Chapter 6, Energize Your Space we will look at how to deliberately charge the area where you sleep so you can receive a more restful night's rest, in which your energy systems will become powerfully refreshed and recharged, giving you extra energy for another day.

Each day we awake and re-engage our energy field with the fields of all those we know and deal with in our daily life. In this time of satellite communications, we also engage with the energy fields of people all over the planet as we bring their lives into our consciousness. It is no wonder we often feel fatigued or stressed out. Our energy field becomes connected to so many people, places and experiences in such a short space of time that it can be overwhelming.

In these energetically busy times it is a wise person that reserves a little time each day to recharge their own field and internal energies. This can be done by connecting into sources of energy that are nourishing fuel for our body, mind, soul and spirit. This is how we develop our attachment to certain pieces of music, colors, art and even people who become our anchors of sanity. We know their frequency will be there for us when we find ourselves in need. They help to recharge our energy field so we can continue to engage with life.

Through the choices we make we generate signals into the energy worlds. As a consequence of our actions these signals radiate and send out invitations for other signals of a like kind to come and join them. Thus, when we emit a signal of care or of love, this energy signal sends out an energetic invitation to others of its kind from the energy field of the planet to come and join it. By generating increasing signals of love we increase its presence in the world and also attract more love to us. There is no dynamic in which this is truer than in that mainspring of human relationships: the energy transference and flow of passion between men and women.

We are the current generation to be working with these two great powers and to have these great powers work through us. The generations that came before us—our mothers and fathers, grandmothers and grandfathers—experienced this great dance of attraction and repulsion, as will our children after us. The fundamental powers that make this great mystery possible remain the same, undiminished, untarnished and perpetual. It is only the individual human faces and expressions that change.

Now it is our time and turn to perform our individual dances within the permissions that these two great powers allow. Tomorrow this permission will be granted to others. You and I are part of this great dance of possibility, here for now but not for long, in which we have the opportunity to work with the gender power to which we are connected by our birthright, whether that be the masculine force of Mars or the feminine force of Venus, the acid or the alkaline, the red or the blue.

The Unseen Worlds of Energy and the Laws that Govern Them

Our lives will be played out in the fields of opportunity that planet Earth offers us. All the energies, powers and forces that make our life possible are governed by definite universal laws which determine all energetic possibilities and results. By understanding the laws that affect the planet and her energy fields, we can enhance our life's possibility as well as our relationships with ourselves and with each other. We can work to become more conscious of these forces and the laws that govern them or we can be content to get by with a lesser level of consciousness. The more enlightened our consciousness becomes, the more effective we can be in the journey of our lives and in our relationships with others.

When we understand how the laws of energetic love work in our relationship fields, we can deliberately apply them to win for ourselves and others a higher quality of energetic relationship. It is from an understanding of these core laws and principles that the need to balance the powers and energies between men and women becomes absolutely obvious, as one detaches oneself from the partisan view of either gender and looks to how the system was designed for the maximum benefit of both.

Understandings from ancient mystery schools teach us that we can either live our lives in ignorance and be in unconscious subjugation or we can develop our understanding and consciousness of these powers, forces and laws at depth. The Ancients knew that the transmission and reception of energies between people works according to definite laws and principles that can both be studied and understood.

Twin Views

To be on the road to more evolving and conscious relationships it is vital to have inner understandings of what the forces that work between men and women actually are and of the inner properties of the laws that govern them. Seven core laws of energetic love are contained in the final chapter of this book. These fundamental laws determine the exchange of energies between men and women and how passion is multiplied or diminished accordingly within the relationship field.

If you wish to approach the rest of this book from the framework of these laws, you are welcome to turn to Chapter 15 and read it through before continuing on this journey. By doing so, you will be able to approach the following chapters through the seven viewing windows that the seven laws of energetic love offer. This approach offers a "laws first" view of all that is to come. If you prefer a more organic journey, you can continue to read this book sequentially and wait to go through the seven laws of energetic love at the end. You will find everything that is written in the chapters to follow leads naturally to the seven laws of energetic love. I offer this choice because some readers will prefer the right-brain approach of finding the framework of the laws at the end, whereas others will prefer the left-brain approach of reading the laws in advance.

There are always two approaches to everything here on Earth and then there is the third way which actually is the most effective and is born out of a combination of both the left and right, the red and blue, the clockwise and counter-clockwise. In this instance, the third way is to read through all that follows sequentially for the right-brain, discovering as you go; then read the book for the left-brain, looking through the viewing window of the seven laws of energetic love; then read the book a third time so that on the third reading the two parts of the brain, the masculine and the feminine (yes, both genders are contained within our brains!) can exchange views. It is on this third reading that the greatest understandings will reveal themselves.

I leave the choice of which of the two chapters you will read next up to you and will meet you on the next page of your choosing.

Chapter Five
Energy Dating

In its origin all dating is energy dating. The attraction between man and woman always begins in the realms of human electricity and magnetism. In exploring energy dating techniques we will be looking at ways and means to magnify the power and multiply the passion so that our man/woman relationships can yield maximum mutual satisfaction.

Whenever our energy field touches that of another person, transference of power takes place. When we think of someone, we send a transmission of energy that connects with their energy field at distance and draws some of their power back to us as, at the same time, we send power from our energy field to theirs. We are all energy traders drawing energy into ourselves and transmitting energy out to others every day of our lives.

Much of this energy trading is casual and non-specific. It happens with people we associate with in the course of our daily lives and is part of the general energy trading of life. Every time we get into an elevator with another person or walk by them there is some degree of transference between our personal energy field and theirs. When we shower, many of these transferred signals are washed away as the water streams through our aura. These signals are also flushed out of our energy field when we sleep at night. There are techniques that can allow us to consciously introduce specific colors into our aura to reduce the amount of these general signals we take in.

Energy dating is a more specific process of energy exchange than this ongoing energy trading of general life. In the process of energy dating we decide that we want to invest further energy and time in developing a particular relationship. In deepening the strength and power of the exchange between ourselves and another person, we deliberately thicken the energy connections we have with them by spending more time together. This usually follows an assessment and evaluation process in which we add up whether we want more of their energies in our life. This is often as much an instinctual decision—following our gut reaction—as it is conscious. It is also greatly influenced by our psychology as determined by our experiences in the past.

When we energy date another person we deliberately bring all that is in their energy field closer to us and cause a closer inter-transference of power between us. We become food for each other. Right now across the world, lovers gaze into each other's eyes. Their energy fields are locked together and the rest of the world, the past and future, fade away. They are powerfully and passionately in the now, experiencing the energy shift that is caused by being in their partner's energetic and physical presence, glued into the moment by the power of the relationship field that is caused between them. Inside this relationship field sparks fly and they wish to be in no other place and time than with each other, in this moment, now.

The eyes are major organs of energy exchange. This is because they are connected directly into the brain. They are the windows of the soul and spirit. Through the eyes the two great powers of yin and yang behold each other and interlock directly. The yin of the woman draws from the yin held within the man and the yang of the man draws from the yang held within the woman. It is the power of this energy transference that compels lovers to reach out to touch each other, hold hands and reinforce the energetic transference that is happening through their eyes and in their relationship field. This is when the atmosphere between them becomes electric and sparks fly!

Some energy dates start slowly and gather power over time, others start with power and then fizzle out and still others never seem to quite click. We may communicate with someone over the Internet for months and then set up a specific place and time to meet for a more intense energy date. We may be in an office with a colleague for several years and then arrange to go on a date with the specific purpose of discovering whether there is a level of mutual compatibility that goes beyond the controlled office environment. We may have not planned an energy date at all and suddenly find ourselves in the middle of one. An accidental meeting can become a powerful energy exchange and the level of intensity may move in a matter of minutes to a level of passion that another relationship of many years has never reached.

Once we start to think of dating "energy worlds first" it opens up whole new vistas of how to think about what dating actually is and offers new perceptions, ways and means to enhance the quality of our relationships at all levels. We can start to open up and discover new ways to power the passion between ourselves and others and enhance the energetic love in our life. Much of what now follows is dedicated to helping you towards becoming a conscious energy worker and a more potent energy date. After today, when you go out with your boyfriend or girlfriend, husband or wife, you are not only going on a date—you are energy dating!

Early Energy Dating Symptoms

In the early stages of a budding romance we feel a natural attraction and affinity to a particular person and an excitement at the prospect of being in their presence. Simply thinking of them may cause our nerves to tingle with a pleasurable electrical pulse. As the time for our date draws near, we can feel a growing energetic anticipation. This can be accompanied by sensations of butterflies in the stomach, tightness in the area of the solar plexus and a feeling of lightheadedness. It can lead us to literally become love-sick; a state in which we pine for the energies the other person gives us and even go off our food. We may become so focused upon our forthcoming date that we fumble the most mundane tasks. This state of energetic anticipation can cause our eyes to shine with a special spark and our skin to become radiant with a glow that emanates from the inside out. Other people may even notice and comment "You must be in love," or "I want some of what he/she is having."

As the time for the energy date draws nearer, our energetic center of gravity may partially shift into the sexual center, which is located in the genitals and can release a high-power charge through the eyes. High-level electrical charges from the sexual center may also be released throughout the nerves, giving a sense of tingling all over. Suddenly hearing a song playing on the radio that you associate with the other person can cause a release of these high-energy signals. These signals can also become linked with the high-power signals of the emotions when they are simultaneously stimulated. The emotions, which are primarily seated in the nose, throat, heart and solar plexus, are easily triggered by the sense of smell and so the scent of a particular perfume or aftershave can release a very powerful emotional and sexual response. When both music and aroma are received in combination and romantically linked, they can become a very powerful aphrodisiac and association in a person's memory for the rest of their life.

These energetic signals being released from the sexual and emotional centers can be of such high power they can override the regular pathways we live by and we may find ourselves impulsively or rashly acting out of character. This is the power of love at work. The energetic signals released from the sexual and emotional centers can be of such intensity they can sweep us off our feet, particularly if we have never felt them in strength before. This is why first love is so powerful as these new, never-experienced-before signals travel through the nerve pathways and over-ride the by then routine signals of everyday life. It is also why a young man who is doing well at school with a bright career in front of him, can suddenly career off the path when he is jilted by his girlfriend and may not recover for years. It is also why someone who may have a high-functioning position can be found mooning about as they think of their newly-beloved. These are very high amperage wires that come swiftly into activation and change the world as we know it from the inside out.

The Power of Love

Think how many songs on the radio are about love. Overpowering love, lost love, stolen love or broken and wounded love. Uplifted by love, cast down by love, smitten by love, struck by love and stuck in love. Love is often referred to as something eternal and infinite, bigger than a mountain and deeper than the sea. Again and again we hear people trying to come to terms with the experience of love sweeping through them. In these songs, those that do not have love are often looking for love, while many that do have it are trying to come to terms with the new sensations it causes in them.

One of the most powerful ways we deal with emotions that overwhelm us is to give expression to them in songs, poems, paintings and other forms of expressive action. This is a prime way of clearing the overpowering emotion of love through our system and into the energy record of the world. So much of human experience and expression is driven by the attraction between these two great forces of masculine and feminine and its manifestation in our lives. From theater, to movies, novels, plays and magazines—if everything that gave expression to the inter-play between men and women was removed, how much of our world culture would be left? At a practical level, if all men went to one part of the planet and all women went to the other and we decided not to interact any more, the human race would end in approximately one hundred years!

Energetic Enhancement

A powerful way to enhance the experience of energetic love is to learn how to become more sensitive to the energy worlds in which these passions flow. When you feel fond of someone, you radiate a particular kind of energy that flows from your eyes and emanates from your energy field. This fondness has an energetic wavelength, a particular quality and even a color. Fondness can often be seen as a yellow glow that emanates from the aura and produces a sense of warmth, care and encouragement that is pleasant to be with. Old friends often share a yellow hue between them that represents a deep emotional bond in their mutual relationship field.

Imagine what it would be like not only to feel the subtle effects of these energies but to actually be able to see them. Being able to see into the energy field brings huge enhancement to the energy dating process. It is possible to see the vibrations of energetic love and other emotions which are present in another person's energy field and also in the relationship field you build between you. To produce an enhanced sense of intimacy, you and your partner can practice looking at and sensing each other's energy fields together. This works particularly well after you have energized your space, which we will explore in the next chapter.

One of the surest ways to detect what kinds of energies live within another person is to learn how to read the colors in their energy field. Using our eyes to see into the energy worlds of the aura enables us to do this. Seeing the most dense energy formations in the aura is easy to do with practice and takes only about half an hour to learn. I have taught thousands of people how to see into the worlds of the human aura. It is simply a matter of re-learning how to use the eyes specifically for this purpose. I say re-learning because when we were very young we likely used our auric or energy vision often. When we were babies we recognized our mother not only by her physical appearance but also by the special glow around her head. No one else's energy field lit up like your mother's did when she looked at you! Babies can often be seen reaching for things that are not physically there because they still see directly into the worlds of energy and reach for things we do not see.

If you have a pet cat, you may have experienced being in a room with a cat when it suddenly looks up and fixates intensely upon something in the air that is invisible to you. We may look at the cat and think, "Crazy cat, looking at something that is not there." But if the cat could speak it would say, "Crazy human, why do you not use your eyes to see as I do?"

To see into these energy worlds we use a different part of our eyes than we do for our usual vision. It is done by "seeing through, not with the eyes" as the poet and artist William Blake expressed. He regularly reported seeing things that were invisible to others. Plato spoke of how the Ancients used an inner spiritual fire and caused it to flow through the eyes. This is the technique that we will use to enhance our energy vision and help our eyes see into the realms of the energy worlds. The ancient Egyptians used their eyes to see in this way and their statues and paintings often depict the soft, unfocused, long-distance look that we will be using to enhance our energetic vision. Once you learn how to use your energetic vision, you can continue to practice this for the rest of your life. One of the key domains that we can learn about, both to see and energetically feel, is that of the human energy field or aura.

The Human Aura

The human aura is the energy field that surrounds every single one of us. It extends approximately thirty-two inches all around a person, including above the head and beneath the feet. All of the experiences we have in our life happen within the space of our aura. When we interact with people, we interact through our relationship field which is caused by the interaction of our auras. Our personal energy field contains the electromagnetic record of everything we have done in our life and within it we build energy deposits based upon how we think and feel, what we experience and our attitudes towards these experiences. Thus it is that when two energy fields meet, according to the energies that each contains by virtue of all that has happened in their lives up to that point, there can either be a tremendous surge of energies that pass from one energy field to another or very little exchange at all. When we date someone, it is our auras that first meet. It is our personal energy fields that exchange the first energetic kiss.

Our aura is the crucible of all the energetic processes of our life. Everything we ever experience comes through our energy field before it reaches the physical, denser part of us. We are energetic beings, growing and changing every day, living within a physical body, but occupying an energetic space that is greater than our physical form. Our energy field expands and contracts according to the power within it and changes shape when we sleep. It is the first advertisement of our life for those with the eyes to see it and those with the sensitivity to feel it, demonstrating in color and shape the nature of the person that is to be found within. The aura is our amazing coat of many colors.

When our energy field interacts with that of another there is always an energy exchange that takes place between us. This can be a very minor matter, like brushing shoulders with a stranger, or it can be of such intensity that it changes our life from that moment forward.

How to See the Energy Field

To practice switching on your energy vision so you can begin to see into the realms of the human aura and the energy worlds, ask someone to sit against a pale background in very subdued lighting. Practice letting your gaze gently rest on the center of their forehead, in the region that is known as the third eye. Now let your eyes relax. Do not focus or strain. Let your eyes take on a soft, unfocused look that gazes into forever—through the wall, through the street, through the town and all the way off the planet into infinity. After a while you will likely see a white glow start to form up closely around your partner's head. You may blink, refocus and it may disappear. Don't worry, just let your eyes relax and try again. This kind of vision works not through strain and effort but by relaxing the eyes. Again the white glow will return and this time you may be able to see it for longer. The way to build up the aura-seeing muscles in your eyes is through many little efforts.

The white glow will tell you much about the energy levels of the person that you are with. If it is thin, wan and close to their head, it tells you that their energy levels are low. If the white glow is about four inches thick and has a bright luminescence from within, this tells you their energy level and level of essence vitality is high. This band of energy is called "the etheric" and in some circles the ability to see this level of energy is called "etheric vision." As you keep practicing, you may start to see the bands of energy that lie beyond the etheric. It is here that you start to see traces of color as your auric vision starts to switch on.

Another way to practice your energy vision is to place a flower against a pale background in subdued lighting and by using the long-distance look described previously, you can start to see the colors of energy that surround the flower. You will find that different types of flower have different energy colors that surround them. Flowers of the same species, however, share the same colors. Over time you will find that every living thing has a color signature in the worlds of energy. Whereas the colors of plants and animals are fixed, the colors in the human energy field regularly change according to what we think, feel and do. Anger has a color, so does care and so does love. We will look at these colors in more depth later.

Another way to practice energetic vision is by seeing the energy lines that radiate from your fingers. We all have rays of energy that stream out from our fingers and thumbs. These rays can be very long and powerful or quite small and weak. It all depends upon what is happening in our energy field at the time. When someone is doing energy healing, they often have very long and powerful rays of power coming from their fingers. When someone is in love, there is also an increase in the power that is transmitted through their energy system. This results in an enhanced glow in the whole energy field and additional power being released through their hands. There are even occasions when you may be able to see different colors of energy coming from the different fingers.

The way to see the power coming from your hands is, if you are indoors, to turn off all the lights and hold both hands straight out in front of you at eye level.

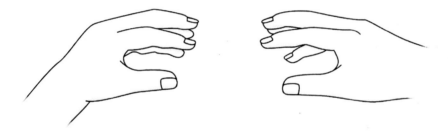

Shape your hands as if you were holding a tennis ball or baseball in each hand. Keep holding your hands out in front of you and then lower your hands down to approximately the level of your solar plexus, turning them to face each other as you do so. Position your hands so that they are about an inch apart, with the thumb of the right hand facing the thumb of the left and so on for each of your fingers. Now, direct your gaze to the one-inch gap between your fingers and let your eyes gently become unfocused. This time let your gaze softly go through the floor, through the planet and out the other side as you gaze into infinity.

Now, very slowly and easily, draw your hands approximately two feet apart, then gradually bring them back together again until they are about one inch apart, as if you were playing an invisible accordion. Keep gazing long-distance through the one-inch space where you began while your hands do this. By repeatedly bringing the fingers and thumbs close together and then drawing them away from each other, back and forth, you increase the power of the energy attraction between the hands, causing the rays of power to increase. As you do this, your long-distance look will cause the power from your eyes to increase and, after a while, you will start to see the streams of energy flowing from your fingers.

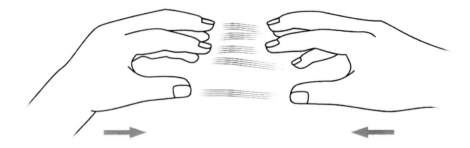

This same practice also causes an increased sensitivity in the nerve endings in the hands, often making it possible to feel an increase in power as the hands draw closer together and a diminishment as they draw apart. This means that by using this technique you are able to not only see into the human energy field but also to feel it at the same time.

Once you have mastered these simple techniques you can practice your energetic vision and gradually increase its power and effectiveness.

Energetic Colors

By practicing, it may not be long before you start to see the beginnings of colors in the human energy field as well as the glow of the etheric. Once you start to see the auric field, then you are on the journey of being able to connect different colors with different energy states.

Just as flowers and animals always have particular colors they radiate, so particular energy states in the human energy field are always associated with certain colors. The color red sends a different message and contains a different energy than the color green or the color purple. Each color offers us a clue to the energies that are flowing through a person. Each of us lives within our own coat of many colors that, like the skin of the chameleon, can change at a moment's notice. When you begin to read these colors, they can reveal to you the energy states of the person that you are with or the energy states of a group of people. You can even use this energy vision to see the energy fields and colors associated with particular places.

When a person is very angry, their energy field literally can go "red with rage." Someone's face really can turn "green with envy" and cowards can develop "a yellow streak" up their spine or become "yellow bellies." Yellow is the prime color of the emotion, which often radiates from the solar plexus and the throat. It can streak up the spine and across the stomach in highly emotionally-charged situations.

The Color of Emotion

Yellow, being the major color of the emotions, is almost always present in an exchange of energetic love and is one of the significant colors and qualities that manifests in an energy dating process. The idea of wining and dining your date is to build a yellow platform in the relationship field between you. This yellow glow can often become tinged with green, which is the color that accompanies high-level sexual energy. Two features that are connected to yellow and traditionally appear during a romantic date are candles, that offer a warm, yellow glow and music that is designed to appeal to the emotions. Traditionally, this music is most often played by violins, the only musical instrument that is held under the chin and played directly out from the area of the throat.

Imagine being on an energy date, calling for music, and a musician appears with a large drum and proceeds to produce a marching rhythm! Percussion instruments mostly produce different tones of red and although this may be excellent to keep time for a marching army, it would not be helpful on an energy date. The red energies of the drum power the blood, the stomach and the pulse of the heartbeat rather than move our center of gravity into our emotional and sexual energies. This example demonstrates how the science of matching music to the different qualities of the human energy field and the relationship field is a worthwhile study in itself. The music a person likes reveals the nature of energies they like to connect to in the energy worlds and music is a great tool for detecting the nature of places and people.

The throat is a major seat of human emotion and is one of the places you will see the color yellow radiate in strength. This explains why it is that when we get emotional we often develop a "lump" in our throat. The concentrate of yellow force causes us to make a swallowing action as we try to clear our throat. Children sometimes hold a buttercup under the throat of a friend to see if they are in love. According to traditional beliefs, if a yellow glow is seen, then the person is in love. What is interesting here is once again the association between love, the color yellow, the throat and the emotions.

Unless you deliberately want to restrict the emotional content in your energy field, a good energy tip for men is to loosen or remove your tie when dating. Many modern customs first began in the worlds of energy. Originally ties were made of silk, which is an insulator of energies. Ties became popularized in Victorian England and accompanied the growth of the Industrial Revolution. The original idea of the tie was to cause a separation between the heart and the head and to reduce the influence of the emotions, thereby facilitating the ability to make unemotional decisions in the workplace. The tie was literally designed to "put a knot in it" to prevent the release of emotional energy and reduce its influence in the energy field. The tie is an anti-emotion device for hard-headed business people who cannot afford to go soft when seeking to attain maximum profit.

If you can imagine the businessman's prayer when putting on his tie in the morning, it would go something like, "I, as General Sales Manager of the Widget Corporation, will not let my emotions, interfere with my business practices, today." This businessman's prayer would reflect the original purpose of the tie. Ties have retained their place in the corporate world, even though their original energetic purpose has been forgotten.

Feeling the Energy Field

Alongside auric vision, another vital technique to practice is the sense of energetic touch. By learning how to sensitize ourselves more thoroughly to the levels of energy that exist in other people's energy fields and in the places where we go, we can enhance all our energy dating experiences. Energetic touch uses the nerve endings in our hands and arms to feel the nature of force that is being radiated from another person's energy field. To be able to do this, the first thing is to learn how to sensitize your hands to more easily register the energy fields of people and places.

Begin sensitizing your hands by drawing them together and apart as described on pages 63 and 64 in "How to See the Energy Field." Keep doing this exercise in repetition. This practice causes a tingling sensation in the nerves of the hands and it is the awakened nerve endings that give us our energy readings on people, places and things. We soon discover when we learn to feel force fields and energy states with our hands that there are subtle differences between these energies. The force fields of states such as red, hot rage produce a heated, prickly energy, while the energy wavelengths of peace and patience are smoother and cooler.

Some energies are hot, gluey and uncomfortable to be with. Others are tingly, cool and pleasant to be with. Others yet again are cool on the outside, but produce internal warmth. There are many different energy properties to be encountered that cause different energetic responses in our hands and also in our bodies. When we blush or get hot in the face, we are experiencing another energy symptom, just as we do when we get butterflies in the stomach or experience heat around the back of the neck or ears. These are all reactions to energetic signals. Part of the reason for sensitizing ourselves is to become more conscious of what these signals mean and also to become more aware of other more subtle signals we might register. We also need to take account in this practice of our own energetic state. If we are running particularly hot one day in our energy field and we encounter heat in another, we will not register such a stark difference as when we are running cooler and encounter the same level of heat. This is why I insist that in their training EnergyWorlds Practitioners spend a good deal of time sensitizing themselves to the different sensations caused in their energy field according to what is moving in their life on different days. It is very helpful in this study to start with the advice from Socrates, "Know thyself." When you have a good awareness and sensitivity to your own ongoing energetic state, it helps enormously in being able to have accurate perception and assessment of what is happening in the energy fields of others and in mutual relationship fields.

Special Note: If you are interested in finding out more about the training involved in becoming a certified EnergyWorlds Practitioner, please refer to the Resource section at the back of this book.

Sensing the Human Energy Field

Now you have learned how to energetically charge your hands, you can also start to practice sensing the human energy field. "Aura sensing" as this is also called, is using your hands to feel the cortex or edge of your partner's energy field. To do this most effectively it is best to clean, prepare and charge the atmosphere of the place where you are going to do this, unless you are able to practice outdoors in nature, which is best of all. How to clean, charge and prepare an atmosphere is shown in Chapter, 6 Energize Your Space.

Once you have cleaned and charged the atmosphere, you can then ask your partner to sit down and, using your negative hand extended (left hand for the man and right hand for the woman), slowly move towards them from about four feet away. It is best during this process to have your sleeves rolled up, not to wear any metallic jewelry and to remove your watch. Keep your fingers together with your thumb lightly tucked in toward your palm and cup your hands slightly to help your nerve endings feel the frequency of what is present in the energy worlds.

Imagine you are going to hold water in your hands. In many ancient cultures a wavy, water-like symbol was used to represent the energies of the unseen worlds, because these energy signals travel in a wave formation and act in a fluidic way. This wavy symbol can be seen in the zodiac sign for Aquarius which, although known today as the water bearer, is actually the power carrier. Aquarius is an air sign, not a water sign and the Aquarian symbol represents ambrosia, the potent energetic frequencies of the higher energy worlds originally only available to the gods in Greek mythology, until Ganymede released it into the energy worlds of the human race and made it available to all.

As you approach the edge of your partner's aura, you will be able to detect an energy change usually about thirty-two inches away from the body. This is the edge or cortex of their aura, sometimes called the auric sheath. Once you have found the edge of their energy field, you can give it an "evening out" by making small, circular massaging movements with your hand—a little like waxing a car. This energy massage is very enjoyable and is the beginning of energy healing. Doing this regularly is very enhancing to the energy field of the recipient and can remove many of the lower forces that can get stuck inside the energy field during the day. We will look at this in more depth in Chapter 14, Enhanced Energy Dating where we discuss how this technology can be used to enhance your relationship fields.

Once you have learned to use your hands in this way to feel the energy fields of others, you can apply this same method to feel the energetic fields of all living things because everything that lives has a field of emanation that surrounds it. You will be able to check the different sensations you receive in your hands from different trees, flowers and animals, as well as from different people. It makes for a new window onto the world as well as increasing the versatility and range of your energy dating techniques.

The Energetic Edge

The more you can see, feel and know in the realms of force and power, the more you can work to the best energy advantage of all concerned, including yourself. So do not worry that with these techniques you will have some kind of unfair advantage. Yes, you will have an energetic edge, but that is to the best benefit of all concerned, including you. It might help you quickly realize that the energy date you are engaging with is not going to work. By enabling you to bring the experience to a swift close it allows both you and your energy date to move on and not take up time in a not-so-productive relationship.

When you have the energetic edge you can enhance all your dating experiences. It is not so you can win, or in some way cause the other person to lose; it is so that all your relationships can be enhanced, both for your benefit and your partner's. The better the energy date, the greater the generation of energetic love, which is good for the energy worlds of us all.

How do you know if what you are saying is being energetically well received? When you have the energetic edge, you can tell because, for example, if you feel your face and hands become heated and a growing sense of discomfort as you speak, you will know that the energies you are projecting are not finding a good home. Although your date may appear to be listening, he or she will either bored or antagonistic to what you are saying. Obvious physical signs such as crossing the legs and arms, fidgeting, looking away or otherwise withdrawing often confirm this. These physical signals are symptomatic of what is happening in their energy field.

As you practice building your energetic edge by training yourself in the realms of awareness and sensitivity to the energy worlds, you are growing a valuable and permanent skill. So much of what we want to say remains unspoken but is to be found in our body language, our gestures and in the tone of our voice. Practicing reading the unspoken energies in people is a very powerful dating technique and well worth the investment of your time. Once you begin to see and feel the energy realms of the human aura, it is a skill that you will be able to employ for the rest of your life.

Transmitting and Receiving Forces

To be a good energy date, a crucial art to practice is that of energetically listening. Listening does not mean waiting for your chance to talk. It means actually going quiet inside so that you can energetically receive the other person. In this context it is interesting that when we shapeshift the word "listen," it forms the word "silent," which is the best inner energy state with which to receive another person's energies.

Real energy listening means being truly interested in what the other person is saying and in the significant fact of their life. When you go energetically quiet in yourself and genuinely listen to another, then the energies that they transmit to you from their energy field actually transfer and are received into yours. Your polarity moves from the positive, transmitting polarity, to the negative, receiving polarity. In this context positive and negative do not mean good or bad, but inclined to transmit and inclined to receive respectively.

Even when a person appears to be listening, if their energy polarity is in transmissive mode, then the energetic signals their date sends towards them will bounce off their energy field marked "return to sender." Their date will likely feel this and register that he or she is with someone who is interested primarily in themselves. It is not a good start for a successful energy date and certainly does not help to build a strong relationship field.

Deep inside all of us is the wish to be heard and received. When you genuinely listen and quieten your internal noise, your date will feel the energies they are transmitting leaving them and transferring into you. They will feel that you are sincerely interested in them and in their life, which you will have to be to cause this state, and a greater flow between both of you can begin. A powerful relationship field can then begin to form. It is vital, therefore, to still your internal noise and chatter. Do not think about work, or the bills you need to pay, or your next appointment. Listen carefully to the words being spoken and try to hear the dynamics behind the words themselves and feel the energies which they contain. This is a great key to being a good listener.

Many people pay large sums of money to go to therapy so someone will listen to them and draw away the energies of their more unfortunate experiences. It is also an ingredient in the original idea of making confession within the Catholic Church. Confession is meant to be the energetic transfer of what is disturbing a person into the energy fields of another person, who has been specially trained to handle such disturbing energies and is able to rid themselves of them. If they cannot do so, then they build an increasing aggregate of these disturbing energies in their own energy field, with potentially devastating effects. If the training has not been thorough, then the therapist or priest becomes the container of an energetic concentrate of disturbing powers passed on to them from possibly hundreds, if not thousands, of people.

Thankfully, for the purposes of energy dating you are not in training to professionally handle the disturbed energy patterns of others, but are in training to be a good receiver and transmitter of energies with a significant other. This will of course serve you very well not only in energy dating but also in every other field of your life.

The Interplay

There are two fundamental states in the energy dating process: transmissive and receptive. The interplay between these two states gives rise to a third state of togetherness which aggregates between two people over time and becomes their relationship field. It is the sense and feeling caused by the aggregate of the interplay between people that determines whether or not they look forward to, or even want to, meet each other again.

If we feel that the energy process between us and another person has been detrimental to our energy state and our sense of self, that we have wasted our time and have been given back less energy than we had put in, then we may opt to bring the experience to a close and move on. If we feel energetically uplifted, invigorated and more energetically alive from our meeting, then we are likely to opt for another date.

Successful energy dating is a dance in which the polarities regularly switch. It may begin with you making an energy transmission, in which case you would want to be energetically received by the person you are dealing with. Then the polarity switches and the other person transmits and you move into receiving mode. The more you are able to become acquainted with the different feelings of the two polarities in yourself and learn how to deepen them, the more successful at energy dating you will become.

Enhancing the Energy Flow

For maximum energy flow between you and your date, the most potent position of all is standing or sitting face to face, because this way all the energy systems are lined up to each other and you can both look directly into each other's eyes. If this is not possible or desirable as, for example, when going for a walk or sitting in a theater, the next most conductive posture is for the man to walk or sit on the woman's left-hand side. This way there is a positive-to-positive energy connection via the hands, whether or not they are physically touching. The least conductive position is with the man on the woman's right hand side. There may be times when this is deliberately applied, such as after a quarrel when both parties' energy systems have become heated and each partner wants to "cool off."

Although this information may perhaps be new to you, there are systems within you that already have this knowledge and respond to it. There may have been times in your life when you were walking with someone and instinctively felt you were walking on the wrong side of them and felt compelled to switch sides, even if it meant making quite a maneuver to do so. When you did this you were responding to an energetic prompting from your instinct, which already has this knowledge and continuously tries to prompt you to act in the most energy effective way. You wanted to be "on their good side" as the folk wisdom tells us..

Sleeping Partners

Something vitally important to know about sleep is that this is the time in our lives when our energy systems receive their major charge and replenishment. Indeed, this is the prime purpose and function of sleep, which is the cycle of recharge in our energetic processes. When we slumber, our energy fields move from a transmitting, expressive polarity into a negative, receiving polarity. During this cycle of recharge our energy systems, which have become run-down and depleted by the processes of the day, receive a fresh energy charge. This is why we go to bed at night tired out and wake up in the morning recharged and ready for another day.

When we practice looking at the human energy field, we soon discover that by the time we are ready for sleep, the etheric band of the aura has shrunk in close to the body, reflecting a low energy state. In the morning when we awaken, we find that it has expanded and is once again thick and bright with energy. Having "slept tight" we are now indeed "wide awake" and ready for another day.

When we sleep alongside another person, there is a great deal of energy exchange which takes place between the two energy fields. We are actually sleeping inside the mutual relationship field caused between us. This is why traditionally a king and queen would have their own separate sleeping chambers so that in the re-charging process their energies would not become confused.

If there are times when you instinctively feel you want to sleep alone, this does not mean there is something wrong with your relationship. It means your inner energy systems need some time in which they are able to recharge without being in the direct presence of someone else's energy field and what that field contains. It is perfectly all right to be in a relationship with someone, even for many years, and to sleep alone from time to time. This is particularly true in times of stress within the relationship because by sleeping inside your own energy field and not directly inside your partner's it gives your mind, brain and inner energy systems a chance to sift through the issues that are up front in you, without adding the energies of your partner and their issues so directly into the mix.

Understanding about the polarities in your hands also influences the decision as to which side of the bed to sleep on if you and your date decide to spend the night together. Sleeping positive-to-positive causes maximum energy transference during the night, while sleeping negative-to-negative reduces the amount of energy transference.

Sleeping Tips

When you sleep, the quality of the energy charge you receive is a vital factor in determining your energy levels. Therefore, it is best to keep your energy field as clear as possible from any electro-magnetic fields that are not natural to you. If you have an electric alarm clock, keep it out of your energy field, switch off the electric blanket, do not go to sleep with the television on and if possible, keep your bed against an inner wall in your apartment. Energy fields can go through walls and if you sleep against a wall that joins someone else's apartment, you may actually be sleeping directly within their energy field without knowing it, because there could be another bed just on the other side of the wall. If this is the case, then you may not be sleeping with that person physically, but because your energy fields are joined together at night, you are sleeping with them energetically! This can cause you to experience dreams that are not yours, as your energy field receives images, powers and forces from theirs. We will look more at how to prepare your sleeping area in the next chapter, Energize Your Space.

The Look of Love

The energy phenomenon known as love at first sight describes an event where there is transference of such power between the force fields of two people that it produces an instant energy connection and passionate knowing between them. It usually begins with a look in the eye, but sometimes it can be so powerful that even this is not necessary.

Leopold Infeld, a professor of physics, was at a conference in the United States and needed to go to a particular office. When he entered the room he found himself standing in the energy field of a woman who was working there at the time. She had her back to him and was going through some files. He described how upon seeing her, even though he could not see her face, he had an instant knowing that this was the woman he was going to marry. She, on her part, described how she felt something change in the atmosphere behind her and that she knew something significant had happened in her life, though she did not yet know what. He introduced himself and they were indeed married a few months later and remained together until his death in 1968. Being a physicist he could use his knowledge of quantum and particle physics to cast light on what had happened to him and the energy waves that had passed between himself and the as-yet unknown lady. To someone with a different background it would simply be described as love at first sight.

I had a similar energetic experience when I first met his daughter, Joanna Infeld. I was with a group of friends that both of us knew and Joanna offered to drive us home. We had not spoken much that night and had only recently met. As I got out of the car and leaned in to say goodnight and thank her for the ride, our eyes met and something tangibly traveled across the space between us. I perceived a powerful glow and received an instant inner knowing that a powerful passion had passed. It was strong enough to cause me to change all my pre-set plans and spontaneously appear on her doorstep the very next day, bearing gifts. We have been on an energy dating journey together now for over thirty years and have, during this time, continued to construct our mutual relationship field on an hour by hour basis.

Dating Secrets of the Ancients

The Ancients had deep and powerful understandings about the transference of energies between men and women and how to construct empowered relationship fields. They integrated these understandings into their artwork, both for their own benefit and also so these understandings could be carried forward into the future. Many Egyptian statues and paintings demonstrate how the transference of forces works between the genders by depicting special hand positions, colors and symbols.

In ancient times we find that much of the platform for living was based on viewing human life energy worlds first, a view that is again growing in power and popularity today. Many of these understandings are now re-surfacing in the West under names such as Tai Chi, Reiki, Qi Gong, Feng Shui, therapeutic touch and dowsing. All of these energetic modalities are based in the idea that life begins energies first and that by changing the energy field of a person or place, we also change his, her or its material reality and possibility.

One of the greatest energy transference processes is the act of sex. Particularly in India, records are to be found from long ago of intricate methods of working with these sexual energies. In the West we mostly refer to these fragments of understanding by the name tantric or sacred sex. At the core of these understandings is the fact that the physical act of sex explored in, for example, the *Kama Sutra*, is a physical confirmation of the powerful exchange of energies that takes place as the great masculine and feminine principles find each other through the gateway of individual human beings.

The Ancients knew that the act of sex could connect people to very powerful energies that could then be released into the ecology in which it took place. This idea is at the root of all so-called sexual magic and magical practices. It is why the act of sex is such a focal point in modern witchcraft. It is all about the energies that are released and not about the act itself. By contrast, the practice of celibacy seeks to use the reverse technique and, by the denial of sex, to increase the energetic power of the individual by transforming sexual energy into higher illumination. Refraining from sex, however, is no guarantee of spiritual development. Indeed, if the individual becomes sexually frustrated, it is more likely to impede than help their spirituality.

One of the colors that the Ancients often related to sexual activity is green. The particular shades of green vary according to the level and power of sexual energy being released. Major radiation points for the green sexual force in the energy field are the eyes, sexual organs and hips. The green color of sexuality often centers on the hips, though it can also appear in other parts of the energy field. It is not by chance that the hippies, with their philosophy of free love and sexual revolution, were indeed called "the hippies." At moments of high sexual transference, the whole of the energy field can go entirely green. Belly dancing was designed to cause the release and transference of concentrated green frequency from the hips of the dancer to the energy field of the audience. In ancient times when a sheikh may have had a hundred wives or more in a harem, the ability to release this powerful green aphrodisiac would have been particularly important!

When both the yellow of emotional energy and the green of sexual energy are powerfully and visibly present in the aura at the same time, an energy date is likely to be particularly powerful.

The Magic of Sexual Exchange

There is far more to sex than a physical act. The physical coming together of the rod and the cup are symbolic of an even more powerful energetic fact. In the act of sex the energy record in the aura of the woman and the energy record in the aura of the man exchange at depth. Consensual sex is one of the greatest energy exchanges possible, and when a couple make love they carry a growing content of each other in their aura.

In the act of sex the original forces of yin and yang can exchange in great power and at times even find temporary completion within the human being. It is this sense of completion that gives us the inner feeling of sexual fulfillment and satisfaction. It can be of such an energetic potency that it overwhelms the conscious mind, giving respite from daily worries and pre-occupations, taking us to a different level of consciousness. This is why the moment of orgasm, in which the two energies move towards their fullest energetic blending and coming together, the French call *la petite mort* or "the little death."

It is this sense of connection to powers bigger than ourselves that also explains why people have the sense of being swept away or swept off their feet by the power of love—by a power that is bigger than they are. It is also why people become addicted to love, which can often be more accurately described as addicted to sex. Like a powerful energetic drug it connects them to forces and energies that they cannot access in their usual day-to-day state. This is also why in the ancient worlds ritual sex on the altar of the gods, for example the moon god Sin in Babylon, was a regular ingredient of religious practice and celebration.

When couples engage in sex, tremendous sexual energies are released throughout their bodies and souls. These energies contain a greater or lesser power and illumination according to the level of the energy worlds that the participants connect to during their love-making. During this time together major energies are also released into their energy fields which can cause both their auric vision and auric sense of touch to become heightened. It is not unusual for someone who has been trained in the ways of energetic vision to see intense waves of energetic color during sex. These waves of color vary in intensity and shade according to the nature of energy that is being transmitted and received. Even energetic faces can be perceived on the face of your partner, as we will discuss in more detail in Chapter 14, Enhanced Energy Dating.

As you practice your energetic vision and touch, there are many new experiences for you to encounter in the realms of energy dating and sexual transference. To see and feel the energy fields of your partner is every bit as natural and as real as to see and feel your partner's physical presence. As you enter into these realms of the unseen worlds of energy you are entering a whole new realm of possible experience which you will be able to explore throughout the rest of your life.

Sexual Transference

In addition to the raw, elemental powers that can be unleashed through both the man and woman in the act of sex, there is also a tremendous transference of energetic content between all levels of the energy fields of both individuals involved.

The energies involved in the sexual act, and particularly within the powerful energy release of the orgasm, become a kind of energetic carrier wave along which other energies of the person, where they have been and what they have done in their life, flow and transfer from one energy field to another. This is why sometimes after sex a person may feel uplifted and energized as they have received energies that are enhancing to them, while sex at another time or with another person may cause them to feel unlike themselves and may even cause a sensation of being in some way energetically dirty. This is not based in what has transferred physically but what has transferred in the realms of energy.

When you have sex with your partner you open yourself to what is lodged in their energy field. There is a tremendous transference of their life history into yours. This is why it often happens that after making love, couples find themselves sharing intimate experiences and personal secrets. There has been a tremendous energy transference and now they seek the words and understandings to put with the energies they have exchanged.

To know and understand these matters makes a profound difference in approaching energy dating as, when dating another, it is like two universes meeting whose energies and forces are organized differently. When sexual exchange occurs, the level of transference between these two universes magnifies. When we have sex with another person it can change both our destiny, and theirs.

Chapter Six
Energize Your Space

There are definite steps we can take to increase the level and quality of the energy fields in our life. We can, for example, do this by enhancing the energies we attract to the spaces where we live and spend much of our time and, by so doing, increase the level and quality of energies we bring to any potential relationship, firstly with ourselves and then with others.

To better understand the kind of person we are and the energies we attract, we need look no further than the space we live in. This offers us an instant energy portrait of ourselves and reveals many of the connections we like to keep close by. Having this awareness helps locate where to begin as we seek to better understand the energy field we have constructed around us through our life thus far, build our personal power and enhance our energy dating possibilities.

In the same way we can study our home energy portrait to reveal much about our own nature, we can employ these exact principles and techniques to understand more deeply the nature of the people with whom we are dealing, what makes up their energy portraits and whether we want to bring them closer to our life and invest our time and energy into building a mutual relationship field with them.

Energy Homes

What is the difference between a house and a home? A house has four walls, a roof, floor, heating, lighting and other utilities which support our life. A home is a place where we have built an energy field that supports our life and it contains the unique blend of energies we have assembled therein because they energetically feed our body, mind and soul. The physical objects we arrange around ourselves in the place where we live are energetic radio sets tuned into the frequency of particular powers and people.

Every physical object we have in our personal space is tuned to an energy frequency and it is one we reinforce and power in ourselves every time we look at the object, feel it, think about it or are in its presence. It does not matter whether we call it over to ourselves consciously or not. Our semiconscious remembers where it came from, the reason why we bought it or accepted it as a gift, when we bought it, who gave it to us and what was our energetic feeling when we brought it into our space on the day that we did. These objects become anchors within the field that we nurture within our home.

The energies we have collected around us and we are connected to are also reflected in the space where we work, the contents of our car, and the purse, wallet, case or knapsack we carry. These energies are also in the music we listen to, the places we like to go, the books we read, the movies we watch and the way we decorate our bedroom. All of these offer us energetic food from the energy worlds that can nourish our soul and feed us with signals we draw energetic support and sustenance from. Sometimes, however, we might inadvertently bring into our domain objects that are not nourishing at all, but, for example, remind us of someone whom we did not like but who gave us a wedding present we feel obliged to keep.

Even our friends are people whose energy fields we like to feed from and who enjoy feeding from ours. If we want to know what we are like, we need only to pause and consider what our friends are like. In part, we are like them and they are like us. We are like energetic spiders, spinning our energy webs and drawing energetic food from wherever we make our points of connection.

Have you noticed how, when the going gets tough, the tough go home? This is because home is usually the place where we build the prime, sustaining energy field for our life. It is the place where we paint the walls in colors that feed our soul and where we have mementos that remind us of our past successes, souvenirs of places that we have enjoyed visiting and music that makes us feel good even after a bad day. All of these are ways of reinforcing our sustaining and supportive energies.

The key difference between a house and a home, therefore, is in the realms of energy. A house is a potential home. It offers us shelter within the walls, ceiling and protection it provides. What turns a house into a home are the energies of the people who occupy it and radiate their energies and energetic connections into it. A home is, therefore, an anchorage for the energies that support our life. Home is a place where we lodge our energies and where we turn to in order to seek comfort and be recharged.

Have you ever met a person who paints their home the colors they like the least or who collects mementos of their worst days? "Oh yes, that was from the day I broke my leg and that was from the day the love of my life left me and over there is the souvenir from the day my favorite pet died." Have you ever met a person who displays souvenirs of the most distressing places they have visited, while they play the music that irritates them the most? In teaching thousands of classes and workshops about energy fields, neither have I.

Every person I have ever met has a prepared space, however small, in which they create their personal radio set to the influences, powers and forces they find are most supportive to their life. These include family photographs, mission statements, pictures of favorite musicians and actors, diplomas and trophies, favorite music and books, whatever confirms the person in what they feel to be the intention and purpose of their life and causes them to feel their life is confirmed, supported, upheld and wanted.

These can range from objects, sayings and music that connect with very high energy frequencies to objects, films and music that connect to very destructive energies. It all depends upon what the person's energy field is tuned into and what they think of as their "at home" energies. A person who is into the Goth lifestyle and dresses in black, wears black nail polish and has vampire pictures on their walls has a very different idea of home than the person who follows Martha Stewart and seeks to make their house into a model home for Christmas. There are as many personal energy fields, and the energetic eco-systems which they create, as there are people on the planet, as we will explore thoroughly in Chapter 7, Energy Mapping.

Talismans

Many people also have personal radio sets or talismans which, for example, connect them to the energies of their particular religious faith. The Christian cross, the Jewish Seal of Solomon, the crescent symbol of Islam and the shrines of Shinto are all examples of using physical tokens to attract and anchor particular religious energies.

Other examples are to be found with people who entirely dress themselves in the regalia of their chosen religion and become themselves a talisman to anchor those forces as the prime commitment in their life. In so doing, they make a statement that they are not open to energies outside of what these preset religious frequencies allow. The saffron robes of the Buddhist monk, the clerical collar of the priest, the bright red robes of the cardinal and the habit of the nun make clear energy statements both to themselves and to others about their priorities. They also make a clear statement in the energy worlds that they wish to anchor the powers and forces associated with their particular religion and no other.

People also make specific actions at preset times in an attempt to cause themselves to become energy homes for particular forces and powers. Muslims bowing five times a day in the direction of Mecca are an example of this. All religious activity is rooted in the endeavor to attract particular energies and forces that live in the energy worlds of the planet into the energy field, mind and heart of the individual, so they can become permanent residents therein. This is obviously very determining in respect of the partners in passion such people are prepared to build mutual relationship fields with.

World religions are particularly fascinating when we view what they are from the standpoint of the energy worlds and the energetic frequencies they are attempting to connect to. All religions, rituals, beliefs, ceremonies and religious rituals originate from the worlds of energy and we can trace all their practices and regalia back into these worlds, when we know how. When energy dating, the religious energies that each partner subscribes to (or not) are very determining in whether a relationship is possible at all, as they can become one of the prime settings of the frequencies that people's energy fields are tuned into.

It is rare indeed that a fundamentalist Muslim would fall in love with a fundamentalist Christian and each become tolerant of the other's ways. This example illustrates the way in which we have two prime overlays in our energy field. The first is set by the date, place and time in which we are born and the genetic inheritance we receive. This determines, for example, if we are born a boy or a girl, an Aquarius or a Leo. The second is set by the energetic belief system into which we are born. Few people choose to become Muslim, Christian or Jew. The majority of believers are born into their faith and are subsequently branded by the energies and practices of their parents, teachers and preachers between the ages of one and eleven. It is very hard to overprint and reset these energy settings once they have been established in our youth.

Making Radio Sets

Most of us do not live in the entirely preset and prescribed way of the nun and the monk. Our homes include many different talismanic radio sets to many different kinds of energy, some of which may be recognized as belonging with an established organized religion and many of which will not. Particularly in this time of secularity and globalization we may have in our home items drawn from all over the world with the only connective thread or tissue between them being that they are things that we like, in other words, things that supply us with some kind of energetic food.

Imagine if you were to die today and someone had to come to your home to deal with all your possessions. What would they learn about you and what you are like? It is very unlikely that all your belongings would remain together once you were gone as the presence of your force field was the binding influence that kept it all together in one place. After your passing your belongings will almost certainly go to different destinations. It is likely that no-one loves you so much that they will declare the rest of their life to be committed to being the living museum of your material and energetic stuff.

Your energy environment will tell you much about yourself, not only by what is in the ecology, but also the manner in which it is ordered. Here we reveal the inner patterns of our mind, brains and emotions. If your drawers, closets and cupboards are higgledy-piggledy with stuff that you are not aware is even there, so are your mind and emotions. Everything that is in our life, that is within our stewardship, gives us back to ourselves an exact reading of what we are like. To understand our nature we can learn much from the domain that is in our "charge." This word is particularly accurate, as we energetically charge up and receive a charge from everything we come into contact with. When we regularly go through our belongings and ensure they have a current reason for being in our life, we keep the energetic field around us fresh, current and well charged. When we allow a build up of material possessions that we no longer have a current reason for owning, this is a clear indication that our energies have also become stagnant in our mind and emotions.

Energy Partners

In our home there may also be a partner who nourishes and feeds our soul with the energies they generate. In a home where two people have chosen to live together this is a major feature that can offer enormous enhancement to both lives or, conversely, act in major detriment to their life's energies. There is no more powerful energy choice in our life than the person we choose to partner with, bring into our energy field every day of our life and construct a core relationship field with. As long as we live with our partner, their choices directly energetically affect us and our choices affect them.

Energizing Your Home

Our energy dating possibilities entirely depend upon the energies we connect to on a daily basis. The most important home of all is our inner space, the inner temple of our heart, mind, emotions and our personal energy field. As this is often a place we may find too intangible to start into directly, what I recommend is to first tackle the apartment, house or room where you live and work from there back inside to your inner temple. In the Western world we are more used to working with the outer space that surrounds us and from there working inwards, rather than trying to engage directly with your own inner space. An excellent place to begin is by re-energizing your home ecology, as this is usually where you spend the majority of your time, including both waking and sleeping. The techniques that are offered in this chapter for energizing your space are techniques that work from the outside in, having made the decision to give them a try, which you make from the inside out.

There are techniques in the world that begin from the inside out, such as chanting and meditation, for example, as used in some of the spiritual practices of Tibet and the ancient mystery schools. However, starting your energetic shift from the outside in is every bit as valid and is often more comfortable and easier to get to for a person raised in the traditions of the West. In addition, when we have cleared the energetic pathways and processes in our outer life, it is easier to have access to the pathways and processes of our inner life.

Energy Clearing

The process of energizing our home begins with making space for new energies and improving the flow of existing energies. It works by clearing out old and unwanted energies that are simply there because they have been there so long they have become familiar and we no longer even think about them. It is amazing how much of our life's energy we can block and lock away in things that are there for no remembered or known reason. To improve our energy dating potential we need to improve the levels of energy that are available to us in the present. If our energies are locked up in the past, it reduces our energy flow and our current energy dating possibility.

In the same way that when we do not clean physically, dust bunnies accumulate and things become dirty and unattractive to be with, so it is in the worlds of energy. When the reasons for things we possess are not thought about and energetically refreshed, energies surrounding them get stuck. These energies then gather to themselves other stale energies. By analogy, on a city street, what begins as one piece of trash that is not attended to and is left outside a building is joined by others until it becomes a trash dump for the local neighborhood. It is a dramatic example, but this is exactly how it works in the energy realms.

A law of energy is that like calls to like and if the space where you live is energetically unkempt and unattended, the residual energetic fug of yesterday becomes joined by that of today and after several months the place will contain a great deal of stuck, stagnant or static energy. When we use our energy vision, we can actually see this static or stuck energy as a murky red or murky orange color that gathers around electrical appliances such as televisions and little-used areas of the home such as in the corners, around the back of sofas or under tables and other furniture.

The idea of energetic clearing and cleaning is to use very specific energy clearing techniques to break up these low level energy fields and to get a good current of energy flow on the go again. Causing the energies in our ecology to become faster moving, fresh and current will in turn help the forces and powers in our personal energy field to move more vibrantly, increasing the current and passion in our life. This helps us become a much more attractive proposition in the realms of energy dating.

Before we get to the specific program for energy clearing, however, we need to focus on the physical aspect of the place where we live. What is in there and why?

Clearing Energetic Clutter

Everything within our home that is not there for a fresh and current reason acts as an energy blockage that gathers stale energy to itself and impedes our energy flow. Our outer life reflects the state of our inner life. To have a powerful flow of energies available to us so we can have energy available for greater passion, we need to clear these arrested or stuck energies.

To thoroughly energetically clear the place where we live may take some time, depending upon how long we have lived there and how much stuff we have accumulated; however, it is easy to make a start. The place to begin this process is the place where we spend more time than any other. This is the area where we sleep. As sleep is the prime energy recharging process in our life, the ecology within which we sleep is particularly important to our ongoing energy levels.

It is vital to look around the area where you sleep and think about what you want to bring into your energy field at night. Anything, and anyone, that you bring into your energy field during the hours of sleep transfers energy into you and will influence your life. As mentioned earlier, it is important to clear away any electronic equipment you can and make sure you are not sleeping directly inside your next door neighbor's personal energy field. But now have a look under the bed. Do you use this area as a storage space for old stuff? If so, then this is in your energy field when you sleep at night and you will be processing through your energy fields what it is connected to all night long.

Try to bring into the area where you sleep only things that uplift you and make you feel well. This also applies to the thoughts and feelings you bring to bed with you, for these too will be with you all night. Try to go to sleep with positive uplifting thoughts and feelings. When you go to sleep with worry, you will wake up with worry, because you had put it there in your energy field the night before.

Once you have physically cleared and cleaned the area around and beneath your bed so you have an island of clarity to work out from, start to go through the rest of your home, cleaning and clearing away your physical stuff as you do so. If you start in your bedroom, which is recommended, open the closets and evaluate which clothes make you feel good and which you wear. Discard the others. If you need money, possibly organize a yard sale. You may start to put things in piles. For example, one pile to sell, another to give to friends, another to keep, another for the thrift store and another for the trash. How you organize it doesn't matter so long as you do it. Keep what you need and what has a currency of connection with you and discard the rest. If you are still hesitant to do this, put all the clothes you haven't worn for a year (four seasons) and place them in a bag in an out-of-the-way place. If you do not miss them for another four seasons, you will then be ready to get rid of them. By doing this you are setting about making space for better energy dating in your life and if your energetic container is already full, how will new passion be able to find a home in you?

If there are family heirlooms you have inherited but don't like, give them to another member of the family who does or sell them. Do not spend possibly days of your life looking at objects whose history energetically disempowers you. A client I visited who has lived in the same apartment for over twenty years told me how the largest piece of furniture in the room, a very large and impressive looking cabinet for the television, stereo, souvenirs, glasses and all kinds of other stuff was given to him when he first moved in and how he had actively disliked it every day since. He told me that somehow he had never quite felt at home in the space but was not sure why. I advised him to let the cabinet go and thereby make space for energies he does want in his life and in his space.

If you have stacks of books you cannot bear to part with, donate them to the local library where you may still be able to access them. In these days of eBay, you may also be surprised how much money your old books and other items may actually bring you. However, do not let the idea that you need to learn how eBay works delay you. It is vital to start the process while you have the fresh energy intention to do so, otherwise the energy itself will go off, just like old milk in the fridge, and then you will have another unfulfilled intention to deal with! The idea is that over the course of a month, possibly two, possibly even six, depending upon the size of your house and how much stuff you have accumulated, to only have things around you that are there for fresh and conscious reasons.

You will be amazed how this causes you to feel energetically lighter in your day-to-day going on because, as these things physically leave your house, so the strings that are attached to them will energetically leave your energy field, enabling you to be more in the present, with a new level of vitality and passion. This energetic feeling of "lightening up" can also translate into physical weight loss and a sense of greater energy and vitality throughout your whole body. Remember also that your energy field extends into the contents of your car, office, garage, the bags you carry with you and the contents of your computer. How many credit cards do you really need? How many magazines do you really have time to read and want to subscribe to? Do you actually want a newspaper on a daily basis?

Everywhere you invest your energy and time calls for your attention, which is itself an energetic payment from your field into the field of someone or something else. This is why we say we need to "pay" attention. The more dispersed your energy is over things that don't really matter to you, the less you will have for the core content and purpose of your life. This does not mean becoming narrow as a life. It means deliberately making your life simpler so you have the energy to work with and focus upon what you really want, rather than being so energetically stretched and pulled in different directions that you become energetically fatigued. To be a good manager of your own energies and also to learn how to conserve energy for what is important to you is an excellent starting place. Winston Churchill, Prime Minister of Britain during the Second World War, was once asked the secret of his success and how he could achieve so much in his lifetime. His answer was surprisingly simple. "Energy conservation," he replied.

As you groom the ecology outside of you so, in the process, you will begin to groom your inner energetic ecology as well. It is important to update and regularly sift through the energies of your mind, which is connected to and has to remember all the stuff you have "on your mind." When you give away something you have an emotional attachment to, say a gift from an old boyfriend or girlfriend, you are also giving away from your energy field this emotional attachment, releasing emotional energy back into your current life. This energy retrieval system by which suspended energy is released from the lock of the past into the present is now known as "soul retrieval" and it can work at shallow and also very deep levels. Understanding how this works and how to effectively help another in this process is part of the Energy Worlds Practitioner training..

The person you give the emotionally charged object to does not have this emotional attachment and so they begin a life with this new-to-them object that is free of any draining connections from the past. By doing this you will release energy for yourself and at the same time light up another person with an unexpected surprise. As the other person is lit up, they will pass some of this energy back to you.

I cannot over-emphasize the powerful effect that energy clearing your home will have in your life. You can only discover this by actually doing it. Until the first suit of clothes goes in the thrift box and the electric radio gets moved away from the bed, this will remain a theoretical, abstract idea. Once you apply it, it will change your life. Then, once you have around you only the things you want and use, you will be able to turn your clutter clearing into a monthly exercise and once a month go through the ecology, deciding if there are items you now want to give or throw away. For additional effectiveness you can even deliberately time your clutter clearing to coincide with the twenty-eight day cycles of the moon. It is always a good time for clearing away clutter and tidying up your space, but you might find that it is easier to do during or close to the time of the full moon.

The enhanced energies you want for your energy dating experiences start at home. Once you re-evaluate what is in your life and why, inevitably you will find that having made space, new contents and energies will be attracted towards you. Now you can exercise your power of choice about what you will bring into your energy field and what you will not. Simply by clearing away the old material goods that clutter your life and clearing from your energy field the old energies that are attached to them, you will make space for new energy dating. You may not even be aware of it but if you do this, there will be a new twinkle in your eye and lightness in your step that will reach out and attract others in new ways.

In the section above I have focused upon the individual energy field, but the same applies to a house and home shared with a partner or even a large family. It simply takes a greater co-operative effort to energetically clear and clean a space in which many people live and it is of course vital to do this with the full participation, permission and co-operation of other members of the household. If your partner comes home and you proudly announce, "I have taken the initiative and energetically de-cluttered your space. I was sure you would want me to do this as I have already started on mine," you will likely find that the generative effect of de-cluttering is more than overcome by the detrimental effect of not asking them if they were clear with this in the first place!

Energy Clearing Techniques

By using the techniques that I am about to describe, you can make the place where you live into a specially prepared, cleared and charged space. The level of power from the energy worlds that you attempt to charge it with will be up to you. If you perceive yourself to be on a spiritual journey, you can try to spiritualize your space. In history this has also been called creating a sacred space.

People still travel the world today in search of sacred places where the atmosphere carries a special electricity or charge. The great cathedrals of the world were designed to support just such charged atmospheres. The pyramids, Stonehenge and other great sacred sites were all places that contained special energies. They were built on the principle of energy worlds first. It is unlikely you will be able to design your own house in the next few months on such principles, but you can certainly set about making an energetically cleared and charged space in the place where you live. The tools you will need to do this are very simple and inexpensive. You do not need to employ an expert to come and do this for you. You have everything you need to do it for yourself.

What follows are simple and effective techniques which, when applied, will make an enormous difference in your life. These techniques have been thoroughly tested thousands of times and are guaranteed to work. The more thoroughly you are able to physically clean and prepare the space before starting this five-step-program the more effective it will be, but it will still help and make a difference even if the physical preparation you have done has been quite minimal (for whatever reason). The more clutter, however, you have been able to clear from the space and the more current are your reasons for everything that is within it, the more effective these techniques will be.

Initial Preparation

The first thing to do is to physically prepare your space. This calls for the application of work, by which I mean specifically the application of energy towards a desired result. By putting work into preparing our home we not only clean, clear and organize it physically but we put our energies and the energy of our intention into it. The more thorough we are able to be in clearing the clutter out from our home, the better will be the platform that we can work upon in the next phase. Also, when we intend something and then offer the payment of work to cause it to manifest, we begin to draw to us the energies we need from the field of planetary energy to help us do it. In this respect work is an active and effective form of prayer—it is an energy transmission toward a self-chosen direction and a petition to the universe for extra energy to come and help us in what we do.Having cleaned and prepared the place physically, our energies are already being printed into the ecology during this process and we can now begin to prepare the ecology energetically. The following five-step procedure, using the tools of sound, incense and mental intention will enable you to energetically clear the atmosphere in your home and any other space which you want to clean and charge.

The Five-Step Energy Clearing Program

First, roll up your sleeves so the sensitive nerves in the forearms can register energy changes as you go to work. Then use the five techniques in the following order:

A. Clap

Energy fields are affected by sound. Stagnant or static energy gathers in corners, around electrical equipment and in places where there is little or no flow through of air and energy. To break up the residue from the energy processes of previous days, weeks and months, go around your home and, using your hands, clap loudly. Clap at high, middle and low level. In other words, down around your knees, at chest height and above your head. The clapping sends out an energy vibration that breaks up the lower stuck energies. If your hands become tired, you can also bang lids of pots or pans together! You may have seen Chinese people banging pots and pans to see the old year out—this is why. They are breaking up the vibrations from the old year to make space for the new. We can use this technique at any time to help clean the energy fields around us. You can enjoy yourself while you do this. You are breaking up the old to make way for the new. But do not worry about dispersing the good vibrations from your home, because these vibrations are at a higher energy level and will not be broken up by your clapping.

B. Bell

Bells have been used from ancient times to clean atmospheres. They produce sound and vibration, which again break up lower energy fields. This is why Christian churches often have bells in their spires. There are many types of bells and they produce vibrations that clean at different levels. I recommend having a number of bells of different tones. A big, old-style school bell is excellent as an overall cleaner and as the atmosphere refines, you can use finer bells, such as a Tibetan-style bell or singing bowl. Go from room to room in your home and thoroughly bell it out. Enjoy the process. You are ringing out the old and ringing in the new. Again, ring the bell at three levels: high, middle and low.

C. Incense

There are many kinds of incense available and it has been used to energetically clean for thousands of years. The ancient Egyptians, Mayans, Aztecs, Incas and the peoples of North America used incense to clear the atmospheres of the places that they wanted to prepare for higher processes. I recommend the pebble-like incense that is made from tree resin as I have found this to be the most effective at cleaning and preparing atmospheres. This is the type of incense that is most often used to clean the atmospheres in Roman Catholic churches before communion. Incenses made from tree resin can often be obtained from church supply and health food stores. Incense sticks, also known as joss sticks (*joss* means good fortune), can be used for flavoring the atmosphere after cleaning, as can aromatic oils. The practice of smudging—the burning of grasses such as sweetgrass and sage—which the Native Americans used for space clearing, is very effective outdoors but I find leaves residue on the walls and too much ash for consistent indoor use.

To use tree resin incense to cleanse your space you will need to purchase a roll of the small, circular charcoal blocks that are made specially for this purpose. These can also be found at church supply and health food stores or other shops where incense is sold. Once the block is glowing red throughout (this will take about five minutes to happen), add a few pebbles of the resin. It is important that the charcoal block is placed in a metal container with a handle, as it burns at a very high temperature.

There is nothing holy about the incense or the container you use to burn it in. You can use a fancy censor like they use in a church or an old frying pan. Go through the place you want to clean and smoke it out. While you do this, keep the windows closed. After you have been throughout the ecology that you are cleaning, go back and open the windows. The way the incense works is that the smoke gathers lower energy into itself like an energy worlds vacuum cleaner and after this has happened, it is vital to release it and let it go. You do this by opening the windows and allowing the smoke to escape.

Incenses come in many pleasant fragrances, however, it is not the smell that cleans but the property of the resin that gathers lower energies into it. It acts as a disinfectant for the energy worlds. In the same way that you put disinfectant into the drains to keep them clean, this type of incense cleans the energetic atmosphere of the place where it is applied. Once you are finished incensing, dispense with the charcoal block by either flushing it down the toilet or breaking it up under running water in the sink. Never throw it in the trash, even if it appears to be no longer hot as it can still be alight at the core.

The most effective incenses I know are those produced by the monks of Prinknash Abbey in England. They are frankincense-based and are available in five different aromas. For basic energetic clearing I recommend the incense called "Basilica" which can be purchased directly from Prinknash Abbey (see Resource section at the back of this book).

D. *Mentally Project and Protect*

What is going on in your mind and feelings while you are clapping, belling and incensing is another powerful energy cleaner. It is no good cleaning the atmosphere while radiating a frequency of being fed up and annoyed and reminding yourself of all the arguments that have happened in the space. If your intention is to energetically clean to make space for new possibility, call this over while you clean so that this is the energy that emanates from you into the atmosphere and into the walls.

E. *Clean Yourself*

Now that you have cleaned and prepared the ecology, you can move into the next stage: the cleaning and preparation of yourself. It is important to do it in this order because as you energetically clean your space, some of the stagnant energies you are breaking up and getting rid of will stick in your energy field. Running water is very effective at clearing away this kind of lower static energy from your aura and so a shower is a very effective next step in your energy cleaning process. If a shower is not possible, then it is important to at least wash your face and hands.

Energy Charging

Now that the ecology is cleaned energetically, we can proceed to flavor the atmosphere the way we want it. For this purpose we can use the energy vibrations of color, sound and aroma. We have created a clean slate upon which to lay down our new field of impressions. We can now select the music we wish and even project particular colors into the atmosphere by using the power of mental projection. If we want a calm, peaceful setting, we may project blue energy into the atmosphere by visualizing it there in our mind and projecting it into the ecology. Yellow will make for a more emotional setting and green for an atmosphere that is more creatively-inclined. Violet is excellent for spiritualizing your space. A bright vibrant red is good for doing your administrative work.

This is also an excellent time for flavoring the atmosphere with aromatic oils. This is a very enjoyable and vast research unto itself, as there are essential oils suited to almost all purposes. There are many companies who produce excellent essential oils. Personally I use and recommend Young Living Essential Oils both for their range and quality (see Resource section). Essential oils that have historically been used to clear and clean atmospheres include sage, palo santo and frankincense.

Energy Clearing Upon Awakening

During the night, while your energetic systems are re-charging, you naturally clean out the electro-magnetic refuse from the day before. This remains in the area where you sleep and if you do not clean it out, it will remain there during the day and await you when you return to bed the next night. The simple technique of clapping and ringing a bell in the area where you sleep when you arise in the morning is sufficient to break up these old energies so that you can sleep in a cleaned and cleared energy field the following night. To help you remember to do this, simply place a bell somewhere in your room where it is obvious upon arising in the morning and make it part of your morning ritual alongside washing your face and brushing your teeth. It is amazing the difference that this small practical exercise actually makes. Like sleeping in a freshly-made bed, it is so much nicer to sleep in a freshly cleared energetic space. This technique really helps contribute to a refreshing night's sleep and a clear start to the day.

Moving Into a New Space

When you move into a new space that you have not lived in before, this is a time when using the techniques of energy clearing and cleaning are particularly important. This is because, although the previous occupants of the space may have moved out, their energies have not.

Everything material absorbs into itself some of the energies that pass through it. This means that when you move into a new apartment or house, you move into the energy record of the previous occupants. Depending upon the strength and level of the energies that they had put into the walls, the floor, the carpets and any furnishings that they left behind, will these energies have a greater or lesser influence upon you. We have all seen depictions in Hollywood movies of extreme examples of negative energetic residues left in a house. But the same principle of energetic residue applies in all houses and all energetic ecologies, good or bad. This is why our instinct is often the deciding factor as to whether we move into a particular house or not. It is the feel of the place that often prompts the final decision.

Once you move into your new place, I recommend going through it room by room and physically and energetically cleaning it very thoroughly. Here is where water comes to your aid because water is a great physical and energetic cleanser. Go through the new place and, even if the walls are physically clean and in good condition, thoroughly wash all the walls, the floor and lightly wash the ceilings. Floor coverings particularly hold a lot of old energy. If there are existing carpets in your new place, rent a carpet cleaning machine or call in a carpet cleaning company and have the carpets thoroughly cleaned. If you are intending to replace the carpets, have the old ones taken out as quickly as you can. It is best to remove the energetic traces of the last occupants as thoroughly as possible so you can swiftly put your own energetic print into the place.

You can live somewhere for ten years and somehow never feel like it is quite yours, as if you are never quite able to print your own energies into the place as the prime influence. This may be true. The energetic ghosts of the last occupants may be stronger than the daily signals you radiate, unless you have learned how to energetically clean and clear the place and then actually do it. The older a place is, the longer this process often takes, as over time, the old energies of the past accumulate in power. I particularly noticed this when living in the historic town of Oxford. The presence of history was so strong there that it sometimes seemed the ghosts of the past were the true occupants, while the current residents were "just passing through."

Having washed the walls, the floors and lightly washed the ceiling, you may even at this stage actually bang the walls to shake up the vibrations in the walls before clapping, belling and following the five-step procedure outlined previously. Do not be surprised if you have strange dreams the first few nights you sleep in your new place, even after you have energetically cleaned it. This is because even as your energies are leaving you and being printed into the walls, the energies that were lodged in the walls before you moved in will radiate out and you cannot help taking some of them into yourself.

How the mind and brain work in this context is that they process these incoming signals and put pictures to them. Because these energies are alien to you, the brain will clothe them with images you do not recognize. A personal example of this occurred when I stayed in a building in Toronto, Canada that had been occupied by people who had emigrated from Eastern Europe. For the first few nights I had repetitive dreams of being chased, caught and questioned by the secret police. I had no reason for these very realistic dreams but on enquiring of the previous owners, I learned that they had had experiences that fitted exactly with these dreams. The dreams were not mine. They belonged with the energies that the previous occupants had left behind. After a few days these dreams diminished, as my own energetic processes became printed into the walls and became the more current and powerful signals.

Many of our dreams are, in this sense, not actually ours but are the mind and brain clearing out energies and frequencies that do not belong with our daily lives through dream images. So do not be surprised if, when you move into a new space, you experience strange dreams. Of course the same thing often happens when sleeping with a new energy partner, as now your mind and brain receive the energy signals and frequencies that are transferring from their energy field to yours.

Preparing Your Space for an Energy Date

When we invite another person to visit our home, we want to energize our space as effectively as possible to give the process of attraction and transference its best opportunity. This process will give the inner essences, forces and powers that drive both our own life and our date's life the best chance to appear. It will make it much easier for the other person to be themselves and to give expression to what is within them, because you will have cleared the space to give this the best opportunity to happen. When the space where you live is energetically crowded out, it makes it harder for another person's nature and essence to appear.

Energy clearing before a guest's arrival will offer a better chance for a fresh energy exchange between you. You do not want your date to be influenced by the energetic leftovers of what had happened in your space the day before. Cleaning from this internal motivation is very different from cleaning for the sake of wanting to impress.

Just as the energies of a previous occupant get printed in the atmosphere and in the walls of a place, so do the energies of whatever happens in your space. If there has been a heated argument between you and another person, whether with both of you present or over the phone, an energetic heat will have been generated in the space. This hangs in the air and if your date arrives and you have not been able to clear this away, it will act as an influence between you and you will both be more inclined to be at difference and to argue. By energy clearing the space where you are going to meet, you give the best chance for passion to flow between you in a fresh and current way.

In the process of clearing the energy in your home, you also prepare your own energy field for the coming encounter. You are, therefore, able to be more in the present because you have told all your many internal lives that this is your wish, not only by anticipating the other person's arrival but actually by doing something about it.

Energy clearing makes it possible for us to be both more focused and spontaneous as we move from preparation mode into being awake, aware and alert to the energies that enter our prepared space. The significant other that is coming to the meeting is bringing with them all of the connections and processes that live within their energy field. In our newly prepared ecology we should be able to get an even better idea of what they are like and feel what their energy fields cause in us and in our prepared atmosphere.

As we clean the space, arrange the furniture, select the music and even the food that will be eaten, we begin to set the base note and tone of the energy field that will be present in the space. While the ecology is being externally prepared the inner faculties are brought into focus, ready for the exchange that is to take place.

Regardless of whether another person is visiting you, it is wise to clean and clear your energy space regularly so you can live in a flow of energy that is current with today, rather than being filled with the energetic residues of yesterday. The most regular and important visitor to your energetic space is, after all, you.

Webs of Energy

We can clearly learn an enormous amount about a person when they invite us to their home because we are able to see their personal talismanic radio sets that are connected to the webs of energy they draw upon to sustain their life. The books on the shelf, the music on the MP3 player, the artwork they choose, all tell a story and, above all, there is the aggregate energy feel of the place. By training our soul senses (energetic vision and touch primarily) as well as our common senses, we can become much more alert to the energy webs a person is connected to when putting together the energy map of this new person in our life.

None of us are one thing. We are not creatures of flat-line identity, we are more like energy spiders, connected into many different webs of energy. It is these webs of energy that determine how we behave and ultimately make us what we become. Angry or happy, joyful or depressed, supportive or critical, it is the energies we connect to that make us the way we are. Our energetic compatibility with another person is determined by how well our energy webs and those of our proposed partner complement each other.

This leads us naturally to the need for some way to chart the energies we gather to ourselves and we meet in others. Thankfully, the ancient explorers of the planet's energies passed just such a map on to us for our use and reference. These ancient magi left us a very powerful tool, an energy map of the planet's energy fields and an understanding of what energies live at the different levels. This map is known as the seven levels or planes of the astral light, which I refer to as the energy worlds. It is these seven levels and their contents that we draw upon to energize our space and that determine the currents of energy available for our lives. It is these seven levels and their contents we will now turn to as we continue our exploration of the human energy field, energy dating and how to be better partners in passion.

Chapter Seven
Energy Mapping

The energies and actions of all the people who have ever lived are recorded within the energy worlds of planet Earth, also known as the astral record or the astral light. Within this luminous astral field there are seven levels of energy. Just as our personal energy field contains seven fundamental energies that correspond with the spectrum, so too do the energy worlds of the planet. When we understand how these levels are structured, we have an energy map within which we can locate all our experiences.

Two people can have quite different energetic experiences while being in the same place at the same time. This is because they are connecting into different levels of the planet's energy worlds. The astral record allows for billions of energy states to be happening simultaneously, all born out of seven fundamental levels of power and potential consciousness. Thus, three strangers can be waiting in line at a store; the first person is thinking about their long-wished-for promotion, the second is in a state of depression, while the third is wondering about the spiritual purpose of life on Earth.

The Seven Levels of the Energy Worlds

When white light passes through a prism, seven natures of energy are revealed, each of which is expressed by a different color. The white light is a carrier of these seven energies which move within their own wave motion, but all of which are active at the same time. The seven colors companion each other in their journey within the white light.

Light is a manifestation of energy that organizes itself into patterns of seven. Like the light spectrum that we see in a rainbow, the unseen energies of the astral light also organize themselves according to the great energy law of seven and has within it seven main energy bands.

Each of these seven levels is characterized by the energetic color that expresses its frequency. Red has the slowest wavelength of the seven energies and violet the quickest, as shown here:

Level 1 Violet
Level 2 Indigo
Level 3 Blue
Level 4 Green
Level 5 Yellow
Level 6 Orange
Level 7 Red

Each of the seven levels contains seven energies represented by colors ranging through the rainbow from red to violet. This means that there are forty-nine prime energy variations possible within the map of the seven levels of the energy worlds. This is represented in the following table:

	Energy Worlds 7 Levels	Energy Worlds Each level contains 7 natures						
higher	Level 1 - violet	red	orange	yellow	green	blue	indigo	violet
↑	Level 2 - indigo	red	orange	yellow	green	blue	indigo	violet
	Level 3 - blue	red	orange	yellow	green	blue	indigo	violet
	Level 4 - green	red	orange	yellow	green	blue	indigo	violet
	Level 5 - yellow	red	orange	yellow	green	blue	indigo	violet
↓	Level 6 - orange	red	orange	yellow	green	blue	indigo	violet
lower	Level 7 - red	red	orange	yellow	green	blue	indigo	violet

The higher we go up the table, from level seven to level one, the cleaner, brighter and more illuminating the energies become. These high energies appear in clear colors that shimmer and seem to be lit up from within. The lower we go in the table, the darker and murkier the energies become. The energies at level four and above are expressed by brightly lit colors in pastel shades. The lower energies, within levels five, six and seven, are like shadow colors in comparison. Think of the difference between a bright, clear blue sky versus a polluted pool of stagnant water and it will illustrate the kind of energy differences that are possible between the highest and lowest levels of the astral light.

A very important understanding that this table of seven colors reveals is that none of the seven prime colors in the energy worlds are good or bad. There is nothing wrong with the color red, although it is the lowest and slowest of the seven rays. If we did not have red energy coursing through our human systems, we would be dead in a moment. It is not that violet is a high color and red a low color; it is the shade of violet or red which is crucial. What is most important in energy mapping is being able to detect the level of colored energy that is in a person's energy field or is in the atmosphere of a space at any particular place and time. Being able to recognize the quality and knowing the nature of the different colors which exist within the seven levels of the energy worlds allows us to make this determination and understand what is its significance and portent.

A bright, strong red around the head can tell you that a person is very good at business and is an excellent administrator. A dark, angry red can tell you that the person is close to violence. Both energies are red, but the level of the energy worlds they are born out from is very different. A pale, pastel violet that seems illuminated from within is a color of high spirituality. A dark, murky violet shows a person who loves to shock and is likely to violate friendship and confidences for short term exposure. This could even be called celebrity violet.

It is true, however, that the most toxic energies appear within the seventh level of the seventh level, being the red waveband within the red ray and the highest energies appear in the violet waveband of the violet ray, as shown in the previous table.

When you arrange a date with someone, you are arranging a time and place in which you will transfer energy from your energy field to theirs and vice-versa. Depending upon where their energies primarily reside on the chart of energies, you can be arranging a transfer of illuminated energy from the higher levels of the energy worlds, a transfer of toxic energy from the lowest levels, or anything in between.

Great saints, saviors and persons of tremendous spiritual development and connection have appeared on Earth and have made energy transmissions within the highest two levels of the energy worlds. They have left indelible spiritual impressions within the astral record. In the lowest waveband we find the records of mass murder, genocide, rape and the worst depravities of human behavior. The behavior patterns of Adolf Hitler, Stalin and Pol Pot drew on energies from the lowest level of the energy worlds. These champions of depravity also left lasting impressions in the astral record.

Most of us go on neither at the very high levels nor the very low but find our way in the middle world, which supplies the energies of general, going-on life. Level four of the astral light is the level mostly occupied by children under three years old who are as yet innocent of the energy experiences of the world. According to our intentions, education and experience do we hold at this level, rise above it, or fall below it.

When energy mapping, it is more helpful to think in terms of energies that have a fine or coarse frequency, rather than thinking in terms of good and bad. Fine energy frequencies naturally locate themselves within the higher levels of our energy map. Coarse frequencies can be found in the lower levels. Once we can start to distinguish between energy levels and have a knowledge of what kind of human behaviors they cause, then we can start to place them on our energy map and deliberately decide what kind of energies we want to pursue in the opportunity of our life. It is wise to remember how the lower energies can pollute and even drive out the higher in a mutual relationship field, unless both partners engage in deliberate personal and self-development practices to keep the levels of their energy worlds processes at a medium to high level.

The Forty-Nine Point Energy Map

With this knowledge of the seven levels of the planet's energy worlds and the forty-nine natures of power they contain, we can begin to construct a color map of human energies and resulting behaviors. All behaviors originate from an energetic connection, most often caused by the thoughts and feelings of the individual and the human networks they are connected to. These thoughts and feelings may then gather power to themselves from the energy field of the person, the energies of their mutual relationship fields and the energy worlds of the planet. Thus, a thought and feeling can swiftly be amplified from a fleeting thought or an emotional reaction into a major energy system. If we are not in control of the influences that are caused in our energy field, we can swiftly become subject to whatever storm happens to blow up energetically on any particular day. This will produce, for example, a moody individual who lacks control upon what he or she will do next. When the time is right, what begins as a small energetic spark can cause the equivalent of a forest fire in the energy field, producing wild behavior the individual may deeply regret later. This is where expressions such as "I don't know what came over me," "It wasn't like me to do that" and the like may be heard.

Fortunately, the same pattern can manifest within our higher energy systems and a momentary bright idea, when fueled by the right conditions, powers and connections in the energy worlds can lead to full-on revelation, inspiration, new hope and initiative. So much of our life's journey is determined by the connections we make and the powers we draw to ourselves from these energy worlds that it is well worth investing some of the valuable time and energy of your life into understanding what they are and what behaviors they make possible and cause, both in yourself and others. When we can understand the nature of energies that people process, we can even forecast the kinds of behaviors we can expect from them, and also from ourselves. Much of the fundamental training for EnergyWorlds Practitioners is in understanding and working with these worlds at depth.

Understanding these different natures of energy is a vital context for understanding human behavior, for seeking the kind of relationships we want and deciding what nature of relationship fields we want to generate and construct with others who may become our partners in passion. The higher we are able to connect in the forty-nine levels of the energy worlds, the greater the uplifting energy we are able to connect to. Conversely, the root of all abusive relationships is in the lower levels of the energy worlds.

To increase the power of energetic love in our lives it is crucial we learn how to climb the energy levels of the astral light. The higher we go, the greater the energetic love we can generate. One unit of power at astral level four carries far more energetic love than one unit at level five or six.

High-Level Energy Relationships

If we decide we want to have high-level energy relationships in our lives, the place to start is within ourselves. According to how we think, feel and act, so do we attract and become conduits for different energies, powers and forces. It is no use hoping for a high-level relationship outside ourselves if we do not start within. It begins with the first decision that this is our wish.

Mahatma Gandhi pointed the way to this profound energetic truth when he said, "Become the change you want to see in the world." If we want to enhance the energies in the world and enhance our relationship fields, we need to begin with the energy map of our own life. This is also why in the previous chapter we started in the most obvious of places—cleaning up our energetic act in the place where we live.

The Passion Multiplier

Now that we have a better understanding of the vast differences in illumination, power and love that live at different levels of the energy worlds, we can better understand the importance of the first two shifts of The Passion Multiplier:

Shift 1. To raise the level and improve the quality of the powers and forces of the energy worlds working through you, thereby increasing the level of energetic love in your personal energy field.

Shift 2. To help the people you are in relationship with raise the level and improve the quality of the powers and forces of the energy worlds working through them, thereby helping them increase the level of energetic love in their energy field.

The quantity and quality of energetic love we are able to produce is determined by the level of the energy worlds we connect to and generate within ourselves. The higher the level we connect to, the greater the power of energetic love within our own energy field and the greater the passion potential we offer into any relationship. By becoming better connected ourselves and helping others to do so, we vastly increase the quality and quantity of passion in our lives. We also are able to generate more powerful and illuminated energies into the relationship fields we share with others.

Human Energy Systems

When we connect with powers and forces from the energy worlds (and we do so all the time, as without them we would be dead in an instant), we process them through our multiple human energy systems. There are a number of different maps of the human energy field that have survived into our times from the extensive knowledge of the Ancients. The two we will concentrate on primarily are the systems of the seven chakras and the five seats of the soul.

The knowledge of the seven wheels or vortices of energy called the "chakra system" comes to us primarily from India and Tibet. The system of five energy centers was transported from ancient China through the western esoteric tradition into these times. It is also known as the five color power system of the five pointed star or pentagram. These two systems naturally complement each other and offer, when studied together, an integrated holistic approach by which many of our energy systems can be understood. There are multiple other viewing windows we could use, such as the fourfold system represented by the elements earth, water, air and fire and the threefold system which represents our conscious, semiconscious and unconscious mind, but, as mentioned before, the most widely known systems in use in the world today are the sevenfold system of India and the fivefold system of China, so this is where we will start.

I believe that both of these systems originated from a complete system of energetic knowledge that existed in ancient times, most probably in ancient Egypt. These understandings were disseminated from there to many parts of the world and various fragments survived in different places. One of the marvels of our own age is that we can now begin to recombine these fragments of a great teaching to once again learn how to contemplate the whole picture.

It is vital to have knowledge of both energy systems to develop a good grasp of human energy anatomy and how it works. The chakra system of India is based in the understanding of the sevenfold energetic vortices. The Chinese fivefold or pentagram system is based in the understandings of how our soul energy or chi works through five main centers of power, corresponding with the five senses. Power can pass through both these systems in two directions: from fast to slow and from slow to fast.

Looking at how these systems work together, we find that the five soul centers provide the major power into our energy systems. If the five soul centers offer us the inhalation and exhalation of the energetic breath of life, the seven wheels or chakras are the seven flowings and flowerings of this energy that represent our energetic expression and attract to us further impressions of like kind.

The Seven Wheels of Energy

The word chakra is an Eastern term meaning wheel or vortex of energy. The chakras, like the seven levels of the energy worlds, work on seven distinct frequencies from violet to red. Ancient Indian practitioners placed the chakras in the following order from fast to slow:

1.	Violet	Crown
2.	Indigo	Brow (third eye)
3.	Blue	Throat
4.	Green	Heart
5.	Yellow	Solar plexus
6.	Orange	Genitals
7.	Red	Base of spine (root)

They believed that just as we express ourselves through the spectrum of the chakras, so we can also receive energies directly through them, according to our level of development. This sevenfold chakra system works by the energy law "according to what you transmit so also do you receive," which today is often simplified and referred to as the Law of Attraction.

The seven chakras can take in and give out energies at any of the seven levels of the energy worlds, but they usually are anchored within three neighboring wavebands of astral energy at any one time. These energies are then passed on to augment the five centers of the soul and, over time, cause our soul to become accustomed to dealing in certain levels of energy.

This is how, over time, our soul becomes flavored and we can come to have a sweet soul, a bitter soul or, like Old King Cole, a merry old soul. The word *mahatma* as in Mahatma Gandhi, means "great soul." A great soul is formed by the chakras becoming attuned primarily to the higher three levels of the astral light and drawing their seven frequencies—red to violet—from these higher levels. Because these higher levels are very clean and increasingly illuminated, all seven chakras will then radiate with colors of great radiance and luminosity. The five centers of the soul thus become themselves illuminated, causing a greatness of soul and allowing for the liberation of a great brightness of spirit.

The Five Energy Centers of the Soul

The soul has two prime states: charge and discharge. When we sleep at night, the soul is being charged by the energies of the universe. That is why we go to bed tired and wake up refreshed. The universe gives us the energies for another day when we sleep. When we are awake and active, we discharge and receive energies through our five color power system. These five colored energies are listed in the following table, together with their corresponding sense and energy center, from fast to slow.

Color	Sense	Sensory Organ	Energy Center
green	sight	eyes	sexual/creative
yellow	smell	nose	emotional/feeling
blue	touch	skin	instinctive/intuitive
red	taste	mouth	moving/habitual
white	hearing	ears	thinking/learning

There is much to explore and discover about the workings of this five color power system and what it makes possible. I have written about this in my book *The Tales of Dr. Woo*, which is a series of stories and lessons set in ancient China, containing insights and information about the five color power system of the soul and its correspondence with the five Chinese elements of wind, water, wood, earth and metal, together with many other insights into the energy worlds and the ancient mystery schools.

Two contemporary examples of how the five power centers of our soul work are as follows.

Example 1. You decide to learn to drive a car with a standard transmission. During your first driving lesson you survey the array of controls and are told to look in the mirror, switch on the indicator, depress the clutch and engage the gears while watching out for pedestrians and other traffic. You think, "How can anyone learn to do this? It's all too much." You may get a tingling sensation or knot in your stomach caused by the energetic overload, known as anxiety. Yet, a few weeks later, here you are, driving down the freeway while engaging in a conversation on your cell phone and at the same time adjusting the radio! What has happened? Initially you were trying to drive with your thinking/learning center, which is the slowest of the five centers. After a number of repetitions the learning center passed the information and experience to the moving/habitual center. Once the habitual center has the programming in place for how to drive a car, it installs it as a motor skill that it will never let go of until it dies. Now that our habitual center has the program, we can get on with new explorations, such as learning how to use the Global Positioning System with our thinking/learning center, while the habitual/moving center drives the car.

Example 2. You are walking along the road feeling good about life, enjoying the smell of the fallen leaves. This smell is connecting you to your emotional/connective center and it is conjuring up for you the feelings of previous walks in nature in the fall. An attractive woman/man goes past you on a bicycle and catches your eye (sexual/creative center). You step out onto the road to look at them as they cycle away from you. Suddenly there is a loud honking noise and before you have had a chance to think, you are back on the pavement, shaking and asking yourself, "What happened?" A bus almost ran you down and you did not even see it coming. How did you get out of the way? It was as if a force more powerful than you appeared from somewhere, picked you up and propelled you back to the pavement. The energies from it were so strong that it causes your nerves to shake for minutes afterwards. This force was the intervention of your instinctive center which can override all other energy centers in moments of emergency. It can draw energies from all other centers to save your life and the power it summoned to rescue you from danger leaves your nerves shaking in the aftershock. Thanking your lucky stars, you move on with your day.

These are two examples of the thousands that happen throughout our day as we express ourselves through the five centers of soul energy that operate on different colors, rhythms and speeds. The levels of energy the soul primarily works on can come from any of the seven wavebands of the energy worlds which is in large part determined by how you use the threefold system of your mind and the sevenfold system of your personal spectrum of energies, also known as the chakras.

Energy Symptoms

Because our soul becomes habituated to certain levels of energy worlds connections, if we go into atmospheres that are higher or lower than we are used to, we experience specific electromagnetic symptoms. When we learn what these are like, we can map these symptoms and determine the levels that cause them.

If we are used to dealing in the lower levels of the energy worlds and are suddenly lifted up into higher levels, it causes a kind of energetic altitude sickness as the soul reaches for the energy food it is accustomed to but which is not there. This can cause cold shivers throughout the nerves and yawns that are symptomatic of trying to take in large gulps of astral energy. Highly charged atmospheres can also make us very drowsy as it becomes difficult to stay awake in charged atmospheres that contain a concentrate of higher astral energy, greater than we are used to. These higher energies also often cause us to feel cold, as the higher we are able to travel up the levels of the energy worlds, the cleaner, clearer and colder the energy becomes. In mapping the energies of places you may soon discover that horror movies have it exactly wrong when the actors start to complain of feeling a sudden cold, shiver and go into a state of fear when some frightful ghost or apparition is about to manifest. There is far more to fear if the atmosphere goes suddenly hot and prickly than if it goes cold and gives you the shivers.

If we go into levels of the energy worlds that are lower than what we are used to, the soul induces a feeling of nausea and a powerful urge to get out of that place. This is often interpreted as feeling stifled, hot and needing air. But it is often electrical air that is being called for and it is this urge to get into an astral field that carries a higher level of charge that drives a person from a room where the lower energies are concentrated. Anyone who has ever been in a crowded place and suddenly feels overwhelmed and that they need to get out knows this feeling well.

This can also happen if you go out on an energy date with someone and you feel they "make your skin crawl." If, when you get away from their energy field, you feel you need to take a shower and that you have been "grossed out," or "creeped out," as the modern idioms have it, then you will know that you have been with a low-life and you have been dealing below your level in the energy worlds. It would be wise to take this into account when deciding if you want to be with this person again.

What you are actually determining, decision by decision, is whether you want to invest in building a relationship field with that person. So much of this goes on in us instinctually and semiconsciously, but it is very helpful to bring this information up front and conscious when considering the vital matter of who and what you want to connect your personal energy field to. We take great care with how we invest our money. I am advocating at least as much care with how we invest the five power content of our soul into the relationships we form with others.

Energy Addictions

When we first encounter lower energies in concentrate, we are innocent and ignorant of them. We have not yet had the experience of processing these energies in any strength. We can, however, habituate ourselves to these lower levels by repetitive exposure. Indeed, after a time of doing this, we can become energetically addicted to the experiences that these lower levels offer.

This process explains how people can begin their life's journey with high intentions (energy worlds level four and five), but actually become corrupted and energetically addicted to lower level powers and their resulting behaviors (levels six and seven). These lower level energies, because of their addictive and toxic nature, cause them to keep repeating behavior patterns that bring the same results as yesterday. People can thus become slaves to the addictive energies of their past. This is such an important dynamic in forming relationship fields and deciding who and what we wish to become partners in passion with that we will examine how these addictive processes work and how to win release from them in greater depth in Chapter 11, Energy Addictions, Vices and Abusive Relationships.

Lasting Impressions

Places are printed with astral connections by what happens there over time. Some years ago I visited the Tower of London. I went into a particular room and suddenly felt very hot and uncomfortable. The room seemed physically no different from many we had previously gone into. I asked a guide what the history of this room was and what it had been used for. He looked at me and said, "At one time it is believed to have been a torture chamber." This confirmed my feeling of great discomfort and my instinctive decision to move swiftly out of that room.

In terms of energy mapping it is very useful to know what such atmospheres feel like so you can match any future energetic experiences with a correct interpretation. Deliberate cruelty and evil have has a particular radiation and gives certain identifiable energetic symptoms. It does indeed make your skin crawl and exudes a particular heat and astral smell. Once you have experienced it, you can mark down where it lives on your energy worlds map and decide whether or not you ever want to deliberately deal with it again. For the EnergyWorlds Practitioner building up a record of such experiences at all levels of the energy worlds, knowing what they feel like and the energetic symptoms they cause in our human energy systems is a vital part of the training, so one can make accurate assessment and be diagnostic about what level of the energy worlds one is actually dealing with.

Multiple levels of the astral light can be present in one place at the same time, but certain places can hold concentrations of particular levels. Where level seven of the energy worlds is brought into concentration, as in a gambling casino, the lower levels become so dense that the higher levels are driven out. There are "hot spots" in any city where cooler energies find it hard to assemble. Similarly, where cool energies gather in concentrate, the lower energies have trouble forming up and are driven away. In medieval churches and cathedrals they would actually have a "devil's door" in the church through which the lower influences could escape as they were being squeezed out by processes such as electrical cleaning and communion. A congregation of people generating devotional prayer will produce a charged atmosphere that leaves little electrical space for the lower frequencies and thought forms that tend to occupy a gambling casino or a prison. This is why some people go to churches and places of religion and others insist on making room in their life to take time out from the city and go hiking in the country. They are drawn to the energies that they can find in these places. Indeed, we can tell very much about a person by discovering the places they are drawn to and the level of energies that concentrate there.

It may be that you are with someone on an energy date. You have looked forward to meeting them. Then, as you sit and speak with them, you experience a growing feeling of numbness and nausea. You feel a strange sensation just above the navel, like a dark hole opening that seems to draw your energy into it. You may even start to feel faint. You may also experience a prickly heat at the back of the neck and around the head. What you are feeling may not be food poisoning or the effects of the wine, but literally an astral radiation that makes you feel sick.

If you are a person who is used to processing the energies of level five of the astral light and you are sitting with a person who is steeped in the lowest energies from level seven, their toxic radiation can have this effect. If you persist in taking in these alien frequencies, they will also give you strange and unpleasant dreams and cause you to feel a vague sense of dread, a sense that something is wrong though you cannot quite put your finger on it. It is important in these worlds to follow your sixth sense and your intuition. If you have an inner knowing that there is something not quite right about a person, you are probably right. It is then up to you whether you want to take the time to pursue the matter and find out what it could be, or not. If you repetitively bring yourself into a lower level connection, then your amazing human energy systems will make the necessary adjustments so you can feel well inside these levels. They do this by thickening your astral skin and coarsening your systems so that you can astrally breathe better at these lower levels. For every energetic shift there is a price, and in this instance the price is that it will become harder to live and breathe in the higher levels.

The symptoms caused by a mutual relationship field, as in the example above, can be so strong they can visibly affect your pets. Earlier I gave the example of the large dog which would find our couple every time they hugged. Another example, but at the lower end of the bar, was given to me in my EnergyWorlds coaching practice. My client told me that when her partner in passion became enraged in an argument, the mutual relationship field between them would become so toxic that her small Chihuahua would faint in her arms. This happened not only once, but a number of times and was accompanied each time by the energy sensations I described above. The influence of our mutual relationship fields upon the pets which live in our ecologies is another confirmation of the power which such fields can generate.

Mapping Energies

The majority of life in big cities today goes on at levels seven, six and five of the energy worlds. You may encounter level four in a rare religious or healing setting, in spontaneous actions of kindness and generosity, in high creative endeavors and in young children. However, as cities are dominated by economics and driven by trade, which are focused in level six of the energy worlds, this is the main energy that is anchored there. From this anchorage the energy levels dip into level seven, often for entertainment and time out from the routines that are enforced by economic need in level six, and lift up into level five as people make an effort to find opportunities for greater self-education and self-improvement. The greater the avarice and greed that is at play within the dynamics of trade, the more the energy slips into level seven. Level seven includes deceitful advertising, lying and cheating. Fair trade takes place at level six and the ethics that support fair trade are worked out at level five.

When we are out in nature, we are within the natural balance of the planet's ecology in which the seven levels and possibilities are balanced and blended together. Connection to level four of the energy worlds and above is often easier in these circumstances. We do, however, take our own astral light with us wherever we go. Therefore, if we go to a place with high astral possibility, but we cannot shake our worries and cares, we will carry our own level six ecology with us. Of course, conversely this also means that even within an ecology that is of the lower levels of the astral light we can carry with us our own bubble of something good.

Understanding that there are different levels of energy that can be detected and mapped is enormously helpful in the realms of energy dating. It means that in addition to your instinct, psychology and the fact that you might get a good or bad feeling from someone, you can deliberately add up whether your date is connected to the kind of energies you want in your life. If someone's priority is sex, power and money, then they will use their energies quite differently than someone who is primarily interested in a spiritual journey and a high level of reincarnation or immortality.

The levels of the energy worlds are like a pyramid in which the most massive signals are at the lowest levels and the higher you go, the cleaner and less populated they become. The following is further useful information about the seven prime levels of the energy worlds, particularly levels seven, six and five that are the major energies within modern towns and cities. It is these levels that primarily make up what is commonly referred to as "the world." We will start from the base of the pyramid of energies and work up from there.

Energy Worlds Level Seven

Concentrations of level seven forces in a person are primarily caused by addictions. These include the energies of pornography, violence, brutality, sadomasochism, abuse, severe inferiority and superiority complexes, criminal behavior and more. When you can see the colors that go with these lower energies, you will register dark, murky colors. The cortex or skin of the personal energy field will be very thick, showing a person lacking in electrical sensitivity. In the chakra system, the lower three wheels are usually particularly active and there will be much dark red and orange in the aura. Dark red is a sign of dominance and blame and the person exhibiting this color usually has little sense of personal responsibility. Murky orange shows greed and is often coupled with a murky green that demonstrates a lower sexual energy. The lowest energies of level seven drive the psychopath and the killer, the rapist and the mugger. This is also the level of deep depression and suicide. Energy vampires radiate these colors and can often be seen to have in their aura a dark cloud that draws to it the lower energies of others.

Level seven has been personified as the level of the cunning fox and the rapacious wolf. Many of the great magnates of the world have come out from this level. People here can be very innovative and cunning. In a date they will be looking for personal advantage that usually is expressed through one of three major forms: sex, status and money. The lower three levels all have the hallmark of "What's in this experience for me?" but none more blatantly than in level seven. Here culture is a thin veneer to cloak entirely personally based motivations. You cannot expect any consideration or humanity from this level of the astral light. The amount of the finer qualities and all the great virtues, including compassion rises as you climb the levels. The human manufactured, toxic contents of level seven of the astral light harbor no mercy and people at this level will take whatever advantage they can from any situation. Expect no chivalry or fairness here, as this is the level of the low-life and the pimp. What you need here is a good security system and an awareness that date rape drugs actually do exist and there are people who will use them.

Energy Worlds Level Six

The French term *ennui* belongs with level six of the energy worlds. It is the level where people make actions but can hardly remember why they are doing them any longer. "Obedience without thought" is the motto of this energy level. Armies march on level six energies and companies rely upon them. Most schooling in the western world is still designed to prepare children for a daily, numbing routine in the commercial world. The lower end of the education process helps children adjust to the daily boredom of level six of the energy worlds by insisting they sit in it for many hours a day. Higher forms of education lift into level five of the astral light and inspire children with the wish to learn and improve. Very often the difference between the two levels is in the passion and quality of the teacher. If a teacher has been ground down by life to the point where they are teaching only for the money and because it is their job, their teaching will be imbued with the frequency of level six of the energy worlds. When a teacher maintains a love and passion for their subject, they are able to imbue their teaching with level five of the energy worlds and sometimes even higher.

Government offices often have a strong radiation of level six as people "watch the clock" and look forward to closing hour when they can go home. Level six is ruled by the law of inertia, according to which a person does exactly what they are expected to do and no more. Those who are "compliant" to external authority in this manner often make "complaint" as they do so—it is no coincidence that these two words shapeshift into each other. The idea of doing extra work for no return does not exist at level six of the energy worlds. It is the level in which general habitual living is the strongest signal. The programming and enforcement that allows a person to do the same things over and over again without thinking about the reason why is the ruler here. Charles Dickens most accurately personifies this level and the never-ending bureaucracy and red tape that occupies it as the "Circumlocution Office" in his novel *Little Dorrit.*

The person whose life is anchored in level six of the energy worlds is the great conformist to the rules of others. If level seven is the level of the wolf and the fox, level six is the level of the sheep. They will work in the office, the factory and the shop taking instructions from an external authority. This is the main band of so-called normal behavior in the western world, in which the trading of time for money is a main feature.

An important feature of level six is the sense of boredom that it produces in the mind, brain and human energy systems. While being acceptable to the older person who has settled to it and accepted that this is their lot, it is usually unacceptable to the young. The young often want something better and revolt against the level six atmosphere that may be established in the routine life of their school, their parents and in their parent's house. In their quest for something better they may set out to raise themselves into the higher levels of the energy worlds. However, because there is little education on how to make a spiritual development journey, the young person often plays energetic roulette with their life, as they experiment with different levels of energy, not realizing what the consequences might be.

In rejecting what they see to be boring routines and a going nowhere existence, they are more likely to get caught up in the addictive energies of the lower levels than they are to make the journey into the higher elevations of energy worlds level five and above. I would offer this sentence to a young person caught up in the boredom trap, "Personal development and evolution are the most effective forms of rebellion." Personal development often begins with the intention to improve and "the power of intention," a concept popularized independantly by both Dr. Wayne Dyer and Lynne McTaggart, author of *The Field*, is the prime hallmark of level five of the energy worlds. What the power of intention ultimately connects to, of course, is determined by the quality and level of the intention. If the intention is to heal, then it can help a person connect to level four of the energy worlds and above. If the intention is to get rich, regardless of any adverse effects upon others, the power of this intention will swiftly bring a person into the toxicity of level seven. So much of our relationship with the energy worlds is determined by the reasons why we do what we do and what our real intentions actually are.

At level six of the energy worlds the prime power of intention can well be characterized as "to make it through another day." At this level of our energy map we meet the energies of convention and general habitual life in concentrate. Here you are likely to go out on an energy date with someone and find him or her rather dull. Your date will seem to want only to talk about the office where they work, what is happening to others and to regurgitate the latest news from the media without having really thought about it for themselves. Most gossip and social talk hangs at level six, unless it is malicious gossip designed to run other people down. In this case it moves from level six to level seven.

The moment someone does something because they have an inner love of it and they lose themselves inside it, they rise above level six of the energy worlds. If it is an intellectual passion that drives them, it will lift them up into level five, but if their feeling life is also involved, it can take them to level four and above. An energy date with a person who has a passion for what they do immediately becomes more stimulating than a date with a person who is bored by their daily job, but whose energy field is filled by their thoughts about it.

An advantage of an energy date at level six, when compared with level seven, is that your date will be restrained by the decency of convention. It may not be an inner property at this level, but unlike the criminality of energy worlds level seven, which is looking for personal advantage through whatever methods it can get away with, the level six person will be held to the workings of the laws and conventions of society. Not because they have thought it through for themselves, but because they do what they are told to do. They are the unwitting champions of convention. The normal behaviors of society are anchored at this level. This may not be the most inspiring of dates, but at least you are not in danger of date rape and robbery, as you are at level seven.

An important consideration here, however, is that you can start off the evening with a date at level six, but after the addition of alcohol and/or other drugs, your date can swiftly move into level seven energies and behaviors. This is because the darker energies that are held back by level six conventions and programming are able to become dominant under the influence of alcohol and other drugs. This is why people who are acting "under the influence" later make statements such as, "I don't know what came over me" or "I don't know what got into me." Drugs and alcohol change our energy states very quickly, allowing us to make actions we would never make while our lives are within our conscious control. This applies to all parties in the developing relationship field, including you. It is vital to realize that the map of energies changes from moment to moment according to the energies and physical substances we introduce into ourselves.

As you use your energy map, realize that energies are changeable and all people click up and down levels of the energy worlds according to how they use the radio set of their mind and emotions. It is how we were designed. Trust between you and your date will grow as you come to depend upon the levels of their energy connections and behaviors. This is why, when someone acts out of character in a relationship, it can cause so much mental, emotional and sexual pain. These energetic pains are every bit as real as the pain you experience from a physical injury, such as breaking a leg. When you come to expect a certain level of energetic conduct from your partner and then their behavior unexpectedly changes, it can lead to a deep sense of disappointment, pain and betrayal.

Energy Worlds Level Five

When we approach level five, we enter into a different order of energy. This level incorporates a whole world of self-improvement, thoughts and ideas, of exchanging views, of discovering with interest what another person thinks and feels. As we climb the levels of the energy worlds, we become more interested in what something is unto itself, rather than how we can gain from it or not be threatened by it.

One of the key understandings about this level is that it is the primary base of the academic and the intellectual. The person whose main fixing is into level five energy tends to be proud of their knowledge and their intellectual attainment. They may have the financial focus of energy worlds level six or seven, but they are also very committed to the development of their intellectual prowess. Their ego is often as much tied to their knowledge as to their possessions and they tend to be more concerned about what other people, who they view to be their peers, think of them. They count the quality and quantity of their knowledge as avidly as someone anchored in level six counts the quantity and quality of their possessions.

In energy worlds level six a person tends to be concerned what the world at large thinks of them. This is why there is such a fear of standing out at this level and people will prefer to hide through conformity and by being part of the masses. It is the level of general social conformity. The real level seven player doesn't care what anyone thinks so long as they can get away with it. Their fear is in being caught and being punished in some way. At level five concepts such as personal honor, ethics and decency come much more on screen. The person often does not care so much what the world at large thinks of them, but they do care very much what others they regard as their elite set think of them. An example of this can be found in the academic community in which being published is such a necessity.

In levels six and seven the quantity and quality of possessions is a vital feature and often a person will use their social standing to advertise themselves during an energy date. In level five the ego is more likely to be roused by the need to be right at any cost, including to the detriment of their date's feelings. You will know that your date is like this if they heatedly fight for the correctness of their position, regardless of the facts. They simply cannot bear to be wrong, because it would hurt their intellectual pride.

The Ego and Personal Identity

People whose energetic center of gravity is in levels seven, six and five of the energy worlds are personally based and are driven by the energy of what marketers describe as Radio WIIFM, otherwise known as "what's in it for me." This is the theme that marketers specifically seek to aim at and also to engender. It is at its most crass in the energies of level seven and reaches greater refinement in level five. The ego and what it connects to is the most powerful driving force in people in these lower three levels of the astral light. People and their energy processes in these three levels have the hallmark of being self-focused in different ways.

Level seven based people have the lowest standards and will do anything to get ahead in life. Their only morality is "Will I get caught? If not, anything goes."

Level six based people are mostly focused on being able to get by and live to see another day with as little confrontation and hardship as possible. The focus here is also having personal enjoyment, but usually in the ways that are prescribed by the mass media and the marketing industry. Keeping up with the Joneses is a powerful force here, alongside not wanting to be seen to be different to one's neighbors. "To conform and to be seen to conform" would be an accurate motto for the behaviors that stem from the energies of this astral level.

Level five is focused on self-improvement for personal gain and advancement. Colleges and universities are centers of level five activities, as they have at their core the idea of improving oneself and becoming a more educated person. The core motive for doing this these days is often economic—to be able to get a better job and have a better material life. This motive is born out of level six, which is the level of fair trade. People based in level seven are not interested in fair trade, only in the profit motive. This is where the bright young things graduating from colleges mostly get sucked into a general going-on, level six job that may be perpetuating a level seven based, profit-serving, mega-corporation. Academics in the universities continuing their researches often struggle to hold at level five, but are usually financed by power brokers in levels six and seven.

The core story of many Hollywood movies today is based in level seven, because its level of degeneration is the most dramatic and violent. Level six energies are more routine and produce entertainment such as soap operas, while level five energies produce highbrow films that are targeted for the intellectual audience. Movies that even attempt a connection to level four energies are very rare and hold a focus upon spirituality and the deeper meaning of life.

News broadcasts primarily focus on the happenings of violence around the world (7), movements of the financial markets and politics (6) and breakthroughs in health, science and technology (5). There are no news media concentrating on level four happenings, such as acts of spontaneous love and kindness.

Woundology

An idea that has taken strong root recently within some spiritual circles is that of "woundology." I have been asked at many workshops what I make of this idea, which essentially says that people are drawn together because they share similar energetic wounds in their energy fields and that karma brings them together so that they can heal each other's wounds. My response is that woundology of this kind works in a rehabilitation center, but is not a core reason for energy dates to be successful and progressive in the long term. I have chosen to touch upon this subject here because woundology, the attraction of one person to another because of what is out of balance in their energy fields, works within the lower three levels of the energy worlds where the ego predominates. Above these levels, in level four and above, what takes over is the mutually agreed quest or purpose of the relationship.

Energy Worlds Level Four

At level four we break into a different nature of astral signal. Level four is the level of the natural man and woman. It is the level beyond the intellectual (5), the sheep (6) and the fox (7). Here there is a natural empathy from one person to another. At this level there is a wholesome and natural respect for the planet and for all forms of life. Judgement and criticism are not welcome here, as there is an appreciation that all lives are born of Creation and are interconnected in the great web of life. The powerful feelings that live here are accompanied by a sense of the sacred. Much of the surge towards spirituality taking place today is an urge towards these higher energy worlds and the spiritual illumination they contain.

At level four the center of gravity of our consciousness and energy worlds process make a spiritual shift and we again become children of the universe with strong feelings of care and respect toward the planet and all her organic life. Our behaviors here are driven by less personal motivations and we find our life motivated by a sense of higher than personal mission and purpose. It is this feeling that has given rise to the ecology movement, for example, and the wish to be better stewards of Mother Earth.

If your date has no feelings for planetary life, but sees the planet solely as a means towards personal wealth with no concern for what something is unto itself, then you know that you are with a person whose energetic center of gravity is rooted in the lower three levels of the energy worlds.

It is at level four that the real breakthroughs in thinking are made and the potential for change in the human condition opens up. These new discoveries are then intellectualized upon, commercialized and made into profit-serving businesses at levels five, six and seven. The illuminating energy that comes with all great human breakthroughs is born out of the higher energy levels of level four and above.

The emphasis at this higher level now shifts from material and intellectual possessions toward becoming a light-bearer, a carrier of spiritual illumination. The level of energetic love that can be generated at this level is far greater in its intensity than at the levels beneath it. This reflects the exponential nature of The Passion Multiplier. The quality of energetic love and the finer human passions increase with each upward movement in the astral light. One unit of energetic love at level four of the energy worlds is many times more potent than one unit at level five, and so on, all the way up the astral levels. Thus it is that a person who is connected to level one or two of the astral light can produce a spiritual beacon of such intensity that it still inspires the human race thousands of years after their physical death.

At energy worlds level four and above we start to meet those rare moments in the relationship field that a person will treasure for the rest of their days. Energetic love at level four gives a person a great sense of internal buoyancy, which can literally sweep them off their feet. This is because relationship fields at level four can only occur when two people actually lose much of their ego connection in the presence of each other. Their egos become "muted" at this level, in the words of certain modern therapies. They no longer think of themselves first but consider their partner in passion and his or her well-being as a priority. Their mind is often on the other person during the day when they are apart and is focused upon them when they are together. They radiate that special emanation of a couple lost in the moment, a couple in love and they share that unique sensation of simply being glad that the other person is in the world.

Level four energies produce a charged atmosphere in a place and between people. Two people deeply in love at this level carry their own level four energy worlds charisma with them wherever they go. They carry a bubble of something good, a bubble of higher energy that others are attracted to and notice. In the same way that a pregnant woman often carries a special level four energy in her personal energy field, which changes and charges the atmosphere around her, so a couple at level four radiate an energetic charisma that makes others feel good, unless their own field is so toxic it causes in them an opposite reaction.

The higher energy system of two people in love need not be limited to newlyweds and newly engaged couples. It is possible for couples of fifty years to maintain such an energy system around them, though it is no longer the radiance of young love, but it becomes the luminosity of sustained love and respect in mutual partnership over time.

Two people can build an energy system between them that is of a higher nature than the general going-on of life. Indeed, this is one of the great potential benefits of two people coming together to form a relationship field and partnership between them. They can deliberately build an energy field between them that targets the higher levels of the planet's energy worlds and create an ecology which is highly energetically charged, rare and powerful. They then radiate this out into the world and increase the amount of energetic love that exists, so there is more of it in the world.

At level four of the energy worlds the suppression of women by men disappears, as this is the level of the natural man and woman. At level five a person may have intellectual arguments about why they feel that equality should be legally enforced. At level four it is no longer an intellectual argument but an inner knowing. At this level it is impossible for a man to subjugate or abuse a woman or vice-versa because this energy level will not support the energies of suppression, domination and abuse. The moment a person thinks of dominating another, they become connected to a lower level of the energy worlds. This is also why the society that confirms the subjugation of women cannot rise into the higher levels of the astral light and energetically prevents its own possible development and evolution.

Astral Level Three

Level three of the energy worlds lifts our energetic experience and possibility up again. Powerful planetary healing energies, elementals and nature spirits live here. This is the realm of the healer, the sage and the shaman, the person who acts as a bridge between the realms of the higher unseen worlds of power and the visible worlds of everyday life in extraordinary and supernatural ways. We now move from the level of the natural man and woman at level four to the level of the enhanced man and woman at level three. The amount of compassion and energetic love that a person radiates naturally increases here and the lower properties of level seven are naturally repulsed.

An energetic partnership at this level is always engaged in some kind of mutual quest. It is a quest that is of benefit not only to the two participants but also to the astral light of the world and all who live within it. If lower level relationships are largely dominated by the psychology of the individuals involved and it is these psychologies that contain the wounds and hurts of the past, relationships at level three take place within cleaner, clearer energies where natural passion and humor are able to be expressed.

At this level a person is careful to keep their energy field clear and clean by regular maintenance practice and when two such people are in partnership, they will spend many hours getting into the exploration of the reasons why they think and act the way they do, as it is very important to them to understand the reasons for things, including their own actions and the actions of the person they are in relationship with. Humor is a vital ingredient here because laughter is a great cleaner of the energy fields and can be used as a way to help sustain a high level relationship. This laughter is of a particular kind, caused by self-humor and not by the deprecation of self or others.

Energy worlds level three is also the beginning of the supernatural occurrence in which extraordinary events begin to take place. These happenings often manifest in what the medieval Celtic Christians called "a thin place." This is a place where the veil between heaven and earth is so thin that heaven (the power and glory manifest from the highest two levels of the energy worlds and the dynamics they are connected to) is able to appear on earth.

The Celtic Christians continued the beliefs of their non-Christian ancestors that there are certain places and times in which strange things could happen. When they encountered such a place and time they would celebrate it, for example by raising a small cairn of stones or giving the place a special name of power and endearment. Thus they would mark out places where they met nature spirits and devis, elementals and angelic forces on a kind of energy map of the lands they lived in and traveled through. Stonehenge, for example, was constructed in just such a "thin place."

When the relationship field between people becomes spiritually charged, it becomes a nomadic thin place through which special charisma, healing energies and new revelation can appear. This is a very special and rare kind of relationship field, but one that is certainly possible for two or more people to build between them.

At this level of the energy worlds an individual person can radiate an energy field of such a fine nature that it causes unusual effects around them, which others may refer to as "miraculous." One of the best documented of these effects was in the life of St. Francis of Assisi. According to tradition, animals would gather to him, rather than running away as they do from lower energy fields. A useful clue in this when energy dating is to take special note of how animals and very young children react to your energy date. This will tell you much about the energies that are lodged and loaded in their personal energy field.

Astral Levels Two and One

Levels one and two contain the highest spiritual expressions of the human race, recorded throughout world history. The energies of the saints and saviors, the origins of the great world religions have all been in these levels. All quests for higher spirituality and illumination have been an attempt to connect to these highest levels of the energy worlds and the treasures they contain. These are the levels of miraculous healings and revelatory teachings, the levels connected to and occupied by Jesus the Christ, Mohammed, Moses,

Gautama Buddha and other great religious bringers and teachers. It is also the realm of higher healing powers and angelic forces.

The quest of King Arthur Pendragon for the Holy Grail was to connect to these higher two levels of the astral light, as was also the expedition of Jason and the Argonauts. Their quest was not for physical silver and gold but for the energies of silver and gold. The search for the Holy Grail and the Golden Fleece were spiritual quests to reach the silver and gold energies of the highest levels of the energy worlds. These levels have always been associated with the power and glory of the sun and the shimmering stars of the Milky Way.

The solar disc in Egyptian art and the halo in Christianity are symbols that were designed to show a person who had reached the level of what has been called an avatar—the embodiment of these highest energies in human form. This is the level of true human royalty, occupied by kings and queens of spirituality, rather than magnates of power. At these levels miracles can and do happen. Miracles are energetically caused events that happen rarely on planet Earth because very few people lift themselves to the levels where such things can occur. Jesus the Christ was able to produce such a concentrate of energetic love that miracles happened around him. This was true also for the Buddha, Mohammed, Merlyn the Magus and many other great spiritual people throughout the history of the planet.

To engage at these levels has always been the quest of the spiritual seekers of the world who value the qualities of enlightenment and illumination above all others. It is true that the higher we go on the magic carpet of the astral light, the greater the illumination and the greater the property of living light that we invite into our life.

Navigating With Your Energy Map

A map is most useful when we know where we want to go. If we know we want to build relationship fields that can lift us into the higher energy levels of the energy worlds, we can use our map accordingly. If we decide we want to excel in living in levels seven, six and five, we can also plan and target accordingly. Someone who is intent upon more spiritual relationships is not going to hang out every night in the casino because the energies generated there will work against what they have decided they want. It is important to make a conscious decision about where we want to target our life in the realms of energy, just as we do in the material world when setting out on a particular career.

When we spend time with another person we are literally spending the energy of our life on them and with them and it is only reasonable to add up if the projected experience is worth the investment, both of energy and time. In this context it is vitally important to be regularly adding up what it is you want with your life at core.

Some of the most wealthy and powerful people have the most toxic radiations and are also the most unhappy. If you decide that material wealth and power are the top priorities in your life, you may need to be prepared to pay the price of processing dark astral forces. If, however, you seek a life of spirituality and development, you will no doubt choose a different path. This is not to say that material wealth is incompatible with spiritual wealth. The two can happily coincide together. The question is whether you are able to control your wish for material wealth or whether it controls you. The urge for possessions is hazardous because very often it turns around and possesses the person who then becomes subject to it.

With our map of the seven levels of the energy worlds we can navigate our way through the options of life with greater awareness, consciousness and skill. We can now start to view people and their behaviors not so much according to who they are, but what they are. What energies from the seven levels of the energy worlds are they connected to and primarily represent? Are they energies we want to bring into our personal field and be associated with? Are they people with whom we want to be partners in passion or partners in purpose? Do we want to build a mutual relationship field with the energies they represent?

The energy worlds map contained in this chapter will help you view your past, present and even your potential future experiences energy worlds first. With it you will be more able to see people as representatives of the energies, forces and powers they are connected to. It is these energies and the compound nature and density of force and power they create in your personal energy field that will ultimately determine your destiny, which is a matter even more core to your life than the quality and nature of the relationship fields you construct with others.

Chapter Eight
Reading People

Perhaps you have met someone that you took an instant dislike to for no apparent reason and, somehow, their mere presence caused the hair to rise on the back of your neck. If you have had such an experience, the question arises: what causes this and why does it happen?

The answer sits within the mystery of the exchange of energies between auras and the antagonisms that can occur between the energetic contents of different personal energy fields. The energies in your aura and someone else's can immediately go on the offensive without either of you having spoken a word. This unseen worlds conflict then triggers a release of power through your instinct into your physical systems, to prepare you to fight or take flight. Somehow, in that first meeting, you literally rubbed each other the wrong way in the realms of energy and this caused a friction between you, whether it was verbalized or not.

Many different phenomena are caused by the interaction of our energy fields with those of others and they work by definite energetic laws that can be known and understood. When we understand these laws and the phenomena they cause, we are in a much better situation to diagnose the dynamics of attraction or antagonism when they occur.

Using Our Soul Senses

The more we train ourselves to be sensitive to the worlds of energy, the more we are able to feel and understand what is happening and what is transferring into our personal energy field from the people we meet. This is why training our five soul senses is so important. Each of our so-called common senses has an energetic counterpart that can directly detect what is happening in the realms of energy. In Chapter 5, Energy Dating we explored energetic sight and touch. There are three other soul senses that we can develop. These are our energetic senses of smell, taste and hearing.

Some experiences literally leave a bad taste in our mouth. This is so tangible that it feels physical. It is actually a bio-chemical reaction to an energy that is degrading to a person. Energies also emit vapors that can be smelled. Higher astral energies, when we are able to smell them, often have an aroma that is sweet and very pleasant, while lower astral energies can have very bad smells. When a person goes into extreme loss and inferiority, for example, it produces a smell like burning rubber. A higher astral presence can cause a scent that is like rose petals.

Electrical hearing often appears like a high-pitched whistling in the ears when the nature of the energy in the atmosphere shifts substantially. This can help you detect when the energy level in the district changes.

In reading people's energies it is important to take into account the subtle signals you have been receiving all your life, but which you may have dismissed as insignificant. These messages have energetic meaning and it is important to pay attention to them.

Reading Energies

How can you tell if someone means what they say to you? How can you measure if their words are full or empty? Such skills become possible when you learn how to read the worlds of energy and power. You are then able to understand not only the physical clues that you witness every day in words, posture and body language, but also the energy signals that people emit.

Imagine that as well as seeing what your energy date is wearing and the expression on his or her face, you are able to see their energy level and also the kind of energies they emitting into their aura on that day. Imagine being able to know if they are telling the truth because you can see and feel any contradiction between what they are saying and the energies that come with their words.

Some people appear smart and well-groomed and yet something inside us feels something is not right about them. In contrast, we can meet a person who seems not much on the surface, but our instinct accurately alerts us that there is more to them than meets the eye and upon enquiry we usually find this to be true. Physical appearances can be deceptive, but when we can see and feel the realms of the human energy field, we have a much more accurate picture of who and what we are meeting.

Energetic Weather Systems

With practice we can begin to see the colors that are active in the energy field and they can tell us a great deal about the people we are with and what is happening with them. Sayings such as "Are you feeling under the weather?" or "What's eating you today?" become more than figures of speech as we find the evidence to confirm these phenomena appearing in the energy worlds of the aura. There are astral forces that can gather around a person and literally eat away at the energy inside their energy field. This often happens when a person is worried sick and just can't seem to shake the feeling that something is going wrong in their life they cannot quite put their finger on. We have so many expressions in our language that hint at these weather systems and what they cause. Once you start to see and feel the energy worlds, you can then trace where the origin of these sayings actually comes from. They come from a time when people knew these worlds as their daily reality.

When a person is depressed, you will see that they are literally under a dark cloud. Depression is a state in which there is a dark vortex of energy in a person's aura that pushes down upon them and literally de-presses them. Conversely, when we have a bright idea, there is a bright flash in the energy field, usually around the head. When we say that someone is looking bright, that brightness begins in the aura and it is this that we respond to.

When a person falls in love, it produces a definite change in their energy field, which becomes supercharged and even gives them a sense of increased buoyancy. A person literally feels lighter on their feet and sometimes they feel like they are almost floating on air. The energy field of the person in love becomes more charged and the shades and natures of colors in their aura change. It starts to have the look of love and their energy field literally glows from within. This is because when we fall in love we rise above our normal selves. We do not fall in love at all. We rise in love and connect to a higher astral energy than is usual in our life. The challenge is maintaining this higher connection over time.

Detecting Energies

Once you begin to explore these worlds, the doors of perception open up and a new world of possibility is revealed. Developing sensitivity to these worlds will help you in all aspects of your life, from health and well-being, to choosing where to live, who you want to invite to be your current partners in passion and how to refine the levels of energy in your relationship fields. When you become consciously sensitive to the radiations that come towards you from other people, you will sharpen your instinct and improve the readings you receive about who or what you are sitting next to. You will become more sensitive to the vibe they give out.

If you sit within the radiation field of someone who hurts animals for pleasure, you will find that it causes a hot prickling sensation, often beginning in the hands and then creeping up the spine. This hot, prickly reaction is hinted at in Shakespeare's *Macbeth* when one of the three witches speaks about Macbeth, "By the pricking in my thumbs, something wicked this way comes." Wicked is a particular compound energy state that a person carries in their energy field and it generates a prickly heat. A person will rarely become like this overnight; it usually takes many years to build an energy field that has this effect.

When you sit within the radiation of someone who regularly uses healing energy to help others and is progressing on a path of spiritual development, he or she will radiate a very different kind of energy. You are likely to feel this as cool tingles on your hands. It is very pleasant to be with. We all instinctively feel these things anyway and it is why within the first ten seconds of meeting someone we get a feeling or sixth sense reading about them. This instinct is a very accurate assessment tool and it is wise to listen to it.

Our instinct is very alert to new impressions and in the same way that it alerts us to danger in the physical worlds, it tries to alert us to danger in the worlds of energy impressions. One part of our instinct is the instinct of the body, another part is the instinct of the soul. The instinct of the soul also tries to alert us when high-energy possibilities are close by. When we listen to our instinct, curious and beneficial coincidences start to happen in our lives in greater volume. We may even come to rely upon this sixth sense or intuitive inner hunch about things as a natural extension of our five senses. It is the prodding of this intuitive higher instinctive faculty that takes us to increasing synchronicity in our lives. It is very interesting in this context that the word "instruction" when shapeshifted becomes "our instinct" and indeed the instinct will instruct us as to where the higher energy worlds would have us be if we are prepared to listen. Very often synchronicity works by inner promptings from the instinct, combined with moments of higher intuition.

The terms instinct and intuition are often used interchangeably; however, they describe two different natural abilities. Our instinct offers us a sixth sense by which we can be alerted to higher and lower energetic opportunities. Moments of intuition are caused when our mind and emotion come to be "in tuition" to energies and essences in the energy worlds, which are able to download some of their intelligence into us. The word "tuition" itself means receiving knowledge from a tutor. In colleges and universities the tutor is another human being, to whom we pay a fee for tuition. In the realms of the energy worlds, the tuition comes directly into our mind from banks of energy intelligence that offer us moments of intuition. Most often the fee that we pay for these moments of intuition is called "paying attention."

I was living on a houseboat on the river Thames in Oxford in March 1977 and was meeting with a teacher who was showing me various aspects of how to work with the energy worlds. On a Tuesday and Thursday evening he would come from London to meet with me and whoever else I could bring to the gathering. Part of my training was to listen to my sixth sense. I was on my boat one Saturday morning when I had a sudden sense that I needed to be somewhere else, but for no reason that I knew. Because I was training myself to listen to inner promptings, I stood up and put on my coat and began to walk into the city of Oxford along the bank of the Thames. I instructed my inner instinct to prompt me as to where it wanted me to go.

I walked as far as the main street, left the river and turned right towards the town. "Now where?" I asked. I walked along until I had a nudge to go left, so I followed. Then at the next turn I went right. I walked to a café that I sometimes frequented. "In here?" I asked. "Yes," came the internal nudge. As I entered I looked towards the counter and there was my teacher. He had his back to me and could not have seen me approaching, but he addressed the waitress behind the counter and said, "Two coffees please." He had bought one for him and one for me. I then learned that he had decided to come into Oxford for the day to have a look around but had no means to contact me. By listening to my instinct and then my intuition it led me directly to where he was. This is one example of many happenings I have known and I have come to rely upon this sixth sense as an important and natural faculty. It has led me to many unusual encounters in places that I had never planned to be and, of course, other instructions have been about where not to be at certain times!

If we are able to not only feel the energy that is coming towards us but can see it as well, then this offers us further insight into what we are meeting and whether we want to associate with it. Once I was looking for an apartment in London, England. I went to visit a house in Hammersmith that had a room for rent. I approached the door and rang the bell. When the door opened, I saw a large, murky-red egg filling the doorway. It was so strong that it took me a few moments to refocus my eyes and see the physical person inside it. I immediately announced that I was not interested in the apartment after all, turned and walked away.

Once we have trained ourselves to use our energy vision, sometimes it switches on as if all by itself, as in the example above. In my experience this is when our amazing human systems want us to get an important message. The message I received on this occasion was "We do not want to live here" and it made it so dramatic that I could not miss it.

Another warning message arrived when I was about to get on a late-night subway train in New York City. Just as I was stepping on, I received a full picture of the other person's aura that was in the subway car. Their energy field was very dark and murky, striped with an angry red. There would have been just the two of us in the car. I did not get on the train but waited for the next one. I will never know what would have happened if I had got on that train.

There have been numerous other occasions in my life when my aura vision has spontaneously switched on and it has always been with a purpose. Sometimes it has been a warning about getting away from someone or something in the district and sometimes it has been an urge to stay near a particular place, person or energy. It has also developed into an extra faculty that often switches on when I do healing and counseling work with others.

Energy Messages

The energy worlds send us messages every second we live. How much attention we pay to these messages is a matter of the inner credence that we give them and consistent training. Training not only makes us more sensitive to the signals themselves, but also lets our internal systems and intelligences know that we are interested in what they have to tell us. This feature is crucial and is often underestimated. What we tell ourselves on a daily basis is our own call-over or mantra about life. The beliefs we form internally determine the way we view the world around us. When we tell ourselves we want to understand the world of energies and the world really does work energy worlds first, then we we are telling our internal equipment this is our wish and our world view. Whatever we tell ourselves on a repetitive basis is how we order our internal universe, and this then orders our external universe. Our inner views govern how we view the world.

What we say conditions us first and others second. There is only one person who will listen to everything we ever say and we are that person! When we verbally declare ourselves, we are letting our amazing human systems know what is important to us and are setting our internal priorities. When we tell our friends, "I don't like so and so," our inner faculties listen and file that information away. It will condition the energy signals we send to that person the next time we meet. The same applies to how we train ourselves about the energy worlds and how connected we become to our intuition. When we tell ourselves we are interested in the energy readings our system receives, it will work to produce more of them for us. When we tell ourselves, "I believe in my intuition and my sixth sense and will pay attention to their messages," they will work harder for us because we show interest and pay attention.

When we tell ourselves we are interested in reading people and registering the energy signals they radiate, our systems will listen and follow through on our request. By paying greater attention to our soul senses and our sixth sense, they can help bring us to be in the right place at the right time for the unexpected meeting which we do not consciously expect but which our semi and unconscious faculties help to engineer for us. The unexpected meeting and the serendipitous event are more commonly known as synchronicity.

Synchronicity is born out of the energy worlds and is facilitated by listening more attentively to our inner energy guides and following their inner promptings. Once we understand this, we realize that there are no "coincidences" in the traditional sense of the word. What there are, are "co-incidences" of two or more energies that are drawn to be together. How many of us have had the experience when, because we turned left instead of right for no conscious reason, it set into play a chain of events that changed our lives?

Reading the Signals

When you know how to read people, they become an open book. In every moment and movement they advertise their nature to you because everything they are is connected to every other part of them. Therefore, what a person shows you on the outside tells you something about their nature on the inside. The way they sit, the way they move, the colors they choose to wear, the way they pick something up or pass it to another person—every small gesture tells you about the person you are with and the energies they are connected to.

The physical always begins in the worlds of energy. So, if you can see directly into the worlds of the aura, the cloak of many colors will tell you a great deal about what is happening with a potential energy date. If, however, you cannot see their energy field yet, don't worry, but keep training. There are a thousand physical signals that a person offers every moment to tell you about the kind of energies they are working with.

Translating from the Physical

Because we are energetic beings, the physical body is the book into which we etch the traces of the energetic processes of our lives. When we learn to read the physical, we can trace the lines on the face and the postures that a person adopts back into the energy worlds where they began. This is the advanced version of reading body language.

If you want to find out more about what it feels like energetically in another person's world, try copying the way they sit and hold their hands. To give one example, when someone holds their thumbs tucked inside their fingers, it means they are prone to being introverted. If right now you tuck your thumbs inside your fingers and hold them that way for a few minutes, you will start to feel what it is like to be in hiding this way. Trying out this posture will give you more insight than by just looking at this posture from the outside in.

This technique is being taught today as "mirroring" and is proposed as a way to cause another person to feel more comfortable. What I am proposing is for a different reason. It is to help you get inside the other person's skin and understand what it feels like to be them and to look out at the world through their eyes. Inevitably, this will also allow you to become energetically closer to them, as you will have more of their energetic frequency inside you. You can then build an increasing empathy between your energy fields as you bring the energies in your energy field onto their frequency. This is certainly a way to form a relationship field between you and the other person more powerfully and more quickly.

Palm Reading

One of the arts within which you can most swiftly get a feel for what it is like within the energies of another person's world is palm reading. Contrary to a common misperception, palm reading is not for the specially trained or clairvoyant few. Palm reading is essentially the ability to look at the lines in a person's hand and detect some of the major energies that they have processed in their life. Once you have a good idea of what these energies are, it puts you into a position of being able to prophecy what these same energies will cause now and into the future.

When a person gives you their palm to be read, they are offering you a bridge into their energetic world. The shape of their hand, the length of their fingers and the formation of their lines began to form in the womb and include the energies of their genetics, hereditary traits and the astrology of the moment they were born. The lines change through the experience of a person's life, but certain energetic fundamentals remain constant. When someone presents you with their palm, they are presenting you with an energetic roadmap of their life, and even of their ancestors.

Fingerprints offer a powerful example of how certain energy fundamentals are fixed at the time of our birth. Whatever happens during our life, although the lines on our palm may change, the energetic fundamentals represented by the unique spiral patterns on our fingers never change. There has never been another person on Earth before who has exactly your fingerprints and there never will be again. These prints are a material trace of the energies that emanate from your fingers, and there is no other person who has the unique electromagnetic emanation coming from their fingertips that you do. Pause for a moment and look at the palms of your hands. You see the lines that are there? They are unique. These lines have formed in accordance with the unique combination of energies that you alone have processed and also by the way that you hold your hands as you live your life moment by moment, including when you sleep.

Hands will tell you a great deal about a person because hands develop almost a life of their own. They reveal much about what is happening in the semiconscious and unconscious energy worlds of your subject. As stated earlier, when you meet someone and they hold their thumbs tucked inside their folded fingers, so they cannot be seen, you know you are dealing with someone who is hiding from you and the environment they are in. If you want to have a successful energy date, you will need to coax those thumbs out during the course of your meeting. When someone holds their thumbs this way habitually over long periods of time, it causes particular line formations in the hand, which are very different to those that form in the hands of an extrovert.

Palm reading is learning how to read the story of another person's hands and from this learning to read the story of their life and their energy worlds connections. You will discover much about your energy date if you learn how to read their palm. Also, if you are seeking an introduction, it is a great opening—who isn't interested in having a palm reading?

Nine Steps to Reading a Palm

Here are nine basic steps to being able to start palm reading today:

1. Let the other person know that you are offering to do a palm reading for them and then wait a minute or two so that their consciousness floods their

hands with the energies that you are going to read. This happens because the person has begun to mentally focus on their hands in anticipation of the palm reading. During this time you can engage them in a short conversation about the nature of palm reading that you offer. and let them know that this is an energy reading and not fortune telling. During this time you can also try mirroring their posture to help you get closer to their frequency.

2. Ask them to pass you an object and observe carefully how they do it (delicately, forcefully, clumsily or tentatively) because it will tell you about how they do everything else in their life.

3. When you ask for their hand to start the reading (which, of course, has already begun), be very conscious of how they give it to you. If they give their hand to you very lightly so that it can quickly be removed, know that they are careful in their commitments and take time to settle to new companions. If the full weight of the hand comes into yours immediately, know that they are quick to depend on others. They may actually overburden people with the weight of their dependency. They are also very trusting and have probably not experienced so much pain in their life. Pain in relationships tends to make a person quick to withdraw and they will give their hand lightly. Remember, how a person does one thing gives you information about how they do everything else in their life.

4. Check the flexibility of the hand and the rigidity of the thumb. The more flexible the hand, the more flexible they are in their attitude to life. Also check for the feel of the flesh on the hand. The more fleshy and spongy, the more likely they are to be good listeners and absorbers of what others tell them. The firmer and tighter the flesh, the more likely they are to be a person of quick action. They may even be seen to be hasty. Is the hand slightly damp? If so, the person becomes nervous easily and is becoming so even at the prospect of the reading. Also, look at the shape and size of the hand. What can you imagine this hand doing? Is it the hand of a pianist with long tapered fingers or is it the hand that holds a shovel? Does it look fine and artistic or solid and practical? Hands speak out the story of their life, if you will sensitize yourself to what the hand is saying. At this stage observe the hand as if it were a unique entity unto itself. Then reconnect it to the overall picture of the person that it belongs to.

5. When the person gives you their hand for the reading, check if the fingers are close together or far apart. A very open hand with large gaps between the fingers tells you that the person is very open, probably has a generous nature and is not good at keeping secrets. They also may let money slip easily through their fingers. Fingers that cuddle close together show a person who is good at keeping their own counsel and is to be trusted with confidences. They may also be a saver rather than a spender.

6. The four fingers and thumb project different kinds of energy that correspond with the five senses and the five energy centers of the soul as shown in this diagram:

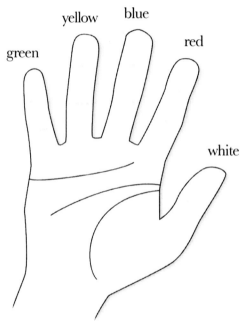

The five colors correspond with the five senses and energy centers in this way:

Color	Sense	Sensing Organ	Energy Center
green	sight	eyes	sexual/creative
yellow	smell	nose	emotional/feeling
blue	touch	skin	instinctive/intuitive
red	taste	mouth	moving/habitual
white	hearing	ears	thinking/learning

Astrologically the five fingers have also been put to the planets of the Ancients, as shown here.

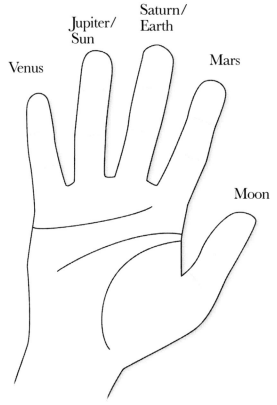

Knowing this you can feel at the base of the fingers for the mounds that are there. These mounds vary in size considerably from person to person. What I have consistently found is that where there are large lumps below the fingers, the person has much of this energy in store. Where there are dips instead of mounds, the person has often generated much of this nature of energy. during the course of their life.

You will often find that where there are dips instead of mounds beneath the fingers, there are often lines of transmission going up those particular fingers. This will tell you a lot about the nature and color of soul energy that they tend to process. When they have a pronounced dip beneath a particular finger, you can even take your reading skills further by venturing to ask if that is one of their favorite colors. Let us say there is a dip under the yellow finger. You might even say they like to have yellow around them.

Having studied the hand, now you can move to the lines themselves. If they have lines of transmission under the red finger, you may say that that they have definite opinions and are mentally strong. A lot of power emanating from the blue finger says they like to be calm and peaceful. Because this is also the finger of Saturn, they will tend to be good at self-discipline. When they take on projects, they tend to see them through. The little finger processes green energy and when there is a line traveling up the hand toward the green finger, this indicates a healing tendency and you may check, for example, if they were always the member in the family to look after sick animals.

Each time you get something right, your energy date will open up to you more. And don't mind getting things wrong—just say up front that you are learning to read palms and would they mind if you had a try. It swiftly moves your energy date into a more intimate setting and increases the energy flow between you. If you want to make an indirect approach on what may be a sensitive issue, you can use the third-person technique of saying that perhaps friends perceive them to be a certain way, rather than directly telling them what they are like.

8. When it comes to the major energy lines, such as the head line and the heart line, as shown here, look for the depth and width of the lines. The deeper they are, the greater the depth of the person's mental and feeling processes. If the lines are fragmented and broken, it speaks of a dislocation in these energies during the person's life. Make comparison also between the heart and the head line. The deeper and stronger

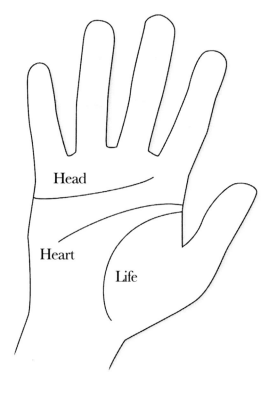

Head

Heart

Life

line will tell you whether they tend to live their life more from their heart or their head.

9. A thick, fleshy mound under the thumb indicates a person who tends to have a strong emotional life. Look out for lines that radiate out from the base of the thumb. These are worry lines and will tell you how the moon influence flows through the person's life. If the worry lines are deep and cross the life line, then their worries interfere with their life. If they are shallow and do not cross the life line, they are not so much of a worrier.

One advice I would give very strongly is never to try and predict the future of the person whose palm you are reading. Tell them this is an energy reading, not fortune telling that predicts their future. It is true that in this process you start to become empathetically linked to the other person and you may even start to get flashes of what their future could be like. I recommend that you do not tell them in specific detail because in telling a person their possible future you can implant it in their semiconscious and make it so.

Advise them that the palm is regularly changing as a person's energetic processes change. If they want to see this in action for themselves they could make a photocopy of their palm today, put it away and then make another copy in nine months and compare the two. They will see definite changes that reflect what has been going on in their life in the meantime. Heart lines can fracture or be mended. Head lines can become stronger or weaker. Life lines can grow. Our palms are a living portrait of our lives and are an open book to those who know how to read them.

Graphology

Graphology is another science based on taking physical evidence and then tracing it back into the energy worlds that give birth to it. Handwriting that consistently lifts above the lines of a page and slants strongly forward to the right shows an optimistic, futuristic nature that may be disconnected from what others see as reality. Backward slanting writing that falls below the line shows a person inclined to live in the past. If the person writes heavily, pressing hard on the pen, they will press hard on everything in their life. Big loops and flourishes show someone who is inclined to live their life with big loops and flourishes, probably with quite a high emotional content. A person who is neat, tidy and precise in their writing is going to be like this in other areas of their life. You can predict to someone from their writing what their socks drawer is like!

This one subject is a whole book unto itself, but even in this small peek we can see how, when you practice reading people, everything they do offers you evidence as to the natures of energies that are working through them.

One other fascinating insight that can be discovered through graphology is if you are able to compare the handwriting of two people who have elected to become partners in passion and are forming a relationship field. To give one example, a couple I worked with in my EnergyWorlds practice gave me samples of their handwriting. When I overlaid them upon each other what was revealed was quite extraordinary. The woman had the most forward leaning writing I had ever seen; it seemed to be straining to leap into the future. The man's handwriting, on the other hand, was the most backward leaning handwriting I had ever seen and seemed to resist being carried into the present at all.

When the two samples of handwriting were cut out and placed together, they exactly leaned against each other to provide a structure that looked like two leaning posts. This was exactly accurate for the nature of relationship field they had formed. He was heavily grounded in the past and seemed to be holding back from expression in the present while she was a choreographer and dancer who was always planning her next dance movement and had difficulty in handling the practicalities of life. They complemented each other exactly. When I pointed this out, they were very pleased and glad to continue as they were. Another couple may have responded very differently and sought to become more individually independent, but for these clients the confirmation of their leaning post pattern was enough and they were happy to find their relationship field thus confirmed in their handwriting.

Faceology

Over time our faces become etched with the habitual expressions we wear. These expressions are caused by the energies we process. Smiling will gradually create smile lines around the eyes, while frowning etches furrows between the brows. The older we get, the more clearly visible these lines become. A traditional saying that holds some truth about this is that under the age of thirty we have the face God gave us, but over the age of thirty we have the face we made us.

When someone has authority over others, they tend to develop arched lines over their eyebrows. These may be a sign of someone who regularly "browbeats" others. Wide nostrils tend to show someone with strong emotions. Thin lips show attention to detail and possibly a tendency towards meanness, while thick lips often indicate a tendency to generosity.

The eyes tell us a great deal. The eyes that meet yours, hold your gaze and do not look away are able to focus on you and what you are saying. The person whose eyes are constantly flicking away into the ecology around you is easily distracted and, therefore, will be prone to not remembering what they have promised.

When people wear dark glasses we often feel that we cannot be quite sure what is going on with them. The glasses block the energies from the eyes and leave us unsure where the person is at. When you are energy dating someone, ask them to remove their shades!

Fidgeting

A person who fidgets has energy they are not using in a productive way. You will often see people who are sitting but whose legs are moving up and down very fast. Their system is producing more energy than they are able to put into words or other means of expression and so their legs shake. This is the equivalent in the human of the tail of a cat, which it uses to flick away excess energies. An example of this is the person who plays computer games that simulate violence. Their brain summons enormous reserves of energy to deal with mortal combat except, because it is really just a game and directly involves only the brain and not the rest of the system, it produces hot energy that is not used and fidgeting is a way their natural energy systems can get rid of it.

Obviously, if you are with your date and they are fidgeting and not focusing on you, then something in them wants to be somewhere else. It is up to you whether you try to bring them back into the space where you are, as in, for example, offering them a palm reading, or just suggesting to meet on another night, or call off the encounter altogether. Another possibility is that they need the washroom!

Reading Clothes

Everything about a person gives clues to the energies they are connected to and this includes the clothes they choose to wear. Clothes may not give such a close-in reading as body language, palm reading, faceology and graphology, as clothes are easier to change in a person's life, but the choice of clothes a person wears gives you another opportunity to connect to the web of their energies. Are their clothes primarily chosen for comfort or are they chosen to impress others? This will tell you a great deal about how they think and how they live their life.

Shoes are often an excellent place to begin when starting energy reading through clothes. Are the shoes comfortable? Do they allow the person to move silently and easily from place to place? How high a price in discomfort is the person prepared to pay so that they can be in fashion? Do the shoes have a lot of non-functional bows and buckles? If so, then the person's life will be like this also. Are the shoes designed to make a statement to others or are they chosen for the functionality of the wearer? This again will tell you about how the person is in their life. Are they shoes that will be worn a few times and then cast aside? Are the shoes well cared for and have they been repaired? In this case the person will probably hold a similar value for what else is in their life. Perhaps they are frugal and they will be less prone to throwing things away immediately when they do not work and will try to repair them. This also means they are likely to be loyal and to value old friendships. Yes, all this and more from a pair of shoes!

The colors a person chooses to wear send another important message. Colors are usually worn for one of two main reasons: either the color reflects an energy that the person is trying to attract to themselves or it reflects a color that is already strong in their energy field and they wish to project it. Often these two reasons are twinned together. Clothing will also tell you whether the person is trying to get themselves noticed or whether they are dressed for anonymity. Some people like the spotlight and others like the shade. It is reflected in the way that they dress. Flamboyant ties tend to be an emotional statement, as are showy scarves and necklaces, because the neck is a prime radiating place for the emotions. When someone likes to accentuate their neck, they usually are subject to strong emotions.

Some people use their clothes to very definitely put themselves on show. They want to be noticed and they draw energies from others this way. This is also true of people who dress to shock. They like to bring other people's energy their way. The quietly dressed person is often more confident in themselves. They do not need external confirmation to prove their importance to themselves and others.

Certain styles of clothing have powerful energy connections. The tweedy jacket with leather elbow patches immediately connects to the essence of the academic. Flared jeans and tie-dyed t-shirts say something quite different to a studded leather jacket. Clothes also often indicate a particular allegiance someone may have to a group, club or association. The golfing trousers and shirt make a mark of energetic association with all other golfers on Earth. This energy association is quite different than the studded leather attire favored by motorcycle gangs.

When detecting energies through clothes, you also need to take into account the ecology. If attending a charity dinner, people will dress differently than for a walk on a beach. Whatever the circumstance, you will be able to tell a great deal about the person by what they wear and how they wear it.

When you are specifically meeting another person for an energy date, the way they have prepared their appearance to meet you speaks volumes about their energetic intentions. Of course, this detection process is always a two-way street and how you have prepared yourself to meet them also speaks loudly to the observant.

Reading Posture

Our human systems are an energetic circuit. This circuit can be open or closed and all stages in-between. When life is read energy worlds first, then body language becomes a series of clues to the energies that are acting through another person. When the legs and arms are crossed, it is easy to see that a person's energy circuit is closed. When someone leans forward, they increase the attention they are paying from the deeper chambers of the brain and are really trying to get what is being said. When someone leans back and looks down their nose at you, then they are more based in their front brain, which is where judgment, criticism and opinion are held at the ready. If a person looks open but has their ankles crossed over, they are holding back some energy to themselves and are not fully with you.

When understanding these basic features about posture, you cannot only read them in others but also use this knowledge for yourself. If you are energy dating and want to maximize the energies that you receive from the other person, then deliberately keep your arms and legs uncrossed, even if it feels uncomfortable to you because you have trained yourself to cross your legs by habit.

Everything about a person in the physical worlds speaks volumes about their contents and connections in the energy worlds and with training and practice you can bring yourself onto the web of a person's energetic connections through the clues they offer you. The value of this is beyond price, as it means that you can get a faster and more accurate reading about a person's nature. This will help you decide whether you want to bring them closer to your life and also if you can assist them in any way.

The art of mirroring, as mentioned earlier, is another tremendous tool in locking onto another person's frequency. When you are able to energetically walk a mile in their shoes, you can move into a level of empathy that can never be achieved working with mental observation alone. By adjusting your inner feelings to another person's frequency, you can read them at many levels, from the inside out as well as from the outside in.

The higher art of reading people's energies is to take the map of the energy worlds from the previous chapter and read what are the prime energies and levels that a person is connected to. In doing this practice you may even be able to ascribe numbers to the different energies you detect to be present, from seven to one. As you practice consciously reading people's energies, you open a book of life that is inexhaustible and lives, breathes and is forever changing. It is a book that never finishes, but offers new energetic experience every day.

Energetic Language

Language is the major medium of communication and energy exchange that we use. Words themselves are containers of energies. We first think what we are going to say in the realms of the mind and we then summon the energies to fill the words from the temple of our bodies. We fill the words with the breath of life and also with electrical energy and power. This power is connected to the seven levels of the energy worlds according to the energy connections of the speaker and the level of what it is they wish to say. When we speak, we make a projection from within our energy field into the energy fields of others. We also project our personal power into the energy worlds of the planet, the astral light.

Words can be used to transmit signals of great spirituality and illumination. They can also be used to denigrate, degrade and degenerate. It all depends upon the quality of the speaker and the energies they are connected to. We can use our map of the energy worlds to detect what level of energy is traveling in the speech we hear.

If you have ever heard recordings of criminal conversations, you will have been struck by the amount of swearing that goes on in them. This swearing is powered by the energies from level seven of the energy worlds.

The quality and nature of a person's language and the energy content that travels with it will tell you a very great deal about them. Like the aura itself, these energies change from moment to moment as they express the energies that are moving through their life. If we are expressing something from the lower levels of the astral light, we will fill the words that we speak with low-level power and energy. If we are connected to the higher levels of the energy worlds, we will fill our language with higher-level energies. When children were heard to swear in times gone by, their mother may threaten to "wash their mouth out with soap and water" because this language was described as "dirty language" and "filthy language," but the filth is not integral to the words; the toxic quality of the words is supplied by energies from the lowest levels of the energy worlds. The mother was not trying to wash out the words, but the energies they were filled with.

When someone is passing on factual information, for example, in giving directions to where you can find the bus, this is usually level six language. This level of language is to be found in most explanatory documents and is designed to inform. It is also used in trade and commerce. When someone asks you to buy their product, they usually pitch the energies of their language at level six. Most discussions to do with trade and finance take place at level six.

Level five language sparks into the realms of ideas, particularly ideas that are to do with trying to improve the human and planetary situation. When you see college students gathered around offering their views on how to improve the world, because of their intent to make things better, they are usually connecting into level five energies.

The energies of language at level four and above contain a mystical, magical quality. Level four language creates a ring of truth that produces a charge in the air. It is never based in personal gain but addresses issues that are bigger than personal.

These are brief indications to show how the energy map of the astral light can be used to detect energies in speech, which is such a crucial medium of energy exchange and so vital to reading people.

Reading Gestures

Gestures tell us a great deal about what is unspoken in a person. Very often gestures are used to reinforce speech and express what the person is not able to put into words. Gestures, like words and postures, transmit energies and are very revealing about what is happening in the semiconscious realms of a person.

When someone is not sure whether to say yes or no to something and has difficulty making a decision, their hand will often go to the back of their neck. This is because contradiction causes heat at the back of the neck and a hand is placed there to draw some of this heat away.

When both hands go on the hips, this is a classic posture of a person either being strong and drawing energy from the power of the hips, or seeking to strengthen themselves by so doing.

When someone adopts "the thinker" position and puts their fist under their chin, they are trying to power their thinking capability by directing extra energy through their hand into their mental systems.

Every posture and every gesture has a meaning and can be explored. It is a physical road map giving indications of what is happening in the realms of energy.

Misreading the Signals

The more we train ourselves to be sensitive to these signals, the better our chances of being able to recognize and respond to the reality of these energy exchanges as they happen, rather than to what we would hope or wish the case may be.

We most often are hurt in relationships because we misread the signals, or overlay the signals of what is really going on with our own wishes, wants and desires. One example of this has been called "seeing the world through rose-colored glasses," which refers to actually producing a kind of energy gas in our energy field which pre-flavors everything we encounter. This may appear to make the world a rosier place, but it does not help us come closer to what is really happening in the worlds of energy and power. Another example is encapsulated in the phrase "love is blind," which is to do with the production of actual love gases in the aura that flavor all incoming energies.

Energetic Disappointment

Disappointment usually happens because we misread or chose to ignore the signals between us and our date, and we project energy into a future that does not exist. In this sense disappointment is caused by the gap between the future we are projecting toward and what the case really is.

When a young man proposes to a young woman, he may already have built in his mind the projection of where that romance is going, including children, a house in the country, a happy old age and much more. If she has in mind a short term relationship because she feels that her true love is elsewhere, then there is going to be acute energetic disappointment coming his way in the near future! This energetic disappointment is caused by his not living in the real worlds and not checking what the other person wants and how they actually think and feel.

If we misread the signals that come from our partner in passion, we can swiftly become prone to building castles in the air. One partner may be ready to move from being a partner in passion to becoming a partner in purpose for the long term, but if their partner is not ready, it simply cannot happen. It takes two to make a contract and it takes two to decide to build a long term relationship field.

As we become older, experience teaches us to be more careful, whereas in the young, the flood of passion that early romance unleashes can easily overpower reason. This is why in many ancient cultures young people would receive careful training in these matters at the time of puberty, so they would not ruin their lives through early disappointment. They would also receive counsel with their partner in passion when they decided to commit to a long term relationship. The second book in this series, *Partners in Purpose* will include many practical exercises a newly engaged couple can do together in preparation for this next step in their commitment level.

The danger of disappointment is that when a person projects energy into a future that does not happen, these energies then return back to the source of their arising in the present. If they have been projecting toward marriage for three years and then the engagement is called off, three years of energetic projection comes back upon the person in one day. This produces real grief because all these energies then need to be processed through and away for the person to be able to move on. Some are so emotionally hurt and distraught they cannot do so for many years, if at all. Miss Havisham in Charles Dickens's tale *Great Expectations* offers us a classic example of energies that could not be processed through and which arrested her life. In this process forgiveness is vital.

The first person we need to forgive is ourselves, because we were the one who misread the situation and invested the energies of our life into something that turned out to be unreal and non-viable. Forgiving the other person is secondary and also vital. In this process an important realization is that they likely did not consciously set out to do us harm. Most probably they also misread the signals and did not know any better. It is best not to blame them personally and go into energetic vengeance, but to realize they did not know themselves and their own desires and acted out of ignorance. Vengeance can quickly connect us to level seven of the energy worlds and all its toxic contents, while forgiveness lifts us up toward level four of the energy worlds wherein live the healing balms and energetic ointments which help us not only to forgive but also to forget

Astrological Energies

No chapter on reading people would be complete without a brief review of the significance of astrological energies. Astrology today is the most used and popular tool by which people try to read both their own energies and the energies of the people around them.

The magi and seers of old mapped the energies of the universe and studied how they affect all organic life on Earth, thus creating the science of astrology. They made a particular study of how these energies affect human life, both individually and collectively. Their first purpose in doing this was to better understand how the universe works and the interplay of energies between the moon, planet, sun and stars. They knew that the human and all planetary life forms are made of exactly these same energies and wanted to understand the relationships between them. Through studying the influences of the universe they also sought to predict future events on Earth. The charts and observations that they made are still the most popular energy maps that people use today when they try and see what new relationships may be coming their way as they read their daily horoscope in the morning paper—perhaps to try and discover the scope of their horror!

The root of the word astrology is the same as the root of the word astral and indeed the influences of astrology always appear first in the astral light of planet Earth. After they have entered the realm of the Earth's energy worlds, people can begin to connect to them. All new ideas, signals and frequencies come to us via the astral light of the planet. Always remember, all new ideas and relationships begin energy worlds first.

Modern astrology is based on the surviving fragments of this ancient science that investigated the energies of the universe and how they influence all life on Earth, including yours. Astrology was and still is a science that is dedicated to the study of energies. Ancient astrologers drew up charts and maps of how planetary and stellar energies appear in different forms of organic life and also how they appear in the human structure.

These charts were come to by a process of energy matching. By using their physical and soul-senses, the astrologers would detect the natures of energy coming, for example, from the planet Mars. They would then match these energies to the Earth's animals, plants and minerals to discover those that had a similar frequency. They assembled their results into tables such as the one shown here. They would also study the affects of these energies on human behavior as they came into prominence in the heavens.

Their studies indicated that if someone had an energy appear prominently in their astrological chart, they would be particularly prone to making behavioral responses as this energy waxed and waned. They applied this principle to individuals and also whole cultures. The culture of Rome, as an example, was founded by Romulus and Remus who, according to ancient fable, were suckled by a wolf, divinated to Mars (see chart). This analogous story was to demonstrate that Rome was born under the power of Mars, a potent carrier of red martial and administrative energy. We can see how this energy plays itself out in the history of Rome.

The Ancients did not divide astrology and astronomy into two separate sciences. They saw the energetic and the physical to be one integrated study. They were deeply interested in both the energy worlds of all things, as well as the worlds of matter.

Just as the medical profession today studies the newborn child to check overall health, well-being and capabilities, so the ancient astrologer would do an "energy check," trying to work out which influences appeared most strongly within the newborn. This is the information they sought with their astrological charts and energy detection systems.

Every time we turn to the astrology section of the newspaper to consult our horoscope or visit the astrologer, we are asking for an interpretation of our weather map of energies and how these forces are likely to affect our lives. Just as the weather forecaster studies the atmosphere of the planet and tries to forecast what is going to happen, so the astrologer tries to map the worlds of energetic influence and offer some interpretation of what this is likely to cause, whether personally or globally.

Astrology: Fragments of an Ancient Science

Zodiac sign	Zodiac symbol	Ruling planet	Quality	Element	Animal/symbol	Part of body	Metal	Gem	Flower	Dates
Aries	♈	Mars	Cardinal	Fire	Ram	Head	Iron	Diamond	Poppy	Mar 21-Apr 19
Taurus	♉	Venus	Fixed	Earth	Bull	Throat	Copper	Emerald	Violet	Apr 20-May 20
Gemini	♊	Mercury	Mutable	Air	Twins	Shoulders	Mercury	Agate	Lily of the valley	May 21-Jun 21
Cancer	♋	Moon	Cardinal	Water	Crab	Lungs	Silver	Pearl	Larkspur	Jun 22-Jul 21
Leo	♌	Sun	Fixed	Fire	Lion	Heart	Gold	Ruby	Marigold	Jul 22-Aug 21
Virgo	♍	Mercury	Mutable	Earth	Virgin	Bowels	Mercury	Sapphire	Pansy	Aug 22-Sep 22
Libra	♎	Venus	Cardinal	Air	Scales	Hips	Copper	Garnet	Rose	Sep 23-Oct 22
Scorpio	♏	Mars	Fixed	Water	Scorpion	Genitals	Iron	Topaz	Chrysanthemum	Oct 23-Nov 21
Saggitarius	♐	Jupiter	Mutable	Fire	Centaur	Thighs	Tin	Turquoise	Daffodil	Nov 22-Dec 21
Capricorn	♑	Saturn	Cardinal	Earth	Goat	Knees	Lead	Garnet	Carnation	Dec 22-Jan 20
Aquarius	♒	Saturn	Fixed	Air	Water bearer	Ankles	Lead	Amethyst	Orchid	Jan 21-Feb 19
Pisces	♓	Jupiter	Mutable	Water	Fish	Feet	Tin	Aquamarine	Water lily	Feb 20-Mar 20

Many people who are trying to better understand the energy relationships in their lives turn to the astrologer for advice and help. "I am a Virgo and he is a Cancer. Can it work between us? Should we become partners in passion?" is a typical enquiry of the person who is using astrology to help them in their energy dating.

The widespread use of astrology demonstrates the popular belief that relationships are based in energy worlds attraction and that we are keen to try and discover the patterns by which this works, by charting them into some kind of working energy map.

The fragments of the ancient science of astrology we have inherited help introduce us to the idea that energy patterns can determine what makes for successful relationships. However, they do not offer us a complete guide to the energies at play in ourselves and in others. There are so many factors that are active that we need to work it out actively in the field of life moment by moment.

Putting It All Together

After you have your first instinctive reaction to a person and have used the tools described in this chapter, it will bring you closer to the energies of the person you are dealing with. This will give you a sense of what levels of the energy worlds they are primarily connected to. An important addition here is that often the younger a person is, the easier it is for them to move into entirely new for them energy worlds connections.

After forty years of age a person is liable to be more fixed in their energy patterns, as this is one of the main effects of aging. A person becomes more fixed in their energetic connections, unless they have taken deliberate measures to keep themselves flexible.

Something you can do, if you wish to know more about the energies that the people you are meeting are connected to, is to prepare a list of test questions, ranging from the personal to the impersonal. A question such as "What do you do for a living?" will focus into the levels of general energy trading at levels seven, six and five of the astral light. When you ask, "What do you think is the purpose for life on Earth?" or "What do you think about life after death?" you invite a whole different level of dialogue. Whether the person has thought about such questions or not, and if so, at what level and power, will tell you very much about the energy level and connections of the person that you are dealing with.

The process of reading people's energies is something that you can practice and develop every day. Remember, energy dating does not stop after you are married or find your significant other. The energy connections of your partner in passion, close friends and relatives change every day, just as yours do. Why is it that one day you are happy and another sad? Why is it that in the morning you feel a little depressed or down and in the afternoon you become light and inspired? The difference is always to be found in the energy worlds and in the energetic states produced in your personal energy field.

You will be energy dating for the rest of your life on Earth, both with people that you have never met before and with people you have known for many years. The vital key is to become as aware as possible of what energies are at play, both in you and in them, so you become a conscious energy worker rather than an auto-responder to what lives in the energy worlds, often put there without your conscious participation. In learning how better to read people and their energies, you thus become more empowered to write the future you want into the energy worlds of your personal energy field and the astral record of the planet.

Chapter Nine
The Seven Levels of Love and Sex

The spectrum of passion that exists between any partners in passion is determined by the levels of the planet's energy worlds they are connected to and how they have instructed their internal energy systems through the course of their lives. When two people come together, both of whom are connected to particular astral properties and whose energy centers are in differing states of balance and imbalance, the range of possibilities in the energy worlds spectrum between them is infinite.

Like Calls to Like

There is no greater aphrodisiac in the world than two energy fields that are alike. When we say we like someone, it is most often because they are like us in some way. In the natural worlds we can clearly see how like calls to like. The saying, "Birds of a feather flock together" is very true in these realms. We can see exactly this principle being played out in the attractions between people and in the powers and forces that fill their energy fields. It is, for example, a powerful reason why people who carry the loading of energy called "fame" in their personal field are very often attracted to other famous people.

Most social clubs and societies exist because people who share the same energies and interests like to spend time together and transfer these very energies amongst themselves. They form up group relationship fields which can be aptly named "fields of recyclement." There usually is little new influence entering this kind of group relationship field and indeed very often there are definite rules laid down to prevent too much change within the relationship field they form. There is a kind of magnetic satisfaction in encountering behavior patterns, forces and powers that change little and this tends to become more true as people become older, except in rare cases. The members of the group feel safe and confirmed in each other's energetic company and know they can rely upon certain energetic frequencies to be present among their social set. Group relationship fields are another fascinating study for the student of the energy worlds.

Shared Chemistry

When people share what has come to be called "chemistry" together, the real attraction begins in the realms of the energy worlds and in the exchange of power and passion between their energy fields. The chemistry others observe them sharing together comes second; the energetic spark comes first.

The relationship field formed between partners in passion is determined by the charisma of both parties and what those energies in combination then attract from the energy worlds of the planet. Two people will come together if they both are caused to feel better than they could when they were alone. The mutual relationship field they form boosts the performance and possibility of both.

Conversely, the relationship field formed by the combination of two energy fields can also cause two people to come together and block each other's lives and possibility. There is no greater assistance we can have in our life than to find an energy partner who is complementary to our life's purpose. There is also no greater stopper or blocker in the world than to invite into our lives an energy partner who is antithetical to what we are setting out to do with our life.

Ultimately, if the partner in passion we are energetically and bio-chemically attracted to is also able to become our partner in purpose and our partner in evolution, we are most fortunate. At the same time, it is not a matter of chance but also a matter of dedicated work over time.

One of my clients in session with me once said, "I want what you and Joanna have got." She wanted it instantly, right there and then. What I then needed to point out was that the relationship field Joanna and I have formed together has been the product of over thirty one years' mutual work and has certainly not been instant. There was indeed that first, spontaneous spark of attraction that caused us to become partners in passion in the first place, but the journey from there to becoming partners in purpose and endeavoring towards becoming partners in evolution has been long, testing and cannot be instantly transferred. It has been based on living and endeavoring together in the now moment. If we have a successful relationship and a potent relationship field between us, it is in good measure because we refrained from declaring ourselves "together forever" but decided that either of us could leave at any time and we would stay together so long as we could make it work hour by hour, day by day and minute by minute.

Soul Mates

So-called soul mates are two people who are drawn together with great power because the contents of their energy fields, aggregated through the way they have lived their lives and the circumstances of their birth and growing up, have become so like each other that an enormous attraction is caused between them. Soul mates can find each other at any level of the energy worlds and their attraction can be so powerful it defies the conventions of the time in which they live. Bonnie and Clyde, Anthony and Cleopatra, Nelson and Lady Hamilton, Troilus and Cressida, were all caught within such a power of mutual attraction that it became destinic for them. Romeo and Juliet is a tale of two such soul mates who preferred to die rather than be parted.

Opposites Attract

One person can also be strongly attracted to another because they offer in their energy field exactly what the person yearns for but does not have. This is where the saying, "opposites attract" has great significance in relationships. In this instance two energy fields can be powerfully attracted to each other because they complement each other by providing what the other person needs. An excellent example of this feature was demonstrated in the Graphology section in Chapter 8, Reading People. In this example the relationship field is strengthened because both partners bring to the table what the other partner only has in small measure or not at all. Once this has balanced out over time, however, it will be vital that the two partners in passion discover a mutual purpose; otherwise, having balanced each other out, they will then tend to drift apart as the reason they came together will have been fulfilled.

Extreme differences between energy fields often make for a short term infatuation but become a source of frustration or irritation because of non-compatibility in the long term. Unless a mutually agreed purpose is come to within the relationship, it is most likely that the partnership will come to an end once one of the partners has fulfilled their temporary energetic need and received the energy food they wanted. This may be in the realms of the need for sex, status, psychological support, emotional dependency and a host of other short term energetic cravings. These relationships do not tend to last unless the partners can find deeper and longer term wells of attraction that lead to lasting and binding energetic love between them.

The Power of Love

Love is the great expression of the push, the pull and the poetry of the interplay between souls. Energy impressions are the prime food of love. "I can't live without your love," "Your love means everything to me," "I cannot live in a world without love," and similar sentiments expressed in hundreds of thousands of love songs, are mostly statements of how important the fuel of the other person's energy transmissions and physical presence have become to the poets and songwriters.

This power of love is not a solid, liquid or gas, though it can put us off our food, make us cry and change our breathing patterns. Love is an energy and as an energy it has different levels of expression. Like all the great powers that move human life, love is invisible and intangible. If we were asked to carry a bucket of water or a bucket of earth, we could easily do it. But if we were asked for a bucket of love, a bucket of hope or a bucket of fear, we could only look strangely at the asker and explain that this is not possible. But it is exactly these invisible energies that are the greatest powers of them all and move our lives the most powerfully. It was not Helen's face that launched a thousand ships; it was the fact that Paris fell in love with her energetic and physical presence and could not bear to be parted from it.

Of all the invisible powers of life, love is the most often spoken, sung and written about and yet, what is it really? Love is not a singular property. "I love you," "I want to make love to you," "Let's make love," "For the love of God," "I love macaroni and cheese," "Love for sale." These are all very different expressions using the same word. The word describes an energy of multiple levels and natures. Love is an energy food and an energy transmission that manifests differently at each of the seven levels of the energy worlds. It can be so powerful that a person becomes love-sick. They can become temporarily addicted to the object of their love. At this level, love can be a drug, as another popular song tells us. This state of being in love triggers chemical and biological changes within the human body, as numerous scientific researches have indicated.

The state of being in love or "hopelessly devoted to you" can become so extreme that when a lover decides to walk away, it can even trigger the suicide of the other party. Their life has become so fixated upon the object of their love that to live without the other person's presence and their continuing mutual relationship field becomes impossible for them. All other joys and feelings about life become irrelevant and they take their own life. This demonstrates the power of the emotional and sexual fuels in combination. They can overpower reason even to the point of taking the person into an early and self-chosen death.

This is not a higher love but an obsessional requirement in which the ego becomes fixed upon having or possessing that particular energy for itself. The higher level of love is being able to leave the other person free and travels alongside a genuine wish for their happiness and for their progressive future, whether the couple is together or has parted ways.

The Power of Sex

The act of sex is one of the greatest healing and cleansing processes available to us. The higher yang power held within the woman is able to join with the lower yang power in the man, while the higher yin force held within the man is able to join with the lower yin systems of the woman. This process can bring great reciprocal healing to both partners.

Although sex offers one of the greatest healing potentials for the soul of both the woman and the man, when it is abused it also causes some of the deepest and longest-lasting energetic wounds and scars. There is a major difference between abusive sex at energy worlds level seven, routine or diversional sex at energy worlds level six, intellectualized sex at energy worlds level five and sex which charges and refreshes the soul at level four. As the act of sex releases huge amounts of energy, it is also very attractive to particular powers and forces that occupy the seven levels of the energy worlds. These forces are attracted to where there are significant concentrates of human energy released that are on their frequency.

Sexual power can both heal and hurt. The energies that attend the sexual act are always determined by what is in the thoughts and feelings, minds and emotions of the participants.

Seven Energy Levels of Love and Sex

The energy worlds table that follows is designed to help you distinguish between the seven levels of love and sex. It is by no means complete, but is designed to offer help in diagnosing what it is that you feel. In the energy worlds feelings are as valid as thoughts, as the emotions are often more powerful and carry greater energy than the intellect. A still greater power is where feeling and thought are able to travel in harmony together. This is the root of poetry, prayer and song.

The seven levels of energetic love are based on the full spectrum of the planet's energy worlds and its contents. It is very rare for someone to occupy only one of the seven levels. Most of us draw and transmit our energies spanning three of the seven wavebands which are adjacent to each other. If, for example, our energetic center of gravity is in level six, our elevated energies usually come from level five and our lower energies from level seven. If we succeed in making level five of the energy worlds our energetic center of gravity, then our higher energies will tend to come from level four and our lower energies from level six.

As it is with love, so it is with sex. Sex is not made of one energetic state. There are many different levels of possible experience within the act of sex. These different experiences range through the seven levels of the energy worlds. There are many different energies from the energy worlds that can attach themselves to the act of sex. Sex can reach heights of religious experience and bring us closer to God; it can be accompanied by the liberation of the spirit and a surge of well-being for the soul. This is the level of sacred sex. Sex can also be accompanied by essences from the lowest, most toxic attributes of the energy worlds, printed there by the actions of perverse people over thousands of years.

In our human energy systems the contents we draw into ourselves from the seven levels of the energy worlds charge and change our mind, flavor our soul and ultimately determine our destiny. Transformation is the process of gradually lifting our life up this energetic spectrum into the domains of higher energetic love and leaving the more toxic compounds of the lower levels behind.

The following table outlines some of the properties that live within the seven levels of the energy worlds when considered through the energetic powers of love and sex.

Energy Worlds Level Seven

This is the level of the criminal, the gangster, the sadist, the bully, the despairing and the suicidal. This is also the level at which one partner subjugates the life and possibility of the other for their own ends.

The energies at this level are so murky that energetic love cannot shine its light here unless it is carried in from a higher level by the conscious decision of a person on a mission to help another. Anyone deciding to attempt this had better watch out, because the concentrates of darkness here can be very strong and may try to recruit them into its world. There is always an exchange of energies and so there is always a price to be paid for mixing at these levels.

Love

- Starkly stated, love does not exist at this level. What resides here are many compound toxic qualities, some of which masquerade under the name of love, always self-serving and self-focused.
- "I couldn't care less about anybody else" is the motto.
- "Everything is always all about me" is another motto.
- Men who subjugate women against their will.
- Mental, emotional and physical abuse and all other severely abusive relationships.
- Deep depression, self-abuse and suicidal tendencies.
- Chronic alcoholism and illegal drug dependency.
- Deliberate deception and deceit.
- Partners supporting each other in criminal behavior.

Sex

- Lust at this level is an angry, violent energy, separated out from any inter-human respect and courtesy.
- "I will get away with what I can and take anything I want, whenever I want it, by whatever means available, regardless of others" is the motto.
- At this level, "Let's make love" is really, "Let's have sex for my gratification, whether you want to or not."
- Here sex is not attached to love. Sex is a driving need, often accompanied by violent thoughts and actions.
- This level of sex can be highly addictive. It is fed by pornographic content and sees the other gender only as a sex object to be taken advantage of whenever and in whatever way possible. Sex at this level is purely based in personal gain with no feelings of empathy, affection or care whatsoever.
- These energies heat the blood and offer no real satisfaction, only a temporary alleviation of the symptoms until the rising tide of lust compels the next action.

Also to be found here are:

- Sexual magic, love potions and spells to have control over others.
- Sadomasochism, porn shops and prostitution.
- Enforced sex of any kind.
- The energies that drive the rapist and violent sexual acts.

Energy Worlds Level Six

This is the level of routine or general habitual love and sex, accompanied by the initiation of new sexual relationships to break out of the bonds of boredom. Love dwells here as a magnetic, habitual glue between people and is based in mutual need, requirement and expectation. Sex becomes a routine action often restricted to a certain place and time. The lower end of the bar of level six energies is that of being beaten down by life, settling to accept what life has come to be and giving up on higher aspirations and inspirations. Staying together to get by dwells here, as does, "Well, we have been together for so long now that it doesn't seem worth starting over."

This is also the level of using sex as a way to break away from the feelings of routine and ennui that level six bring with it. Sex is seen as an escape from the mundane aspects of living and offers an outlet for bottled up frustrations. Level six is also the primary level of the discotheque and the night club and the traditional Friday and Saturday night social scene. According to the connections then made within such a social scene, partners in passion may discover each other at lower or higher levels of the energy worlds according to what is powered in their energy fields. There is nothing wrong with using the social scene, or Internet dating for that matter, to try to find your significant other. This is a medium through which you are able to meet potential partners in passion and partners in purpose. What counts is where you go from here in the formation of a mutual relationship field, if you and your selected partner choose to do so.

Love
- A relationship field at this level often comes to be bound by economic necessity—two can pay the bills better than one.
- "Staying together because we can't see what else to do and don't see a better option"—and there are the children to think about, too.
- Energetic love here often comes to have a sense of a couple being resigned and weathering life together.
- Love here can be like a spoonful of emotional syrup that gets dished out the same to whatever is being considered without much distinction. I love my car, my house, my food, my husband/wife and my desserts.
- Men's eyes routinely follow women down the street.

- "I love you" greeting cards that someone else has written are exchanged.
- Love as an expected energetic fuel without really thinking about the other person—"You don't send me flowers anymore."
- He or she is mine. "That's my woman/that's my man."
- Love as possession and requirement upon the other person.
- "I need and depend upon you" would often be a more accurate expression than "I love you" at this level.
- "I am habituated to you and must not forget your birthday or anniversary."
- The husband or the wife being characterized as the ball and chain is an unfortunate expression at this level.
- Co-dependency and fear of letting each other go is strong here.
- "I am bored and going out with you is better than staying in on my own."
- Entering the relationship for a sense of gain and not wanting to lose.
- Wanting the other person to stay just as they are—because if they improve themselves they may leave; this is the stay-the-same syndrome.
- Mutual dependency and feeding each other's weaknesses and habits in the name of love.
- The focus often comes to be upon getting by from week to week and trying not to have confrontations, producing a relationship in which both parties can feel comfortable. They agree not to think too much or question each other's motives.
- "Holding within social conformities because it is all that we know" is very strong here.
- Taking the initiative to have an affair out of boredom is also a strong feature here as there is a lack of purpose in the mutual relationship field.

Sex
- This is the level of what can be called general habitual sex in which sex often takes place out of boredom and wishing to escape routine life.
- Automatic sex because you are in the same bed.
- No special preparation for sex.
- Sex with little mutual warmth and feeling.
- Sex as a 'one-night stand' initiative without inter-respect and courtesy.
- 'Hooking up' for the night often under the influence of alcohol and drugs.
- Sex as the expected thing to do.
- Sex as competition and for bragging rights.
- The introduction of drugs and alcohol as a further escapism can quickly move sex from energy worlds level six into level seven.

Energy Worlds Level Five

Love

- The focus here is often upon self-improvement, improving one's lot and supporting each other in career and ambition.
- Keeping up with and, if possible, overtaking the Joneses.
- Improving the home circumstance, sending the children to the right schools.
- If possible, having both a town and country home.
- Mutual intellectual and class snobbery. A consciousness of being part of the elite.
- Mutual confirmation of each other's inttellectual abilities and goals.
- Intellectual preening of each other's ego.
- Relationships for the purpose of elevating one's social position.
- Social climbing and competition with other couples.
- Going out with the coolest guy or girl to show them off, giving ego satisfaction (also at level six).
- Trophy wives and husbands.
- Goal-orientated relationships, offering each other emotional and intellectual support, particular in each other's goals and projects.
- Impressing others is often a feature at this level.
- High achieving political power couples.
- Relationship based in academic and intellectual pursuits.
- A greater allowance for the other person to improve and to change than in the previous two levels.
- An increasing interest in what each other has to say, and in each other's company.
- There is less possession as we climb the levels of the energy worlds and an increasing wish for the other person's success as a life in their own right.
- A greater desire for mental as well as physical and emotional stimulation.

Sex

- Sex within the context of a relationship that is based in ambition and achievement.
- Intellectual sex: "What was it like for you?"
- Performance driven sex: "How was I?"
- Using sex to impress self and others.
- Brain-centered sex. The participants feel like actors on the stage of life due to

over education of the brain, producing "the observer syndrome" in which neither partner is able to fully forget themselves.

- Sex in a semi-detached state because the center of gravity of consciousness stays in the brain. The brain will not still its chatter.
- Self-conscious sex surrounded by lots of words.

Trading in Sexuality

Whereas "the skin trade" resides at level seven of the energy worlds, trading in sexuality is a powerful feature in both levels six and five. Consider the time and effort invested in preparing for the exchange of sexual power that takes place across the world each evening—particularly on Friday and Saturday nights! This is not the sex trade for money but the trading of sexual power for energetic and physical stimulation. In level five of the energy worlds this trading in sexual power is often accompanied by an agenda of personal improvement, social climbing and ambition, as well as searching for Mr. and Ms. Right.

Energy Worlds Level Four

Love
- Level four love is less common, particularly when people are in a relationship over the long term, as it takes special effort to keep a relationship fresh at this level.
- Genuine altruistic love begins at this level.
- There is less self-consciousness in matters of love and sex.
- The couple is no longer trying to impress others, but is more interested in what the relationship really is unto itself.
- The couple is more prepared to be honest with each other and offer each other genuine reflection at this level.
- There is a greater sense of freedom and energy flow in the relationship.
- A greater mutual trust is present together with little sense of possession upon the other person's life.
- Being glad to let the other person be themselves.
- There is a natural allowance and permission for the other person to improve and change.

- A continuing effort by both parties to improve their mutual relationship field.
- A natural enjoyment of each other's company and conversation with a greater flow of humor and enjoyable inter-respect and courtesy.
- Love without personal agenda begins at this level.
- There is a rising in, not a falling in, love.
- There is often a sense of everything else fading away when the couple is together.
- Energetic love at this level often brings a destinic feeling and a sense of this being a unique moment in time.
- A high level of passion and a sense of entering a new world.
- There is a sense of discovering a new you in the relationship as the level of energy transference is so high.
- The beginning of what is called true love.
- There is a charismatic power, presence and sense of purpose that grows in the mutual energy field of the partners.
- People often remember touching this level all their lives.
- A sense of finding your soul mate or spiritual kin is often very strong.
- There are spontaneously arising fine feelings for each other.
- A powerful sense of coming home to the other person and feeling at ease in the mutual charisma caused between you.
- A powerful wish to be true and honest with each other.
- The natural love of woman for man and man for woman not tainted by intellectualism (level 5), trade (level 6) and sexual perversion (level 7).
- Love with a spark that lifts us up and makes us feel better about ourselves. It provides a sense of feeling like a better person because of the relationship.
- A powerful sense of simply being glad the other person is in the world.

Traditionally poets referred to this level of love as pastoral love, and would contrast the idealized simple love of a shepherd and his maiden (level 4) with the sophistication of the court (levels 5, 6 & 7). The shepherd's love was shown to have a natural purity scarcely present in the sophisticated court. This represents a relationship between a natural man and woman, rather than the intellectual (level 5), the sheep (level 6) or the fox (level 7).

Most couples that touch level four and marry do so in the hope of maintaining this level four connection. Those that do so tend to stay happily married. This is why the saying, "And they lived happily ever after" should really be, "And then the energy work between them really began..."

Sex

- A hallmark of sex at level four is what is not present, because the personalized ego loses its grip. At this level trading in sexuality has no place. Kinky underwear and sexual gamesmanship are irrelevant. The lower levels play mental games, tease and conceal. Here no such tricks are necessary.
- Sex at level four is a natural process between a man and a woman. No more and no less.
- The self-consciousness of personal identity disappears as the power of the now experience sweeps it away.
- In natural sex there is very little intellectual activity, but rather simply being present in the moment in which thoughts of the past and the future fade away.
- The brain goes quiet and is present in the moment. The background brain chatter that happens at level five, six and seven is absent. Tuning in to the rhythm and power of the soul in a more natural and pure form. Being in the moment, in the power of now.
- There is no sense of disconnection between the brain and the body. There is a sense of being totally inside oneself.
- Mind, body and soul are connected into one harmony and one is able to forget one's identity.
- Supporting the whole of the other person by the joy of touch, mutual companionship and energetic exchange.
- At this level there is a glow of mutual warmth and endearment in which both parties give freely to the other. It is not self-focused as both partners want to ensure the sexual and energetic satisfaction of the other. There is a free and generous giving both ways.

Energy Worlds Level Three

Love

- At level three and above, the power of mutual exchange in the relationship field becomes so high on a daily basis, that the energy transference that occurs during sex becomes an extra flare of mutual passion in the ongoing passionate exchange that takes place in this relationship. High energetic properties such as inspiration, honor and decency anchor in strength in this mutually created energy field.

- This level of love does not happen by accident. Both parties are doing self-work and are on a spiritual development journey.
- There is deliberate cultivation of high creative qualities in each other.
- The partners create an enhanced atmosphere between them.
- There is increased telepathy and clairvoyance at this level and above as the relationship field becomes a highly conductive medium through which telepathic and clairvoyant messages can travel.
- Love at this level and above causes a high level of ongoing energetic connection, even at distance.
- There is a conscious harmonizing with the yin/yang powers of the universe for mutual refinement and increased spirituality.
- The two partners consciously set out to help each other in their mission and sacred contracts in any way that they can.

Sex
- Sex at level three takes place within a powerful atmosphere of mutual love and affection.
- Sacred sex begins at this level.
- There is always a great respect and endearment for the other person present.
- Both partners are able to engage in giving each other pleasure as a mutually purposeful act that is in support of everything else they have mutually agreed to do in their life together. Sex is part of the web and weave of their purposeful lives together.
- There is an attitude that sees the other person as a spiritual being and sex as a sacred transmission and reception of energies both ways. There is increased understanding of the energies at play in sex and its processes.
- Sex is engaged with as an experience that joins the human to the great Creation in a core way.
- This is the level of sex where the spirit floods the brain, mind and body.
- This is the level of what has been called Kundalini sex in which the spiritual power at the base of the spine flares up simultaneously in both partners and allows them both to be bathed in the higher spirituality of indigo and violet energies.
- Spiritual sex begins here.

Energy Worlds Level Two

Love

- Here we move above personally based love, into a level of love between people which is described as "all encompassing love." This is very rare.
- The love of two people at this level becomes so powerful it beacons out and touches all it comes into contact with.
- This level of love is described in Buddhism as compassion.
- This level is always associated with higher spirituality and enlightenment.
- Mutual love here is always within the context of consciously being part of the universe, with a certainty of continuing life after death.
- Love at this level makes such a powerful impression in the energy worlds that it survives the erosion of time for possibly many thousands of years.
- Here, you cannot not love others. You recognize that the spirit of God is in them as the spirit of God is in you and so you reach out to assist.
- The Christian concepts "Love thine enemy" and "Love thy neighbor as thyself" become no longer an ideal but an unavoidable living reality.

Sex

- Sex at level two is always spiritual at its core. It has religious purpose and connection and always the sense of upholding the purpose of life.
- Sex takes place within the conscious context of the higher purpose of the universe and Creation.
- Some sexually-themed statues in Eastern religions depict this kind of sacred sex. It is the level they described as sex in the presence of the gods.
- Here sex is a conscious technology to offer warmth and comfort on the journey from this life to the afterlife.

Energy Worlds Level One

Love

- At this level love moves beyond language into the realm where we do not have the words.
- Ineffable love, almighty love, compassionate love, omnipotent love, the love of the Creator, the love of God, the love of Allah, are all attempts to express this level of universal love.

- All the great religions of the world were originally dedicated to trying to produce energetic love at this level, in an attempt to influence the human race away from the lower forces of violence and warfare, and onto the path of peace.
- Love here is a direct connection to a permanent universal property, which is all encompassing, non-personal and new every day.
- Here a transmission of energetic love is of such power and potency that it transforms the astral field that it transmits into.
- At this level to live and to love cannot be separated.

Sex

Sex only happens here as a purposeful act, within the mutual sense of the presence of God and Creation. It is known by both partners to be a sacred process that allows them to feel the unity of man, woman and their higher purpose. They know sex to be a very high energetic event that can connect the human to the core powers of the universe, and respect it as such. At levels one and two, sex is a highly religious part of a spiritual journey.

Full Spectrum Passion

Full spectrum passion describes the state in which two people meet and their seven chakras and five energy centers are open to exchange with each other. Full spectrum passion can happen at any of the seven levels of love and sex. The higher the energy worlds level within which it is able to happen, however, the greater the quality of the relationship field and the more powerful the generation of energetic love between them.

When a couple can move their relationship from a center of gravity in energy worlds level six to a center of gravity in level four, it brings a tremendous increase in illumination and energetic love to them both and to all those they deal with.

As you climb the seven levels of the astral light, the love you generate within yourself and with your partner cleans and clears away residual toxins from the lower levels that may be lodged in your energy fields. As you progress together on a journey of spiritual development, the level of energetic love you generate between you refines. This is one of the great rewards of engaging in a spiritual development journey as your mutual relationship field becomes enhanced, empowered and illuminated through the three progressive processes of being partners in passion, partners in purpose and partners in evolution.

Energetic Refinement

In an ideal relationship of two fully evolved people, both parties would live in the highest three levels of the energy worlds, their five soul centers would be fully balanced, they would be in conscious control of their brain, mind and faculties and all seven of their energetic chakras would be fully open and engaged. This relationship would be a beacon of spiritual illumination into the astral light of the world and, because of The Passion Multiplier, the energetic effect of their love would have a tremendous illuminating effect in the energy worlds of the planet. These two people would occupy the dynamics of what it really means to be a king and queen in the worlds of spiritual illumination. The masculine principal would be connected to the gold and yellow energy of the sun, while the feminine principal would be connected to the royal blue and silver of the planet.

Although we may target building such a relationship field, the reality of achieving it calls for a great deal of dedication and conscious application. When we go to work on a Monday morning, for example, we mostly take ourselves to a job that is anchored in the frequencies of trading and is dedicated to a financial motive. We may spend forty hours or more a week inside this energetic ecology. Once we include travel time, fulfilling the many maintenance demands of keeping body and soul together and the rebalancing of our relationship with our partner, there are not many hours left in the day to do the spiritual work we want to do to even attempt a lasting relationship in the top three levels of the energy worlds. Knowing, however, that a higher state exists as a possibility in human relationships can inspire us to set our feet upon the path of seeking to refine the level of energetic love in our relationships. The practicalities of building an empowered and long-lasting relationship field within the exigencies of modern living takes conscious awareness, time and dedication.

Coming to Terms

We have many terms that describe the stages of energetic refinement of the masculine/feminine energies passed on to us from those that have gone before.

At the lower levels of the energy worlds the terms male and female describe the gender power we are connected to at birth. These terms also apply to the animal worlds and belong at levels seven and six of the energy worlds.

The terms man and woman describe the process of connection to the power of the masculine and feminine powers as ascribed only to human beings. These terms belong with people who have a center of gravity primarily at the higher end of level six and at level five of the energy worlds.

At a higher level of energetic refinement, we meet the terms gentleman and gentlewoman, which tell us of a man and woman who have engaged in a conscious process of refinement to lift themselves up to the higher end of level five and level four of the energy worlds.

Another level up in energetic refinement and we meet the terms knights and ladies. These terms in the energetic realms apply to people who are attempting to establish themselves at level three of the energy worlds and are based in the higher end of energy worlds level four and level three.

The next elevation brings us to the terms king and queen which would belong only to those people who had established themselves with a center of gravity in the higher end of level three and level two of the energy worlds.

In level one the terms used are no longer gender specific as we meet names such as savior, deliverer and world teacher which can apply to both men and women. This does not mean that gender does not apply at this level, but that the mission becomes the prime feature and gender is simply a feature of the vehicle it is expressed through.

The Light Bearers

When a full spectrum relationship rises into the higher levels of the astral light, then through the power of The Passion Multiplier, two people are able to produce a level of energetic love that offers an enhanced ecology in the place where they live and to the people around them. Further, through the way they live and the powers they conduct they beacon spiritual light into the astral planes. This beaconing spiritual light causes an upgrade in the astral planes that radiates new energetic opportunity to others.

Light bearers lodge the signals of their illumined energy processes into the energy worlds and influence the occult choices available to people alive today and to future generations. The way is still open for us to become beacons of higher spirituality whose emanations offer new light and hope to the future of the human race.

Chapter Ten
Occult Choices

The energetic ecology in which we live is formed by the seven levels of the planet's energy worlds and the seven wavebands within each level . We are not alone in this ecology. The astral light contains the energetic record of everything that has ever happened here on Earth. The Roman Empire may have declined and fallen sixteen hundred years ago, but its energy record lives on within the astral planes. Everyone who has ever passed this way has left his or her energy impression within the energy worlds to a greater or lesser degree.

The Occult

The occult is a term that describes all the energy impressions that have ever been imprinted within the energy worlds of the planet. Some of these impressions are now long gone into dormancy and are hard to connect to; others are very alive, immediate and easily accessible. The different energies that exist in the occult naturally find their place within the wavebands of the energy worlds according to their nature. Low level energy transmissions frequent the lower levels of the astral light while higher level energy signals and transmissions live within the higher levels of the astral light. This is a law of human generated energies: they naturally find the level of the energy worlds to which they most closely correspond.

Like any other life form, these energies want to live, grow and reproduce. They do this by working through human beings. The lower energies are easy to connect to, as they will enter into human life at any opportunity and there are far more lower energy signals around; the higher energies take more work and development because they can only enter people who produce signals in the higher levels of the energy worlds. The Ancients believed that it took special training to enter the realms of the higher energies and they organized special schools and societies to help make this possible. To connect to these higher levels was a fundamental purpose of the mystery schools and esoteric societies of times past and many of the still surviving fragments of spiritual development practices in the world today. Initiation and graduation practices were designed to confirm that a spiritual shift had successfully been made by a person from a lower level of the astral light into a higher.

The term "occult" itself does not signify good or bad. We mostly have a misconception of the term based upon Hollywood movies, such as *The Exorcist*, that show these unseen forces to be mostly evil. This is only true of what lives in the lowest waveband of the energy worlds. The occult also includes every decent action that has ever been made. Qualities such as care, honor, courage and humility are also occult powers that live in the planet's astral light.

The occult is the total of every signal, power and force that has ever been generated by any human anywhere on Earth since human life began. The occult contains living powers and forces at all levels that have varying degrees of life energy, power and intelligence. Ghosts are scars in the lower levels of the astral light. Angels are intelligent powers that try to help in human development and spirituality. Demons are intelligent lower forces that try to cause lower behaviors, such as violence, so they can feed from the power that is then released.

The higher we go up the levels of the energy worlds, the greater the consciousness, intelligence and illumination. This is where energetic love is broadcast by the power of individual conscious action. The lower we go, the lesser the intelligence, illumination and consciousness. In these realms the reliance is upon powers such as brute force, mass persuasion, deception and blind obedience to the guardians of conformity. Certain occult energies are highly toxic and once they have entered our space, they are hard to clear out.

In our energy dating and pursuit to raise the level of energetic love in our relationship fields, it is crucial to be aware of these different levels and the powers, energies and forces they contain. When we date another, we open ourselves to the essences and entities they are connected to and the contents that live in their personal energy field, both high and low. This is particularly true when they become our partner in passion and consensual sexual exchange takes place because there is such a high degree of energy transference during mutually agreed sex.

Our Personal Astral Light and Occult

Just as the planet's energy fields contain an occult which is the living record with the associated power of all that has energetically happened on Earth, so our energy field, our personal astral light, contains the energetic record and associated power of everything that has ever happened in our life. This is our personal occult we carry with us wherever we go. It contains the record of our highest and lowest experiences. It is the stuff that our dreams and nightmares are made from. It contains the ghosts and angels of our history. It determines what we are able to think and feel. It changes its nature, grows and amasses energy over time.

In our personal occult we carry the energetic record and the living signals of everything we have ever done. The higher signals try to influence us in our daily actions, as do the lower. This is why we have the traditional image of a little devil sitting on our left shoulder whispering in our ear trying to influence what we do and on our right shoulder, a little angel. The little demon and little angel represent powers of our own creation and our own history. They are the energetic signals of our past, living in and influencing our present. Our past actions provide the energetic platform with which we move into today.

When we make a charitable action, we send an energy transmission via the energy worlds of the astral light and occult and link to all the charitable actions that have ever been made. We both confirm the existence of that energy and send an invitation for it to come into us. When we make a violent action, we transmit a signal to the record of violence in the energy worlds and to all violent acts that have ever been. We support the existence of violence thereby and help its record, power and influence to grow into the future. We also invite it to come closer to our lives. This is why the original Christian teaching of non-violence and "turn the other cheek," which Mahatma Gandhi practiced under the name *ahimsa* is such a powerful refutation to the forces of violence. It is a refusal to recycle this force between two warring parties, the process by which it would continue to grow and become a greater influence in the world.

What we do today for the first time is easier for us to do tomorrow, because we have planted the seed of its signal in our energy field. With every thought, feeling and action in our life we are issuing invitations to the occult powers and forces that live in the energy worlds to come and join the energy combination that makes up our life. We are the ones who are in ultimate control of what invitations we issue by the power of our occult choices.

In making an action today, we can connect to an occult power that began forming thousands of years ago. The birth of violence on the planet is symbolically told in the story of Cain and Abel. Once the first murder happened, that power was released, that particular genie was out of the bottle and has continued to grow ever since. Alternatively, when we make an action powered by love, we connect to the energetic record of love in the energy worlds that has also been growing for thousands of years. The occult choice of which path to take is always ours and is always decided and re-decided in the present moment, in the power of now.

All the great spiritual teachers have tried to teach us to view the world "energies first" and make occult choices from within this context. When we see the world from this perspective, it makes absolute sense of the doctrine taught by Jesus Christ to love your enemies. When you love your enemies, you refuse to power the lower vengeful entities of the astral light which can otherwise take control of your life. As Mahatma Gandhi said, "An eye for an eye will make the whole world blind."

The energies in our personal occult are alive and seek to influence us, both directly and through our relationship fields with others. Once something is established in our personal energy field, it uses us as its home base through which to influence others, as is also the case with them. We become keepers and carriers of different energies through our life and these energies seek to grow through us. "Grow or die" is one of the great laws of energy and we are the field in which these essences and entities can grow. To them, we are the field in which they plant themselves—a living human energy field.

The Seven Chakras and the Occult

There are seven full spectrum possibilities from the energy worlds that a person can be processing through the inward and outward flow of their sevenfold chakra system. It is not necessary to have in-depth understanding about the chakra system to understand this basic concept. If you take out the word "chakra" and simply think of seven levels of energy in your personal energy field, consisting of the seven levels of your personal energy worlds which you carry with you, it will be sufficient to understand what is being said here.

Using terms from other languages often presents a further barrier to what can be quite simple to grasp. I use the term "chakra" only because it is so well-known. In my live seminars I speak of seven wheels or vortices of energy through which we give expression to the seven levels of the energy worlds and receive impressions according to what we give out. I try to use terms in language that can be readily understood, while holding true to what needs to be transmitted as I believe it to be the duty of a teacher to bring what is being transmitted as close as possible to those seeking to understand, while holding true to the essence of what is being taught. To obfuscate matters by using hard to understand technical terms distances people from the professionals they turn to for help, as can so clearly be seen in the field of modern medicine.

 The sevenfold chakra system always works in conjunction with the fivefold energy system taught in ancient China. They are two parts of the natural charging and discharging systems of human life and in living reality cannot be separated. We draw energy into ourselves and release it through ourselves according to how we use our mind and these seven and fivefold systems of charge and discharge.

One way to think of this phenomenon is that it is like an aquarium in which different kinds of fish live at different levels. There are the top swimmers which live closest to the light and air. The middle swimmers prefer the water in the middle strata and the bottom feeders like to stay at the lowest level. When we look at human beings we find there are those whose life endeavor is to live in the highest energy levels they can. These are the people who embody spiritual development and illumination. They charge and discharge energy through their sevenfold and fivefold energy systems in the medium to higher levels of the energy worlds.

Then there are people who settle for a middle-of-the-road life within the norm of accepted standards of conduct. They charge and discharge energy through their sevenfold and fivefold energy systems in the low to middle levels of the energy worlds, where so-called "normality" predominates.

Then there are others who are the low lives or bottom feeders. They charge and discharge energy through their sevenfold and fivefold energy systems in the lowest levels of the energy worlds. These people thrive on low energies and may live by supplying the middle swimmers with what they want to amuse themselves with in their leisure time such as illegal drugs and strip clubs.

A vital understanding of our human energy anatomy is that our systems are designed so they can function at all seven levels of the energy worlds. We are not forced to go high or low. We are given a wide range of options and the choice of the levels of energy we process is left up to us. The power of choice is the power by which we ultimately choose our destiny, day by day and decision by decision. The level of energetic love that we generate in our life is a vital factor in determining this.

Remember that all seven levels of the energy worlds contain all seven colors, as shown again in the following table. When someone spiritually develops to be at the high end of the planet's energy worlds system, they will process all seven energies at the high end of the planet's energy fields. This means their root chakra, as it is called, will still process red, but at a high level of illumination. Their sexual chakra will process a high level of orange and so on up the system.

If a person is a bottom swimmer in the planet's energy fields and commits acts of sadism and murder, their chakra system will still receive seven natures of power, but the energies will only be drawn from the low, murky end of the planet's energy spectrum. When someone is based in the energies of the seventh level of the astral light, they will draw in and give out energy through all seven colored chakras within this lowest energy plane. At this level violet is not a color that is automatically "spiritual" as some energy workers claim. The level of spirituality depends upon the shade of violet. Dark indigo and violet within the energy field can represent a person capable of breaking through existing convention to come up with new kinds of degeneration. Conversely, if a person is tuned in to the energies of astral level three, then all colors, including their red energy, will be of a vibrant, clean nature.

	Energy Worlds 7 Levels	Energy Worlds Each level contains 7 natures						
higher	Level 1 - violet	red	orange	yellow	green	blue	indigo	violet
↑	Level 2 - indigo	red	orange	yellow	green	blue	indigo	violet
	Level 3 - blue	red	orange	yellow	green	blue	indigo	violet
	Level 4 - green	red	orange	yellow	green	blue	indigo	violet
	Level 5 - yellow	red	orange	yellow	green	blue	indigo	violet
↓	Level 6 - orange	red	orange	yellow	green	blue	indigo	violet
lower	Level 7 - red	red	orange	yellow	green	blue	indigo	violet

When these energies are processed through the five centers of the soul, the power of these energies is multiplied. The first letters of the thinking, instinctive, moving, emotional and sexual centers (which correspond with the senses of hearing, touch, taste, smell and sight) when read in sequence, spell out the word "times." As in the five times table, they multiply whatever energies they receive through the power of five. The energies are then multiplied again by seven as they leave us through the full color spectrum of passion. As human beings, we are an energy amplification and broadcasting system, planting impressions into the energy worlds of the planet which then influence our contemporaries and future generations. The higher and greater the level of energetic love that we are able to broadcast, the more beneficial our influence will be.

This is where The Passion Multiplier becomes even more significant. Not only are the powers in the man and the woman multiplied by each other, they are multiplied again through the energetic powers of the five centers and the sevenfold color spectrum. This means that two people can meet and one person can have over a thousand times more energetic love in their life than the other. This is not such an alien idea, as we can see it clearly in level six of the astral light with monetary energy. Just as a billionaire can have a million times more money than another person, so too in the higher realms of the energy worlds one person can have and radiate a million times the energetic love of another.

The idea of all people being equal is nonsense in the energy worlds. While two people may both have the physical and energetic systems of human beings, the difference in their energy worlds process can be staggering. The energy fields of a saint and a sadist are not the same. Their pre-occupations are different, their ways of thinking and feeling are different and what lives in their personal energy field is certainly different. This is why you can sit next to one person and feel well due to the energy that comes from them, while when you sit next to another person you might feel hot, irritable and argumentative. It is all about the energies that have gathered in their personal energy field day-by-day through the course of their life. Who you share mutual relationship fields with and invite to become your partners in passion will certainly make a difference in your life. Think of the difference between sitting next to Mother Theresa or Charles Manson.

Through the process of energy mapping, as set out in Chapter 7, we learn how to spot with greater energy worlds clarity and awareness who is who and what is what. This is not so we can judge other people but so we can assess what energies they carry and decide whether we want our life energies to be associated with theirs. This is not about a moralistic sense of good or bad, but is about measuring what is energetic food or poison to us and our chosen life's purpose. Our choices of which energies we will bring into ourselves and which we will not affect not only our todays but also our tomorrows, as the occult connections we make now determine our possibilities in the nows that are yet to come.

In the Company of Angels

There is a vast spectrum of possible energies, all of which are open and accessible to human life. Some of these are very elevating and pleasant to be with. Indeed, they can cause in us sensations by which we feel like we are walking with the angels. There are other kinds of energies that are like hungry ghosts which steal away our vital energies to feed themselves, leaving us spiritually bereft and emotionally bankrupt. The energy worlds are both a jungle and a scented garden. They contain enchanted places of high connection and dark places that snare and soil the soul.

The lower energies take very little work to connect to and are easily available. Greed, anger, lust, violence, apathy, despair and a host of their friends are always close by, waiting for the opportunity to enter our energy field and plant themselves within us. It takes very little effort to attract these low-level energies. Like weeds in the garden, they grow easily and need no special planting, care and attention. The higher energies of patience, care, love and compassion call for a conscious effort and deliberate cultivation. The rarer the energetic plants we wish to grow in our energy field, the higher the price we will need to pay. This price is not financial, it is energetic and is paid in the realms of commitment, deliberate choice and maintenance of our self-chosen standards.

A vital key to understanding these different natures of energies is in knowing that the lower energies always suggest we surrender our ability to make conscious decisions and give up our faculty of choice. It is exactly this feature that allows individuals to surrender their individual power of choice to the power of the mob or the tyrant. It is why a group of friends, while individually not dangerous, can come together to create a gang that does things the individuals would not do on their own. It is why well-meaning parents warn youngsters about getting in with a bad crowd or coming under bad influences. Like the common cold, attitudes are contagious and the attitudes of the people you hang out with can soon get into you.

A client of mine who worked in a mental health facility once asked me an unusual question. "Is depression contagious?" he asked, "I have observed the staff in the facility where I work and it seems to me that depression passes from the patients to the staff." We moved into a long discussion about the nature of depression in the energy worlds and how it can pass from one person to another through the relationship fields formed between them.

I believe that treating patients who are encountering difficult mental and emotional states without understanding the nature of the energy worlds is like traveling in a strange country without a map or compass. This is why I am collaborating on a new model for therapy called Energy Systems Therapy and Energy Systems Play Therapy which focuses upon the importance of what lives in a person's energy field and energy systems in the therapeutic process.

Response Ability

If we are to consciously enhance the level of energetic love in our relationship field and with our partners in passion, we first need to make the decision that this is our intention. For this to be effective, the first step is to take responsibility for what we generate and collect within our personal energy field. This is our sacred space and is the only sanctuary over which we have ultimate mastery and control. Whatever passes from us into the energy worlds of the planet, travels through our sacred space first. The first place in which we can increase energetic love, therefore, is within our own personal energy field. It all begins from here.

By connecting from our personal energy field into the higher levels of the energy worlds, we immediately begin to increase the power of energetic love we radiate to others. Development in these realms is often not so much a matter of doing more as refining what we do. If we wish to bring remedy to the energy worlds of the planet—which are far more polluted than the physical worlds—we can only begin by refining the energies in our own personal energy field, as this is the home base to which we return and from which all our energetic transmissions are made.

Prayer is an energy transmission we consciously make by directing our thoughts, feelings and the power of our energy field toward a particular end and in a particular direction. The power of our prayers depends upon the power we have access to in our personal energy field and what levels of the energy worlds we can connect to. The energy transmissions we make, consciously, semiconsciously and unconsciously—including those of prayer— then influence all the people we meet. The more we mix with particular people, the more we will influence them.

By changing the energy worlds within us, we start to change the energy fields of those around us. We have the opportunity to consciously take on our lives and our relationship fields as works in progress, in which we are primarily responsible for the outcome. We are responsible in part for what we bring into ourselves and above all for what we release from ourselves into the energy fields of the planet. The planet's energy worlds are highly populated and we are the gatekeepers and decision makers about the kinds of energies we will allow into us from the seven levels of the astral light. We are also the gatekeepers and decision makers about what signals we will generate out into the planet's energy worlds, which will then influence others. We have been given the sacred gift of choice, which is built into the design of our human systems and it is we who are able to determine the nature of occult forces that will work through us.

When someone decides to hold a séance and calls out "Is anybody there?" the real answer is "Of course, it's as busy as Grand Central Station at rush hour up here!" Sending out a general invitation to the worlds of energy, which is what a séance can be, is like standing on a busy city street holding up a hundred dollar bill and calling out, "Will anybody take me home?" Someone certainly will. The question is, would you want to go home with them? Would you open yourself up to such a random date? In the realms of relationships, dating and love, a valid question is, "What am I going to invite to share my life and why?"

There are thousands of powers and forces of different levels that want to lodge and take up residency in our personal energy field. Are we going to be particular about what we invite in or are we going to be a drop-in shelter for whatever energies are looking for a place to bed down for the night?

Energetic Roulette

Basic understandings of the energy worlds of the astral light, the occult, the human aura and the calibration of energies are crucial if we do not want to play energetic roulette with our life. When it comes to understanding energetic love, energy dating, selecting our partners in passion and building mutual relationship fields, putting in a little time to see, feel and understand these energy worlds now will enhance our relationships and save a great deal of time and grief later.

It is vital we understand that all energies are not the same. Some energies are very enhancing to our human energy systems and will lead us toward a deeply meaningful life. Others are highly corrosive and will rob us of our soul energy and our possibility. Energy mapping helps us determine which energies are which, so we can make more conscious choices in our lives. Whereas some energies are uplifting and bring us closer to our true selves, others are addictive and lead us away from our inner spirituality.

The people we meet and date are carriers of different energies and are connected to the enormous variety of essences and entities that live in the energy worlds of the occult and the astral light. There are energies that are obvious and easy to read and others which we may only discover after months, or even years.

It is vital to have a foundation of self-belief and self-worth so you project into your personal energy field a radiation of being a no-messing person that knows they have intrinsic worth and value. If this is the case, you will naturally attract to yourself others who share this internal belief about themselves.

Energy Worlds Concentrates

In Places:

Different places contain different kinds of energy in concentrate. A prison is a place that contains a powerful concentrate of low energy, while a church is a place dedicated to higher energy. If we make a map of places and put them to different levels, then we can see that prisons belong with level seven, most offices of trade and government with level six, colleges and libraries with level five and places of religious concentrate with level four. To go above astral level four we need to find those places in nature and within the charisma of illuminated human beings where special energies gather, as these are the elemental and angelic levels and they rarely come inside human-made structures.

Once we understand how these different ecologies actually contain different natures of energy, we can deliberately choose the ecologies to which we decide to take our personal energy field and also in which we wish to meet our energy date. If we are selecting a place for a honeymoon, for example, we may want to choose a place with a high level generation of negative ions, which is very healthy for our body and nourishing to the soul. An example of such a place is Niagara Falls and, indeed, anywhere there is a large body of moving water.

In this context it is interesting how many popular holiday and honeymoon resorts are by the sea, where there is also a vast production and release of natural negative ions. These ions bring us closer to the sacred blue feminine frequency of the planet, which is very healthy for us. As we "vacate" the "ions" from the city that we do not want and our daily stresses, these health-giving negative ions recharge and replenish our systems. It is interesting that the word "disease" shapeshifts to "seaside" and, indeed, this is a place that it is excellent to go when your systems are energetically depleted and run down.

When considering where you would wish to go on a date, you may well come up with certain restaurants, cafés and concerts. When you think to yourself why, you will find they have a certain energy ambience that you believe is both conducive and conductive to the dating process and to building the nature of relationship field you want to cause between yourself and your partner in passion. Night clubs are organized primarily to heighten heated sexual energy, while a walk under the stars is likely to lead to a more spiritual encounter that can also include a powerful exchange of sexual and emotional energies.

In People:

The mind and brain are like the captain and first officer of the human ship. The five energy centers are like the crew and the seven chakras are like the ship itself in all its different aspects. Our consciousness is the singular "I" that issues commands to the captain, who passes them to the crew, who then direct the ship accordingly into different kinds of experiences on the ocean of life. As we live our lives we bring to ourselves energies of many kinds that gradually build to become energy concentrates in our body, mind and soul.

a) The Higher Case

When a person is operating in the higher three levels of the energy worlds, their five senses draw in high level frequencies and their seven wheels of power radiate high, fine colors. An aura of illumination starts to build around them and their seven wheels not only transmit high energies but also draw these energies towards them. Their brain and mind offer them new revelation and insight into the reasons and purposes of life because their brain is running on the highly powered energies that exist in the higher levels of the astral light. These energies offer supremely enhanced spiritual intelligences for the brain to work with, so life is constantly opening up with new perceptions and realizations from the inside out. The aim of all esoteric religious practices has been to switch on exactly these kinds of states.

If two people who live in these higher energy states come into personal relationship and connection, they will generate a high level of energetic love and charisma between them. Their relationship will naturally be one of mutual consideration and respect. The relationship field between them will naturally have a high level of illuminated charisma which other people, essences and powers will be drawn to. This field is the accomplishment of partners in passion who are also partners in purpose and have become partners in evolution.

It is not that two such people have "made it." They will need to work each day to maintain this level of generation and connection and keep their passion and purpose refreshed. If they do not do so, their relationship field can swiftly lose its charisma and become discharged. If this happens and lower energies begin to predominate, then two people who seemed ideally suited to each other can suddenly be at difference. It is not that they start to find fault and argue, it is that the lower essences they have brought into their field will cause this to be possible and happen between them.

Bickering does not happen at level three of the energy worlds, but it certainly will happen at level six. This is why one of the vital practices in building a successful relationship field is to clear out the lower energies that inevitably find their way in, even into the relationship field of people whose center of gravity is at energy worlds level four and above. Humor is one of the great cleansers in expelling lower energies from a high level relationship field.

In the modern world it is very rare go through a day without dealing with the level six energies of trade. Having to deal with office politics, the telemarketer who calls you at home or the unexpected bill you receive through the mail, bring influences into your relationship field that need to be dealt with.

b) The Lower Case

If someone is living in the lowest two levels of the energy worlds, then their five senses will draw in lower impressions and they will become "thick-skinned." Their aura will start to have a thick, dense skin around it, making them increasingly less sensitive to the energy fields of others. Their sevenfold chakra system will run on lower wavebands of power and, therefore, the colors will be murky and a much higher level of toxicity will be present. The fivefold system of their soul will become increasingly polluted and they will develop a "dirty mind." This is likely to also cause a high degree of "filthy" language. Their whole energy system will become closed down to higher influences and possibilities. Cynicism, dirty jokes and dark comedy will become their stock in trade and there is likely to be a high degree of toxic opinions about any subject on Earth ready to be spouted.

If the person is young, this may be covered over to some extent by the grace of youth, but as they age these toxic states compound and deepen, becoming more obvious and harder for anyone to be with unless they also are pickled in the same kind of toxic broth.

The Spiritual Shift

Fortunately, just as it is possible to change the content of one's energy fields and go from high to low, it is also possible, through personal and self development, to change one's energy fields and go from low to high. When this happens the skin on the aura starts to thin out and the sevenfold chakra system and the fivefold power system of the soul start to expel the lower energetic toxins in favor of the bright, pastel colors of the higher energy worlds.

It is also possible for the mutual energy field of two people in a relationship to refine from murky colors with low energy worlds content and charisma into higher contents which radiate higher energy transmissions into the energy worlds and the people around them. This is the true meaning of transformation and conversion, which I refer to under the idea of making a spiritual shift.

A true conversion is not from one religion to another or from no religion to a particular brand; a real conversion is to go from low to high in the energy worlds and to be able to maintain the new level that is reached. Backsliding is always possible and this is well illustrated by the originally esoteric game of snakes and ladders. It takes time and effort to climb the ladder of the energy worlds, but sliding down the body of a snake can happen in a moment. This applies both to individual energy fields and relationship fields also.

Energetic concentrates build up in people over time, in the same way that they build up in places. The concentrates are caused by the energies we transmit and receive within our energy field in repetition. It is the repetitive thoughts, feelings and actions that aggregate to build our energetic character portrait. We carry this portrait with us when we go energy dating and it is this portrait that forms the authentic inner person we are and become. When our outward portrayal matches this inner portrait then our words and actions carry the unique property called "authenticity." Ultimately, we become the energy concentrate we aggregate within our energy field over time, by how we use our entire human energetic and material systems. Through the time of our lives it is possible to aggregate within our human energy field and energy systems powers that are of great power and spiritual illumination. It is also possible to grow aggregates of evil. The occult choices which bring about these possible results are for us to decide.

The Occult of Evil

Two individuals who are both heavily connected into the lowest levels of the energy worlds can be powerfully attracted to each other. When they come into connection and form a relationship, lower energies, essences and powers will be attracted towards them. In its most dangerous form, such a couple can become a platform for the energies of evil and can commit heinous acts of violence and depravity. They compound each other's worst aspects and invite the dark forces of the occult that reside in the lowest end of the planet's energy spectrum lodged there by evil practices of human beings over thousands of years, to join them.

Evil itself is energetic. There is nothing evil in the physical worlds. Only the energetic intent and power behind something makes it evil. There are evil energies that are looking for humans they can live within and practice through. When their latest host is dead, often through practices that the energy itself has promoted, they go looking for another host.

An evil energy is any energy that has been deliberately created to work against the impulse of life. Imagine a command issued throughout Creation that says "Live." Evil is when this command is reversed and turned back upon itself. This is shown in the relationship between the word "live" and the word "evil." It is no coincidence that the word "evil" is an exact reversal of the word "live." Death is natural, but evil is not. "Death" may be "hated" (which is the anagram of death) because it is not understood, but it is not evil. Evil is an energy that has been caused by people who have done things that are consciously and deliberately anti-life. These energetic impressions are lodged in the lowest levels of the energy worlds and are always on the look-out for new hosts to occupy and take possession of. This is also the true meaning of what it means to be possessed.

When someone begins to process forces and powers that are new to them, then people they know are often heard to say things like, "He's acting out of character" and "That isn't like her." One of the most revealing statements describing this situation is in the common expression "I don't know what came over me" and this is exactly what occurs. Something comes over a person and causes them to act the way they do. As human beings, however, we open and close the gates of our consciousness to the essences, entities and powers that live in the energy worlds and are ultimately responsible for the forces and influences we allow through ourselves.

There are essences and powers trying to influence the world today that first began to form in the times of Egypt, Rome and Babylon. These energies transfer from one generation to the next as they have an energetic life that continues in the energy worlds after the demise of their hosts. History always seems to be repeating itself because these energies occupy and then reoccupy the human race from generation to generation.

It is just this feature and the increasing quantity of low level energies in the astral light which has given rise to the resurgent interest in the theme of vampires in recent years. Physically, vampires do not exist, but in the unseen worlds of energy they certainly do. The original author of *Dracula*, the Victorian Bram Stoker, drew on his knowledge of the esoteric and the energy worlds to create his popular mythic creatures. The inside story of what vampires really are and how to deal with them is taken up in Chapter 11, Energy Addictions, Vices and Abusive Relationships.

The greatest antidote to evil and its partner in suppression, fear, is energetic love. We will only stop evil and its vampiric brood by denying it energetic access to the human race. A certain way to do this is to raise the level of energetic love to such a degree that evil cannot get in. This can only begin in one place: within us.

The Occult and the Power of Choice

In the spectrum of passion most of us do not occupy the very high realms of the saints, sages and saviors, or the very low realms of being vampiric predators upon the innocent. We mostly live somewhere in the middle ground. We connect to level four energies in our very high or "timeless moments" as the poet T. S. Elliot described. In these moments we rise above our usual selves, such as in a moment when deeply contemplating God and the purpose of life, when making an altruistic action to help another or in a moment of high orgasmic love. We live mostly within level five and level six energies in our daily going on, in which level six supplies us with our routines and level five with our progressive thoughts and feelings.

We may dip below our usual standards of conduct when we feel the inner urge to get away from routine and take a break by going into an alternative form of energetic stimulation. This feeling of needing relief from routine may take us to "Happy Hour" at our neighborhood bar and may lead us into more extreme behaviors so we can escape our sense of the walls of routine, level six life closing in.

We can take this urge and inner desperation and use it as an impulsion towards meditation, therapeutic massage, yoga or other practice that gives us a time of recreation by connecting us to a higher energy. Or we can follow this impulse for additional stimulation and allow it to take us to the gambling table, strip club, whisky bottle and illegal drugs. The power to choose which path we take is always ours, although the lower addictive energies can be very hard to separate ourselves from once they have us in their vice-like grip.

The urge to find an energetic alternative to the routine of levels five and six is what often drives potentially addictive behaviors. Once we know this, we can be better fortified to resist the mass media and look for recreations that help to liberate the spirit and often cost less as well. Lower level stimulations tend to draw energy from our energetic bank account and money from our physical bank account at the same time! The lower energy levels mostly give us a short term stimulation and a long term headache. The higher energy levels cause us to feel good now and also put energy into our energetic bank account for later. I am not suggesting becoming a puritan. Recreation need not mean going down the energy levels of the astral light; it is also an opportunity to rise up. One simple technique that helps in this process is to find a special place in nature that recharges your soul and revisit it often.

As human beings we like to think of ourselves as doing the choosing. We are used to the idea of choosing our courses of study, of going to the shops and supermarket and choosing from the items on the racks and on the shelves. So long as we can afford it, we can select it, purchase it and take it home. The range of our power of choice in levels seven, six and five is determined by the power behind our bank account and check book.

When it comes to the realms of the occult, it is not only we that are making the choices. The occult is a living, breathing realm of energy with as many energetic life forms as there are organic life forms on the planet. We are not choosing from inert objects that are on display. Just as we are choosing what we select to deal with from the energy realms of the occult and the astral light, so these energies and entities are choosing whether or not to deal with us. The poets of ancient Greece, for example, would petition the Muses to come and inspire their verse. They knew the Muses to be living powers in the higher levels of the energy worlds and would call upon them for divine inspiration in hope that the Muses would imbue their poetic works with this higher astral content.

When we rise from our bed in the morning, we set our feet upon the stage of the great theater of life in which, by the way we think, feel and act, we make energetic transmissions into the energy worlds of the astral light and occult. These petitions are always answered in the energetic worlds, though often not in the way we may expect. Each moment of every day we send our transmissions and petitions into the occult and it is these energy signals, together with the words we speak, that are answered from the energy worlds.

When we choose to petition for increased energetic love in our lives, we can best do so by generating it within ourselves first. This includes doing everything we can to produce a positive charge in our energy field that becomes a beacon of light to ourselves and to others. It means deliberately developing an attitude of gratitude, calling over to oneself the great gifts we have been given, such as the ability to see, to feel, to move, to speak and to be in relationship with others. By insisting upon the generation of joy within oneself, we call out to the greater joy that lives in the higher realms of the occult and the astral light to come and join our life. This is how the great Law of Attraction really works. It is not enough to ask by words alone. It is when we manufacture a small part of what we seek within our own energy fields that the greater version of that same power, living within the energy worlds of planet Earth, can come and find us. When this power brings with it a quality of illumination, like the sun, it banishes lower formations from our energy field and we need have no fear of vampires and the like.

Sex and the Occult

One of the greatest powers that is used to promote addictive behaviors is the power of sexuality. As it is one of the most potent forces in human life, it is used by the media to sell everything from products to lifestyles. Sexual energy is powerfully connected to the occult and the sexual choices we make play a powerful part in determining our energetic portrait.

Whenever two people have sex, they release energy into and attract energy from the occult powers and forces that reside within the energy worlds. According to what they are thinking, how they are feeling, the nature of their relationship and why they are having sex, will they release and attract different levels of energy transmission, as we saw in the seven levels of love and sex in the previous chapter.

The energies of all the sexual activity of people since the world began is recorded in the astral light. This ranges from the high-level frequencies of the sacred sex of India, to the most perverse and abusive behaviors of black magic, in which the magician seeks to take sexual energy and use it to power the accomplishment of his will for personal ends. Aleister Crowley is an example of such a low level practitioner of magic.

Sex at astral level four and above is a great cleansing and healing property that leaves both partners free and clear inside their own life and also cleans and refreshes their relationship field.

In the lower levels, abusive sex and the energies that attend it can become highly addictive. Lower powers and forces of the occult that have been building in the energy worlds for thousands of years can take a vice-like grip upon a person so they no longer have control of their own life and become the tool of an addictive energy that dominates their energy field.

Chapter Eleven
Energy Addictions, Vices and Abusive Relationships

Abusive relationships are caused by the energies that make them possible. If there were no energies available in the energy fields of individuals and the energy worlds of the planet to power abusive behaviors, they would not be possible. The higher powers of the energy worlds cannot be used to abuse ourselves or others, they will not participate and lend their energies to these low level behaviors.

We access the energies that power the abuse of self and others by dropping down the levels of the energy worlds to the places where lower powers and forces live. These exist in the lower two levels of six and seven of the astral light.

By changing the way we think and feel we can change the energies we connect to and prevent abusive behaviors. This is a real energy field transformation and is at the heart of making a spiritual shift. We may not be in a position to eradicate the energies that power abuse from the astral worlds of the planet, but we can certainly prevent them having access to our personal energy field. By so doing we deny these energies another opportunity to grow. We can also help others to do the same, once we understand the energetic principles involved.

The lower energies that cause abuse are addictive in their nature. Once exposure to these energies has happened and been acted upon it becomes ever easier to experience more. It is important to note that exposure to these energies alone will not cause an ongoing connection to them. Exposure may prepare the ground and open the possibility for connection but it is acting under their influence that confirms their presence in your personal energy field and secures a long term connection. Once abusive energies have been acted upon, they are hard to get rid of, both from your personal energy field and from your relationship field with another person. It is certainly possible, but it calls for real transformative work to climb the ladder of the energy worlds and not slip back into acting out the promptings of lower, toxic energies. This is because these energies can give gratification, short term stimulation and release to the ego, which is most powerful in the lowest two levels of the energy worlds. There are parts of our lower ego formations that can be turned on by such stimulations if wrongly trained and educated. These lower ego formations then look to repeat the experience unless there is some deliberate intervention to prevent and retrain them.

Once we experience these addictive energies and allow them into our energy field they will leave a trace behind them. This trace acts as an energetic beacon or, by analogy, a computer cookie in our personal energy field that calls out to other similar energies because they are on the same energetic frequency. We may begin the day with a particular intention but as we walk past a movie theater or bar, the cookies of our addiction may receive an incoming signal and activate so that, before we know it, we are at the movies although this was not our intention for the day. If these happenings keep growing in number we can find that we are losing control of our life. It can happen with drinking, gambling, pornography, obsessive shopping and always there are people who deal in these lower energies who stand to profit from our giving in to this addictive behavior. Only by superimposing upon and discharging these behavior patterns and connections can we cause these addictions to become de-activated. Superimposure is caused by repetitively processing energies of a finer nature that re-balance the energy field and overprint the previous energetic loadings and programming. As with any addiction, the old wiring remains in the energy field, mind and brain and can be caused to flare up at any time by the re-introduction of similar frequencies. It is a person's responsibility to intervene at such moments and refuse to allow the addictive energy to be re-activated or acted out anew.

Energy Addiction and Education

If you have ever tried a first cigarette, then you know how it produced a feeling of nausea alongside a buzz that was new to your system. The second cigarette produced a lesser reaction, as did the third, until your system became habituated to the new experience and actually came to crave it. The craving is caused because the nicotine offers a short term stimulus to the brain which seeks to have as much stimulation as possible. The brain hates to be bored and will bring to itself whatever stimulation it can to avoid a bored state. The great danger of supplying the brain with stimulants is that once they have been introduced, the brain seeks to recycle the experience repetitively with increasing doses of stimulation regardless of the cost to the rest of the human system.

Just as there are physical stimulants, such as drugs, which bring a rush to the brain, so there are energetic stimulants that have the same effect. An example of such an energy stimulant is gambling, wherein no physical drug is introduced to the system but the sensation of gambling one's material possessions on the throw of a dice or the turn of a card causes a powerful short term stimulation to the brain. An addictive sequence such as this offers short term stimulation but is energetically and physically destructive in the long term.

Energetic addiction goes much deeper than obvious examples such as gambling or compulsive eating. Consider that, as human beings, we should naturally have great confidence and an aura of power and accomplishment. We are a tremendous success, simply by the fact of being born. Yet we are often caused to feel inferior through social conditioning and the modern education process. We then become addicted to the energies of feeling inferior. You may think "No, not me" and it is true that there are also those who are trained to a superiority complex from early youth and who are even sent to expensive private schools that specialize in inculcating such feelings. A superiority complex, however, is as unnatural to the human being as an inferiority complex. They are two ends of the spectrum of the ego, which only exists in the lower three levels of the energy worlds. At the higher levels, the ego transmutes into the realms of higher consciousness and falls away.

It is very rare, indeed, to meet a person who is not addicted to either feelings of inferiority, superiority or more often the bipolarity of both. These two addictions are the tail and head of the same snake: the snake of addictive self-consciousness, also known as ego. Both these states—superiority and inferiority complexes—are exploited by marketing gurus and the media. The message that you will really be somebody if you are seen in a particular make of car or style of clothing is designed to appeal to these addictive energy states that we are educated into over time.

At level five of the energy worlds the ego is still powerfully present and is likely to be the main actor in a person's life, singing its song of "Me, me, me, me" but in a more refined form than at levels six and seven of the energy worlds. Indeed, the ego at level five will preen itself at its social superiority and larger fields of reference than the egos which live in the lowest two levels. The truth is, however, that this is still ego, only in a more refined form.

It is only at level four and above that the ego becomes muted and the person is able to lose their ongoing sense of self-consciousness and me-based thinking and start to feel more closely connected in their energies and consciousness with the planet, the universe and their place and part within this cosmic ecology. At this level, the word "ego" shapeshifts to "geo" which is the name for planetary centered thinking and feeling as in the words geography, geometry and geomancy. I believe that it is the pursuit of this shift into the higher energy worlds and the inner feeling of the needs of the planet it is connected to that drives the ecology movement today, which seeks to be geo-based, rather than ego-based.

Once introduced repetitively, energies that are initially alien to our system take root and become part of our personality. They then come to live inside our energy field and the cells of our body. None of us are born thinking we are inadequate or stupid in some way. It is only by having the idea and the energies associated with it introduced to us from outside of ourselves in repetition that it gradually comes to take root and condition how we think and feel.

Ultimately, the greatest educator in our lives is ourselves. As said previously, there is only one person who will listen to everything you say. With each statement you make, you are educating your inner energy systems as to the kind of person you are and want to become. This is why the inner language that you use when you address yourself is so crucial, as it causes energy states within you and gradually educates every cell of your being as to the kind of person you are.

When you tell yourself you are naturally confident and charismatic, you cause yourself to become so. If you tell yourself you are a loser and do not deserve a high level of energetic love in your life, you cause this to become so over time. It is in just this fashion that we create our own reality out of the vast range of possibilities life on Earth offers us.

When we tell ourselves something once, it has a certain level of power but when we tell ourselves the same message over and over again, we can cause this to become a core belief and make a strong connection to its power and the level of the energy worlds in which it lives. It now becomes harder to change this energy state, as we have programmed ourselves that this is what we are like and it becomes a truth of our inner existence. This is how character is actually created; it is formed by our core beliefs and connections that are acted and re-enacted over time.

The prime purpose of a modern education is to make a person fit for the working world and to habituate us to the kind of energies needed for this. Modern education introduces a person to competition, which is one of the most addictive lower powers that exist. It introduces us to gain and loss, coming first or last, judgment, criticism, failure, the need to be right and the wrong kinds of comparison. To line up thirty children and start a running race is guaranteed to produce twenty-nine losers. We may not be able to run as fast as the child next to us, but we may have a natural gift for storytelling or music. To introduce competition between nations is even more absurd. The major tool of comparison today is based in economics and gross national product, but what of gross spiritual product? Would America then lead the list or would it be India, Bhutan or Tibet?

Becoming an Adult

There is a great deal of difference between growing up and remaining true to one's inner core or essence and becoming an adult. Being an adult often carries with it connotations of being a man or woman "of the world." The expression is interesting; not a man or woman of the planet, the universe, Creation or God, but of the world. "The world" is a term that describes our occult inheritance at levels five, six and seven of the energy worlds, rather than our original spiritual purpose on Earth which is to be found in strength in the higher three levels of the energy worlds.

Becoming habituated to the addictive energies of the world and the powers and forces of the lower occult often goes with the process of growing up. When this happens, becoming an adult is an accurate expression because the word "adult" is the root of adulterated, which means becoming polluted and being turned away from one's original nature by external agencies.

A great part of modern education is designed to introduce us to the adult energy worlds. We are given the toxic stuff of the modern world and its history and taught how to ingest it until we assimilate it to the point where it becomes part of us. We even learn to build our identity upon the extent of our knowledge of these lower realms and our connections to them.

Identity and Addiction

Lower energies work by addictive processes and these lower energies can gradually form up our identity traits and personalities. Our inner essence can then be coated by the cloak of personality in such a way that it becomes almost impossible for it to express itself because it has no energetic room left in which to breathe.

The gradual process of adulthood can sometimes be seen in the difference in the brightness in the eyes from a young child to those of the adolescent. The affected disillusionment that often accompanies 21st century adolescence is not a natural state. It is not natural to be cynical at seventeen. When this happens, it is always because of external agencies that cover up the brightness of youth.

An example of this habituating process is how boys are trained in many parts of the world to think they are automatically superior to girls. Creation demonstrates that girls and boys are equally valuable and desired by the planet, the universe and God. It is the inherited addictive energies of masculine biased economics and tradition that cause parents to value girl children less and in some countries even destroy them at birth while valuing much more highly the production of boys. Boys learn that they are held to be superior in these societies and then adopt the habit of "lording" it over the girls. This is a false view that lives only in the realms of lower, addictive energies.

Both boys and girls are equal in their spiritual possibility and in their spiritual intelligence. It is only the inherited traditions of the world that portray the feminine as lesser. Plato taught that girls were a rung lower than boys in the wheel of reincarnation, while in certain cultures women are seen as fit for breeding purposes only.

In many Muslim countries it is still the case that women do not receive the benefit of equality of education, freedom of movement or career opportunity with those of men. Such a deep inferiority complex, caused by the restrictions imposed from the outside in, makes it very hard for the inner spirit of the woman to be expressed and for her to discover the sacred contract for which she was born.

When a newborn boy and girl look at each other, they know no feelings of superiority or inferiority one to the other. This is trained into them by education at home and at school. False cultural and religious conditioning of this nature causes an increasing disconnection from astral level four and above. A daily saturation in the astral powers of levels five, six and seven gradually habituate children to operating at these levels. Most schools discourage level seven behaviors and encourage levels five and six. Level six is the level of habitual routine and level five is the level of intellectual enquiry. It is interesting how this produces two kinds of rebel at school: those that escape via level seven and go the way of drugs, alcohol and other addictive behaviors and those that escape through enquiry and contemplation into the mysteries of life that school mostly avoids. In youth these two kinds of rebels are often attracted to each other as both share the burning desire to escape the guardians of conformity that are primarily active in level six. They are both on the outer edge of conformity.

Even this rebelliousness of youth, however, is something that is capitalized upon by the mass media and the machinery of commerce. How important was it in your youth to have the right brand of sneakers and to listen to music that was considered cool by your peers? None of these things were natural to your inner essence or genius. They were adopted from the outside in as part of your early identity formation. In our early years we are so eager for identity and to be part of something that we often grasp for identity and acceptance as desperately as a drowning person reaches for a lifeline.

Identity usually plays a huge part in the formation of relationship fields and in the quest for partners in passion. How important is it that your partner is part of the right set and has the approval of your peers? If your life is centered in ego need, then confirmation of your personality and identity will still be a powerful motivation in how you view potential candidates to become your partners in passion. If a person sole quest is in seeking to establish themselves in the role of a successful merchant banker it is unlikely they will set about building their core relationship field with someone whose prime motivation is questing for the meaning of life. They would not be a good fit with the other relationship fields the merchant banker is forming, such as with the board of directors at the bank.

We form many relationship fields with different groups of people in our lives and how compatible these are can be a source of drama, friction and self-discovery, as well as a great support and richness. Many movies have been made based on the theme of a hero who lives within certain established relationship fields finding a partner in passion and falling in love with this person who does not fit the relationship fields they already have in their life. The story then usually revolves around the need for the hero to make a decision and either follow their deeper life and sense of self by going into the new relationship field and separating from their already established fields or holding with convention and losing the love of their life. Although, to make for a happy ending, their existing fields often then come around over time and welcome the strange new relationship field and all is well. However, as in *Romeo and Juliet*, these stories can have tragic endings as well.

These movies are popular because they touch on the triumph of the individual over conformity to the expectations of society and the price are we prepared to pay to form the relationship fields that actually fit with who and what we feel ourselves to be from the inside out.

Energetic Ecologies

Every household has its own unique astral and occult properties, formed by the energy patterns of the people who live there. Members of a household release signals into the energy worlds and, by so doing, tell the occult of that district what is welcome and not welcome to call in. Over time the house comes to have a particular astral and occult content. Certain houses become beacons of energetic love because of the attitude and conduct of the people who live there. Other households become beacons of depravity and yet others may be mixtures of everything in between.

If we could see the stereotypical suburban neighborhood "energy worlds first" we would not see the picket fences and mowed lawns, we would see banks of colors and powers that had been built up over time. Certain houses would radiate energies focused on music and healing, others would radiate energies of financial worry and depression. Some would radiate an atmosphere of people in love and yet others would be surrounded by a murky green of sexual depravity. Houses as well as people have energy fields. In the case of houses, the fields are determined by the aggregate radiations of the people who live there amassed over time.

From Field to Field

We seldom learn how to go on with other people from what grown-ups tell us to do. We learn from the live examples that we see every day. In this context the most formative early relationships we are exposed to are those of our parents. Addictive energies are often passed to children from their parents. If a child is a victim of domestic violence, it is not only that they have the memory of these experiences to deal with, they are also up against the live energetic imprint which is passed on to them in a living way within the astral light of the house. It is interesting how many children of famous parents go on to achieve fame in the same line of work as their mother or father, such as in politics, movies and the music business. The energies that are in the house where the child grew up entered their energy field when they were young and influenced them to continue in their parent's footsteps. Energy addictions, essences and entities can be passed from generation to generation. This is also at the root of the idea of royal blood and aristocracy having inherited titles.

As human beings we become the living containers of the energies we habituate ourselves to. Young children do not have the ability to pick up their belongings and move to another house—though some have tried. They are caught within the energetic properties of the household in which they are born and they become habituated to these energies at a tender age.

From the time of their birth, children are given a powerful starter by the universe by being closely connected to their inner spirit and the higher levels of the energy worlds. This explains children's incredible resilience in energetically challenging ecologies. However, over the process of the years they can be led away from their inner spiritual nature and habituated to the lower levels of the astral light and its contents. This is one way cruelty finds its way into children. If you look into any playground you will see children acting out, in addition to their childish games, the occult influences of their parents and the planet's astral light. Young boys play at being soldiers, for example, because the energetic print of warfare is so powerful in the astral light that, being young and open, they pick up on it and it plays through them.

If you have tried to give up smoking, you know how hard it is to break away from a physical addiction. If you try and break away from your parents' and teachers' ideas about God, you know how hard it is to break away from an energetic addiction. The teachings of the Roman Catholic Church, for example, have strayed from the original teachings of Jesus the Christ, but even when one comes to know this, it can be hard to move away from their influence.

The Victim Cycle

Identity addiction means that a person is addicted to the energies that they have experienced so far in their life simply because these are the energies they have experienced so far in their life. "Better the devil you know than the devil you don't know," is the applicable folk saying here. Identity addiction produces a closed mind, a closed energy field and a life that keeps recycling around the same energetic circuits again and again. This has major repercussions in the realms of finding partners in passion because it keeps causing the same types of relationships in repetition.

A story that illustrates this syndrome is how elephants are trained in India. When the elephant is young and the trainer wants to restrain it, it is tied to a large tree with an iron chain. Try as it might, the elephant does not have the strength to get away. Through repetition, the elephant learns it cannot struggle against the chain that binds it. Over time the size of the chain and the tree are reduced. When the elephant is fully grown, it can then be restrained by only a flimsy rope tied to a small sapling. Even though the elephant now has the strength to pull over full-grown trees, it has been trained in its youth that it does not have the strength to pull away and is still bound by this belief. Even when grown to mature strength, it no longer tries.

In just the same way, the training we received in our youth can still hold us today, even though our strength is full-grown and the real conditions of our life have changed. There no longer is the mother, father and teacher insisting we behave a certain way, but their indoctrination upon us can be so deeply embedded that we do not have the strength or inclination to change. Our conditioning offers us a framework and a feeling of familiarity and security so we do not even try to test it any more. It has become our reality. This is exactly the case with the prisoner who is released but has been in jail so long that he is scared to live outside the prison system and so deliberately commits offenses to be taken back in. We may not live in a physical prison, but our energy field can become our portable prison if we close ourselves off from new experience and insist on repeating the energies and experiences we already know, but with new names and faces.

We tend to stay within the comfort of the known, even when it is destroying us. The punch drunk fighter becomes addicted to being hit. He doesn't know what else he can do because his ego is fixed within the identity of being a fighter. A person who has regularly felt himself to be a good also-ran may think that he wishes to become a front-runner, but the moment he begins to move forward into that position, his habitual programming that sees him to be a second principle comes forward and prevents him. Effectively, this is the person in the now meeting and being arrested by the previous programming that they had received in childhood.

Energetic Habituation

We become addicted to particular energies through a process of habituation. Habits are not only actions that we develop physically. Habits start in the realms of energy; they begin in the mind and in the emotions. We can, for example, become habitually addicted to the feeling of failure so we do not feel ourselves if we have not had our bout of failure energy for the day. We also become habituated to certain kinds of music, food and experience.

One of the biggest energy habits of all is becoming habituated to guilt. The Catholic Church, for example, specializes in producing feelings of guilt in people from a young age and habituating them to these feelings. A person then needs to go back to church to confess and becomes addicted to this cycle of guilt and confession. The danger with this is that it becomes part of a person's energy identity. They start to feel not themselves if they have not had their dose of sin and confession for the week.

Mostly, identity is formed around energies that we come into connection with on a daily basis. A good example of this is the particular job a person does. When those words "I am a...(fill in the profession)" are used, then you know you are meeting an energy addiction. A truer statement is "I am a human being earning a living as a...(doctor, bricklayer, lawyer, etc.)." We are all first and foremost human beings on a journey through life. Only on a secondary basis should we identify ourselves with our particular occupation in the world.

Vices

Vices develop from our habits, which are the processes we engage in on a repetitive basis. Vices, however, are not something that we have. Vices are energy addictions of such an extreme nature that they have us.

We all know what a carpenter's vice is and how it is used to grip a piece of wood so it cannot get away when the carpenter is working on it. A vice in the energy worlds is a lower occult energy that has a grip on us in such a profound way that we cannot shake it off. Talk to the compulsive gambler and you will find a person who is most probably overcome by the need to have the energetic experience of risking it all, even though they know that ultimately they will lose. Compulsive shoplifters seldom need the goods they steal. They are addicted to the energetic buzz of trying to get away with something for nothing under the eyes of the security guards and video cameras.

The seven vices of medieval times were the seven lower powers that were perceived at the time to be the greatest threat to the human soul. An important part of Catholic theology was the need to build an energy content of what they called the seven virtues to overpower the seven vices. The seven cardinal vices were held to be lust, gluttony, greed, sloth, wrath, envy and pride. These were to be energetically superimposed by chastity, temperance, charity, diligence, meekness, kindness and humility.

To be a novice in a religious order at that time was to be in a probationary period. The applicant was not permitted to become a member immediately because the people in charge of the order wanted to see what powers and energies would be caused to appear during the novitiate. They knew that any vices would make themselves known because once an energy is deeply hooked into a human system, it will persuade the person to certain kinds of behavior that give it energetic food. The trained observer can then spot these behaviors. The novice was therefore in a probationary period to check if he or she indeed had no vice that was permanently occupying their energy field.

Part of the dating process involves the discovery of what the other person is really like and whether two people are energetically compatible to become partners in passion for the long term. Can they graduate from being partners in passion to becoming both partners in passion and partners in purpose? This is also what the engagement period between a man and woman was supposed to be about, after which, if they found that they were able to form an effective and loving partnership, they could traditionally exchange their silver rings for gold and become married.

Breaking the Chain

It is a known fact that a child who has been sexually abused is far more likely to sexually abuse other children upon growing up than the child of loving, caring parents. Why would this be? Surely the child who knows the pain and suffering of abuse would not want to inflict it upon another? To understand why such behaviors continue from generation to generation and why it so difficult to break the chain of abuse, we need to better understand the process of how vices transfer their grip in the energy worlds.

When the abuser abuses the victim, the victim experiences not only physical abuse. The energies that cause the abuse transfer into the victim's aura and into their cellular memory. That energy now has a foothold in their energy field and is always looking for the opportunity to cause repeat behavior because it is through repeat behavior that the energy is fed and can propagate itself into another life.

When we are not able to control addictive behaviors, these vices control us. We become possessed or in the grip of entities that are beyond our control. This explains why some people commit the most unspeakable horrors upon others. It is these lower energies working through them. This does not mean, however, that an individual is not responsible for their actions. We are all responsible for the energies we allow to act through us. We cannot be held responsible for what happens to us from an outside energy, but we are certainly responsible for the energies we choose to give expression to through the theater of our lives.

Addictive Relationship Fields

Addictive behaviors show themselves in relationships more than in any other field of human experience. What is called "co-dependency" describes mutual addiction to certain energies that the other person supplies. Why is it that an abusive man keeps finding women that are already printed with the experience of being victims of abuse? Why is it that a woman keeps attracting to herself the same kind of abusive man repetitively? Why is it that a man keeps being attracted to a woman that is going to cause him to feel rejection and pain? The answer in each case is energy addiction. The man in the first case is addicted to abusive behavior. The woman in the second case is addicted to the energies of abuse. The man in the third case is addicted to the energetic feeling of being rejected. They will keep finding ways to recreate those experiences until they are able to rise above that cycle. It is only new understanding that allows the cycle to be broken. By understanding better the worlds of energy and how, like all living beings, energies seek to grow inside our human system, we can elevate our consciousness and make new decisions and new choices that solve the addictions that grip our lives and allow us to build relationship fields of entirely new kinds. Co-dependancy only exists in the lower three energy levels, above these levels shared purpose is the natural way of the partnership.

In this understanding process it also helps to know that the energies of the vices which may grip us are as real as the physical world we occupy. The energy worlds contain tens of thousands of occult forces that are resident therein. Just as we attract different people by how we conduct our energies, so also do we attract different kinds of energetic powers from the seven levels of the energy worlds.

In the Field

The people that we mix with pass to us the forces and powers that are in their personal energy fields, just as we pass ours to them. These forces are looking to plant themselves in our energy field and grow. Some forces fall on stony ground, while other forces fall in fertile soil. The field that they enter is the energy field of our aura, our astral field. The soil that they plant themselves in is the soil of our soul.

Greed, anger, jealousy and other vices describe actual energies alive in the astral light that have been occupying human energy fields for thousands of years. They are always looking for customers and once you have shopped in their store, they mark your aura so they know how to find you again. Similarly, virtues such as patience, hope, generosity and peace also describe actual forces and powers that can be lodged inside the human energy field and grow there. Very few people ever come to contain all virtues or all vices in their energy field; we are mostly a unique mix of many kinds of essences, entities and energy worlds connections.

Our personal energy field is a bubble of energy that has an auric sheath around it and inside this filtering system each of us is a unique experiment of unknown outcome. It is never entirely clear what our energy content and connections will be until the day we die and our particular experiment comes to a close. We are, in this sense, walking, talking Petri dishes in which different powers are planted and different energetic cultures grow by how we think, feel and live. There has never been another person energetically the same as you before and there never will be again. Inside your amazing coat of many colors you paint the portrait of your future and your destiny by the energies that are planted, nurtured and grown there.

We can plant, nurture and grow illuminated energies of a very high nature which bring to us what in the East has been called enlightenment, energies of a middle nature which can be classified as the energies of normal life in whatever age and time it is we are born into and energies of a very low nature, which bring with them names such as criminal, depraved and perverse. Some forces and powers carry powerful healing properties both for ourselves and others; other energies are highly toxic and will corrupt our soul and imprison our spirit. Ultimately, these energies will not only form our personal energy fields and our relationship fields but also our destinies, as we become the aggregate of the energies that form in our aura.

New Habits for Old

Habits are not our enemies, although they are often perceived to be. It is addictive habits which are programmed to bring us results we no longer want that become our enemies. Even here it is best not to use the language of aggression and warfare as suggested by the word "enemies." Old habits do indeed die hard when we fight them; the way to overcome addictive habits is to superimpose new and better habits in their place. To try to remove one habit without replacing it with another is to invite conflict into oneself. It is far wiser to reprogram ourselves with the habits we want, a theme Stephen Covey explores in his book *The Seven Habits of Highly Successful People*.

It is in encouragement of changing the habits of a lifetime that the monk and nun take to "the habit." The habit that they wear is a reminder of the change of daily habits that they have chosen to make. We can decide to change our own habits without needing to take the measure of surrendering our life to someone else's rule.

One of the glories of being alive is that as long as we breathe, we are living within the opportunity to remake our energetic or essence portrait. Just as it is possible to change physical habits, so it is possible to change energetic habits. We can superimpose new habits upon those we decide we no longer want— new habits, with new more positive reasons attached. Our habits thus become our friends and allies in our life as they help bring to us the energies we want. Habits can be used as a very constructive force in our lives. Our habits are like the skeleton that the rest of our conscious life is built upon. When we superimpose a habit we choose and want upon an addictive habit that has had us, we change our character, our future and our energy dating possibility.

Moving on From Addictions and Abusive Relationships

Thirteen vital factors to help you in solving energy addictions and resolving abusive relationship fields are as follows.

1. Forgiveness

Forgiveness begins with forgiving yourself and then forgiving others. If you do not forgive, you will harbor energetic grudges. To harbor a grudge is very damaging, as it means that you keep a poisonous energy in your energy field and allow it to grow over time. You may think that this grudge is going to be delivered to the other person, but it is you that nourishes it, supports it, feeds it and lives with it every day. In the end, they may not accept it and send it back to you! This means that your energy field is taken up with growing this toxic substance that may or may not harm the other person, but will certainly harm you. A saying where this is concerned is "getting your own back," which energetically is certainly what happens, as what you have grown comes back to find you. It does, after all, have your frequency and recognizes you as its energetic home.

The ability to energetically let things go is crucial to forgiveness. When you have made a decision to let a particular thought pattern together with the accompanying emotion about another person go, firstly make the decision and stop yourself from consciously thinking of them. When their image or an associated feeling crops up in your mind, re-mind yourself of your decision and consciously let that energy go. If necessary, pause in whatever you are doing, close your eyes and say to yourself "I release that energy back to where it comes from, with no returns." It is then clear to return to where it came from and your internal systems hear what you say and know that you no longer wish to retain that energy. Remember that there is only one person who will listen to everything you say!

Working with images can be very helpful in letting your inner systems know what you want. If, for example, you wake up in the morning and there is a face that you do not want to be connected to in your mind, you can put a red line through it. The particular image that you choose is not so important. The important thing is that it works for you and that you use the images you choose to instruct your amazing inner equipment as to what energies you want to keep close by and which energies you prefer to let go.

2. Decide What Energies You Want

Make a list of energies that are acceptable to you and another list of energies you reject. This is a very powerful exercise in instructing the many lives within you as to what energetic processes you want to encourage for the future.

Ultimately, this is you deciding in advance about the energetic character resumé that you will build in your personal energy field and also what you want in your relationship fields. A sample chart could look something like this:

MY CHART OF ENERGIES

I ACCEPT	I REJECT
Love	Greed
Hope	Meanness
Patience	Hatred
Joy	Jealousy
Courage	Spite
Generosity	Bitterness
Encouragement	Callousness
Forgiveness	Vindictiveness
Belief	Cynicism
Care	Sarcasm
Gratitude	Anger without reason

This is only the beginning of such a chart. It can continue for many pages. By drawing one up, you are instructing yourself about the energetic processes you want to encourage and grow in the garden of your mind, soul and energy field.

Each of us has such a garden and we decide by what we plant what kind of fruits we will ultimately produce. Even though you may not remember your list in detail, your subconscious mind will remember it for you and can bring it to your attention when you need to be reminded.

3. Tackle Specific Energy Addictions

There are two key ways to tackle specific energy addictions that you deliberately target for treatment. They are called "starvation" and "superimposure" and are best used together.

Addictions are maintained by being fed. This can be seen in the workings of the brain. Between the brain cells are synapses and the more electrical traffic there is between brain cells, the stronger the link that develops between them. Thus, if you wire up two words such as "stupid" and "me" in your brain, the more traffic there is between these two, the more they become identified with each other. If this becomes a major link, then one of the prime associations with the idea of "stupid" will be "me." This is usually caused from the outside in, by schoolteachers, parents, friends and associates when growing up.

Try calling out into a crowd "Hey, stupid" and watch which heads turn toward you. They are the people whose identity is linked to being stupid. As they may not be happy to be so addressed you can then say, "I wasn't talking to you" to get yourself out of what could otherwise be an awkward situation. Try calling "Hey, handsome" or "Hey, gorgeous" and you will see a different form of self-identification.

When you decide that you are not stupid and will not allow yourself to think this any more, it becomes necessary to starve this thought to death. This means to feed it so little that the connective tissue between the two ideas "me" and "stupid" withers and dies.

To do this, the most effective way is to build a new connective tissue while starving the old. You might start a morning and evening affirmation process such as, "I, (name) am a talented and intelligent person." Do not say, "I, (name) am not stupid," because by repeating the "stupid" word, even in a negative sense, you send energy around the old circuit. Your brain, the most marvelous organic computer on the planet, does not hear "not stupid" it hears the power word "stupid" and fires that circuit up again.

In doing this morning and evening affirmation, you are deliberately deconstructing and disempowering the circuits you do not want, while building and empowering the circuits you do want. This is another way in which you are taking control of your life and building the person that you decide you want to be. This way of reprograming who and what you are and how you perceive yourself is at the root of such popular practices as Neuro-linguistic Programming (NLP), which basically consists of reprogramming the connections of the nerve cells of the brain (neurons) with language (linguistics). This has been a consistent human practice for thousands of years and is at the root of all mantras, spells, prayers and affirmations. An excellent introduction to the science of using affirmations to influence the subconscious mind and the personal energy field can be found in Napoleon Hill's *Think and Grow Rich* and also in Shakti Gawain's *Creative Visualization*.

A way to make this creation of new circuits even more effective is to add the payment of deliberate action to your decision. Let's say you discover, when evaluating your life and behaviors, that you are a rather mean person in your habitual way of going on. You may find this first in your attitude towards money but then, as you look deeper, you might find that this is also true with all your energies.

You may decide to make an affirmation in repetition and start to tell yourself, "I am a generous human being." This is a good start. However, to make the change more profound, decide that you will give something away every day or at least once a week. Then keep the promise you have made to yourself and practice being generous by actually giving things away. Buy things for others and turn your energy from being inward into yourself into being someone who gives to others. Leave a quarter on a park bench for someone else to find. The size of the act is not so important; what is important is that you are backing up your affirmation with action, thereby amplifying the new signal that you are beginning to anchor in your energy field. After a while other people will start to notice and you will begin to build a reputation as a generous person. What others will not realize is that this is because you have decided this is the kind of person you want to be and are deliberately making it so. You are starving out the "me first" attitude of meanness and replacing it with outgoing generosity.

You can take any of the list of qualities that you draw up in the exercise mentioned earlier, form them into affirmations and then add the payment of action. By combining two properties—one that you decide you want to starve and another that you decide you want to grow (for example, meanness and generosity)—you can deliberately cultivate the garden of your own life and energy field making it a conscious work of art, rather than a collection of energy addictions over which you have little or no control.

Perhaps you are the person who is always making up the bill at a restaurant when a group of friends meet, not because you decide to but because somehow you are the one that lacks the power to say "No." You may do an affirmation to say, "I (name) am a person who has a powerful ability to say 'no' and speak my mind." Then you practice, possibly starting in small things, until you are able to speak up and say that you will not pick up the remainder of the tab. This is you changing the patterns and the energies that you have been addicted to, so you can be in fuller control.

It is crucial, when doing an affirmation, to repeat it on a daily basis for at least twenty-eight days. This is because you want the change to be more than skin deep and you must complete a repetition for longer than the twenty-eight day cycle of the moon for it to be established in your life. The more intensively you repeat the affirmation through this period, the more deeply rooted the new property you desire will be. By repeating your affirmation upon awaking, throughout the day and before going to sleep, you will cause a deeper printing and superimposure than if you make the affirmation only once a day.

To superimpose upon an old energy print always takes work. Work is a conscious application of energy towards a deliberate end and as such is one of the highest forms of prayer. To work at reforming yourself in a new way is far more effective than praying for forgiveness by words alone. It is a practical prayer in that as you ask for forgiveness, you also do something to put yourself in better order.

4. Clean up Your Energetic Act

It is important to be neat and tidy in your energetic affairs, just as it is in your material affairs. Each night before going to sleep, mentally go through your actions of the day. Have you left any energetic promissory notes outstanding? Are you happy with how you have acted? Do you feel that you have done an honorable day's endeavor toward your chosen purposes? By doing this, your sleep will become more deeply charged and you will have a growing sense in your energy field of a life that is going somewhere and will awake less cluttered in the morning. In the same way that you groom your body, it is a wise practice to energetically groom your mind and emotions.

Do not think you can be perfect and have no addictive behavior patterns any more. If you starve your addictions for a week, watch out the following week because they may come roaring back with a vengeance! It is best to proceed slowly in changing your habits, otherwise your big habit-changing intentions can backfire. Ask the smoker who proudly proclaims "I have given up smoking sixty-three times this year!"

Do not make promises you are not able to keep, firstly to yourself and then to others. When you make a promise, always try to fulfill it. A promise is like a commitment to give someone energetic money. They will remember and your account with them will be outstanding if that promise is not fulfilled. I am sure you can remember people from years ago who promised you things they did not deliver. Realize it is the same with others remembering your unfulfilled promises.

People most often make promises through over-intention because they mean well and want to be liked. But when you energetically overextend yourself and promise what is not possible for you to achieve, you disappoint both yourself and others. Then think, is this happening because you are addicted to wanting to please and is it a repeating pattern in your life? In this case you need to deal both with the over-intention and with the addiction that causes it. Over-intention can be a chronic energetic disease that prevents you from building power in the now.

If this seems like it is getting too much, there is a vital saving grace. As soon as you become aware of an addictive behavior, it means you are now in a position to start to change it. Also, by becoming conscious of it, you already begin to change the ecology in which it grows. Think of it this way. There is a fungus growing in a dark cupboard. You open the cupboard and discover the fungus. By so doing you already let the light into the cupboard. The fungus starts to retreat. By analogy, once you become conscious of how these things work in the energy worlds, you let in the light of consciousness and the addiction starts to weaken.

5. Clear Away the Clutter

One of the greatest addictions we have in the "developed world" today is the addiction to clutter. Clutter consists of material and energetic properties that live in our energy field which we are connected to on a daily basis and are not directly relevant to the purpose of our lives.

In a materialist culture, identity is often built not so much upon what we are but what we possess. Possession, however, is a two-edged sword. When we possess something, it may also possess us. Take the example of a cottage in the country. We may be proud to possess one. However, part of the energetic trade-off is that we need to think about it, maintain it, insure it and carry the fact of it in our energy field. We need to constantly be giving energy to it. This is energy that we no longer have available for other pursuits in our lives.

Everything that we possess costs us in the energy worlds. So be careful your possessions do not possess you in such a way that they block the free flow of energies through your life. There is nothing wrong with having a cottage in the country, but there is everything right about being aware of the energetic cost of whatever you take on in your life.

Another example of possessive processes is the image of ourselves that we like to project and sustain. Our self-image, which by the art of shapeshifting says "life's game" takes a lot of energy to maintain particularly if it does not represent our actual character. To maintain a life of pretense in which we want to appear a certain way to others costs a huge amount of energy. We may think that we are self-possessed and choose our external image but, again, our image may possess us. The extra energy that it takes to sustain this life of pretense can prevent us from being authentic and mean that our words, gestures and energy field lack the throughout radiation that goes with the ring of authenticity. When you are an authentic person, you radiate the fact that you are comfortable inside your own skin and this is a very charismatic property.

6. Be Current

We can think of ourselves as a whole series of pipes through which energies flow. If the pipes are blocked with unresolved residues from our history, then the energy is not able to transfer from us to another person whether in the boardroom, bedroom or elsewhere. Things come to live and breed underneath our clutter. Think of an unattended woodpile in the country. It is not long before snakes, spiders and other creatures begin to live inside it. Some of these creatures can be highly poisonous and bite when disturbed.

There is physical clutter and there is also mental, emotional, soul and sexual clutter. Try to bring yourself increasingly into the now so you can be more fully alive today, rather than dragging yesterday's luggage around with you. The simpler we can make our life, the happier we very often are able to become.

Being addicted to collecting stuff is one of the greatest addictions of our times. Can you make do with less? Can you donate those books to the library? Can you get more interested in your own mental and emotional processes or do you need to always be stuffing in more and more external references? Can you bear to be quiet or are you immediately reaching for some kind of noise stimulation, whether from the television radio or satellite service?

Every time you discover something that is no longer relevant and move it out of your life or update the reasons why you keep it, you release further energy into the currency of yourself. You can then apply this energy to what it is that you are doing. This will increase your charisma and give you better control over your addictive energies.

By taking up the practices recommended in this book, you can help keep yourself and your energies better focused in the present so you do not become locked into what has been but are able to be with the flow of energies that is moving on the planet today.

7. Boost Your Electro-Immune System

The bio-chemical immune system is now known as the system of self. It works by rejecting invaders that do not fit with the integrity of the whole. As the immune system breaks down, so the resistance to alien invaders weakens and the body has increasing difficulty recognizing what is native to itself and what is not.

The human electro-immune system works in a similar fashion. We build an ecology within our own personal energy field by the way we live, the way we think and by our pre-occupations. This astral field naturally rejects powers and forces that are alien and destructive to it. If we get emotionally upset, we can cause a tear in our energy field which then allows in energies that normally could not affect us. This is why, when people experience emotional trauma and especially when more than one stressful event occurs at the same time to sap their energies, they often become physically ill. The trauma lowers the power of their electro-immune system, which in turn impacts the physical immune system.

To be healthy and to maintain a strong level of energetic current, it is important to keep powering our electro-immune system. We do this by taking the energy equivalent of vitamins, minerals and other supplements. These energy supplements come in the form of reminders of our belief system, who we are and what we are doing with our life. To remind ourselves often that we believe in ourselves and our capabilities is vital to keeping our level of resistance high to corrosive features, such as doubt and depression. Empowering our own self-esteem is to empower our energetic system of self. The higher up the levels of the energy worlds we can establish ourselves, the greater the energetic resistance in our immune system.

In respect of energy dating, one very important call-over is that you have value in your own right as a life. Your value does not depend in any way upon being in relationship with another. There is a great cultural pressure, particularly upon women, to define their lives as being worthwhile only when in relationship with a significant other. This is due to the false loading of the astral light over thousands of years by masculine dominated world history. We all have an innate, inbuilt value regardless of whether we are in a sexual relationship or not.

8. Clear Away Unwanted Connections

Look around the place where you live and ask yourself why you have surrounded yourself with the different objects and pictures that you have. Realize that everything carries with it energetic connections caused by its origin and history, as well as the reason that you brought it into your home. If you have a painting by Toulouse-Lautrec it is connected to *fin de siècle* Paris and the Belle Époque of the nineteenth century. Nazi helmets and regalia connect directly to the occult record of the Nazi party. Photographs will instantly connect you to the people and places that are portrayed. Therefore, surround yourself with items that give you fine connections in the energy worlds, rather than coarse ones. Clear away stuff that is no longer relevant to your life's purpose and particularly any objects that connect you to times and experiences that cause your energy fields to weaken. Do this in addition to the space clearing practices given earlier. We are now talking about what we introduce into the space where we live and why, not only from the standpoint of personal taste and what something looks like but according to what it connects to in the occult and the astral light.

9. Astral Protection

One of the most effective ways to deal with energy addictions is prevention. This means not letting lower energies in to begin with. One effective way to help is with the use of energy shields. An energy shield is made by deliberately projecting energy from inside your energy field using the power of your mind and then projecting it to fill your aura or a particular place that you want to protect.

Energy shields can be formed of different colors, such as pale blue which can create a cool ecology inside your aura while all around you may be hot and can be put in place inside your energy field before you enter a subway or a crowded room. Energy shields can also be used to refine the energy field in the place where you sleep to help you have a refreshing cycle of recharge.

10. Defend Yourself Against Energy Vampires

Energy vampires do exist. There are those you can see with your physical eyes and those that exist in the unseen worlds. They are not the blood-drinking, sharp-toothed, cloaked figures portrayed in movies.

The first kind of vampires are people you meet who leave you energetically drained, feeling as though your life energy is being sucked out of you. Sometimes we can meet a friend that we have known for many years and discover that something has changed in the relationship and that after each meeting we feel energetically debilitated. If they are going through a difficult time, we may deliberately decide that this is the price we are prepared to pay for the continuance of the friendship and we contribute our energy to help them out. If, however, it becomes a continuing energy drain, then we may want to address them about this and try to reset the energy balance.

When someone receives a deep emotional hurt in their life that causes them to indulge themselves in continuing destructive emotions, they may connect to the lower energies of the astral light, which will consume not only their own energies but the energies of all those around them. At this point the person moves into becoming an energy vampire upon others. Sometimes it will even cause them to seek out new friends who are also processing lower energy levels. A person who takes to drink will start seeking out other drinking companions and other people addicted to drinking will start to find them.

The second kind of vampires are those occult forces that draw away our life's energies and can take up residence in our own energy field, so it is we who start to become the energy vampire upon others. These lower forces are often classified as negative thinking, negative emotions and the like. Worry is an example of a cloud in the energy field that draws away some of the power of your life. Depression is another. They are, of course, related. Worry in sufficient concentrate leads us towards depression and this can bring us into despair. Despair represents a dark occult connection in which the energies are so thick it becomes very hard to think in a purposeful way. It can lead into mental derangement and even suicide.

The mythology of the vampire reveals much about the human condition in relation to the energetic formations that live in the lower energy worlds. Bram Stoker, the author of the gothic novel *Dracula*, was absorbed in esoteric studies and poured some of his understandings of the human condition and the energy worlds into the vampire myth he created. In our time, as the astral light continues to become increasingly filled with signals in the lower occult, stories of vampires are more popular than ever before. It is as if, at a collective subconscious level, there is an awareness that these tales speak of something in the darker realms that truly lives. Somehow, these stories resonate deeply in our psyche and cause terror, fascination and arousal in our souls. In truth, most of us have probably come into contact with some form of these vampiric, lower energetic forces that live by feeding on the life force of human beings. Whether through becoming entangled in toxic intimate relationships, friendships or work circumstances, many of us know the feeling of having our energy, optimism and enthusiasm for life siphoned away until we are compelled to end the situations we have helped create and, in extreme cases, run for our energetic lives. The mythology of the vampire offers enough genuine insights into the workings of the unseen worlds and practical technologies available to repel the lower forces that live therein, to be worthy of examination.

Folklore tells us that vampires cannot be seen in mirrors because they exist in the unseen worlds of force and so do not cause a physical reflection. They can also shapeshift their form as they are not physical beings but live in the energy worlds and so can change shape from human to bat at will and back again.

Vampires cannot cross running water as this causes the breaking up of static or stuck energy and is why showers are so effective when cleaning and clearing the aura and why lower energies, which vampires represent, are broken up when an atmosphere is energetically cleaned. Further, vampires are said to be destroyed by sharp stakes being driven through them. One method of energetic cleaning involves jabbing a sharp object into the corners of a room, where lower energy formations tend to accumulate and grow in power. The sharp point breaks up these low formations, enabling a space to then be cleaned by the use of bells and incense (see Chapter 6, Energize Your Space).

Another component of energetic cleaning that appears in the vampire myth is the placing of garlic, also traditionally known to be a great cleanser of pollutants from the blood when eaten, in windows to keep vampires at bay. Again, in energetic cleaning and clearing, garlic and other members of the onion family can be used to absorb lower forms of energy. It is not that the garlic would destroy the vampire, but that in passing through it, part of the lower energies grouped by Bram Stoker under the name "vampire" would be absorbed and thus this lower energy formation would be diminished. When garlic is hung in the window, it is designed to absorb lower energies into itself, thus making the house repulsive to lower energies. Dream-catchers in the Native American tradition are also employed for just this purpose.

Dream catchers cannot catch bad dreams; their purpose is to absorb and deflect the energies that cause them. In the Eastern tradition mirrors are traditionally used to reflect and deflect lower energies and keep them out of any protected space.

The rays of the sun combat disease and lower energies that corrupt the human system and are used as a component in the therapeutic treatment of conditions such as depression and the prevention of breast cancer. Vampires, being powers in the lower occult, are destroyed by exposure to sunlight, which is the direct issue of the illuminated power of the sun and has healing and disinfectant qualities.

Vampires drink blood, which is a special kind of liquid that holds the energies of life. This is true not only biochemically but energetically as blood holds the energetic charge of all our actions, experiences, connections and aggregated soul power. Indeed, the ancient Egyptians understood the astral body, or "Ba", to be built and domiciled within the blood. This is why, in the rite of communion, Christians drink the blood of Jesus the Christ as through this, a person brings into themselves the special or holy energies that filled Christ's blood and are given some of the high energetic content that was held within it as a power boost to act as an assistance and pathway of connection for the devoted to help them make a religious connection for themselves. In this sense, Jesus' statement "I am the way, the truth, and the life. No one can come to the Father except through me" may provide a deeper insight into this remarkable ritual which is of such importance in the Christian tradition that it was one of the fundamental disagreements that brought the schism between the Catholic and Protestant churches; the Catholic church maintaining that the wine turns into the actual blood of Christ during communion and the Protestant church holding that transubstantiation is symbolic.

Vampires retreat from the power of the cross. Although representative of the feminine power of the planet, the cross is now predominantly used as a symbol by the Christian Church. It was adopted by Christianity at the time of Constantine in the fourth century, but prior to this time the prime symbol of Christianity was a fish, representing the onset of the astrological age of Pisces. Energy formations which live in the lower astral worlds live at the levels in which moon force is the predominant power. These lower level formations are caused to retreat when brought into the presence of higher powers such as those of the planet and sun, as represented by the cross, particularly when made of silver. Vampires retreat from silver and can even be destroyed by silver bullets. In the unseen worlds, silver is an energetic property that lives primarily within the highest two wavebands of the astral light. The metal silver represents a connection to this high energetic silver power and is its physical manifestation. Silver, therefore, represents an energy that can banish energy formations in the lower occult. Silver is also known as a natural disinfectant and antiseptic and can be used in colloidal form for this purpose.

Vampires are burnt by holy water, which is a combination of water, salt and a special energetic charge transmitted from the person who is mixing it. In the Christian tradition, the energetic charge is that of silver. Vampires are burnt by charged water because they represent lower energy formations and when brought into contact with the high energetic power of silver contained within holy water, are broken up. Perverse astral formations cannot retain their form in the presence of higher planetary forces. It is not, therefore, the silver bullet, cross or holy water that cause the lower energies to retreat, it is the higher level planetary power that they are connected to, together with the intent of the individual using them.

Vampires have extra power at the time of the full moon and are associated with lunar power. Mental derangement was originally called "lunacy" as ancient physicians perceived that "lunatics" were particularly prone to outbursts at the time of the full moon when the effects of lunar power were at an increase. In addition to attracting all liquids on Earth by the force of its magnetic pull, the moon attracts the lower orders of the energy worlds in the astral light, which the western esoteric tradition has described as a "magnetic fluid." This pulling influence of the moon also extends to the lower powers and contents which are held within the liquid of our blood. Thus, we have the cycle of blood, the moon and lower energy contents which are strong components in the vampire myth. In ancient times, the energies of the moon were also associated with sexual energy and desire, which is also a strong element within the vampire ethos.

Vampires can live forever as they represent lower powers that leach energies from the human soul generation after generation. They do not physically die as we do; they simply pass from one host to the next after they have drawn the life force from them. True vampires, therefore, are not creatures that sleep in coffins filled with Transylvanian dirt but are the entities of war, violence, greed, hypocrisy and their kind, which pass from generation to generation and pollute the human energy field and soul. There are specially trained people, such as the character of Van Helsing in Bram Stoker's novel, who are able to exorcise the power of vampires. When a person is connected to higher planetary and solar powers, they can direct these higher powers toward lower energetic formations and cause them to retreat, like shining a light into a dark place. Many of the stories of miraculous healings and exorcisms of demons which are to be found in the religions of the world are exactly this. Jesus the Christ, as an example, was so powerfully connected to the spiritual power of "My father who art in heaven" that he could draw on this power to cast out mental and psychological diseases from people and the energies that caused these diseases. Similar tales are told of many saints, sages and even kings and queens in world history.

The core principle of an exorcism of any kind is that lower formations cannot bear to be in the commanding presence of the higher occult. In dealing with energy addictions, what we are trying to do is superimpose higher powers upon the lower energies in our energy field. In effect, we are trying to exorcise the lower from our personal energy field by calling upon the power of higher connections and forces to superimpose upon and push out the lower.

If we are addicted by habit to relationship fields in which we are the abuser or the abused, we can change our way of thinking and being so we attract a different order of energy. By changing the contents of our personal energy field we change our behaviors and our life. There are many helpful technologies given in *Partners in Passion* to help us make this spiritual shift, particularly in the use of positive affirmations, tests and energetic clearing and cleaning. By making a spiritual shift in our personal and relationship fields we can slay the vampire within. Aside from external vampiric energies, it is often the vampires within us that are the most dangerous of all.

11. Exorcise Personal Ghosts

Ghosts can live both outside and inside our energy field. In both cases they are scars from the past that drain energies from the present.

The energy worlds hold the record of everything that has ever happened here on Earth. The more powerful the energy impression is, the longer it holds. Whereas the Heavenly Host refers to energy impressions of a very high nature released into the higher levels of the astral light and held within the astral record, ghosts are powerful impressions released into the lower levels of the energy worlds. This is why they are always associated with traumatic happenings and are living scars within the planet's energy field. People who are psychic and particularly sensitive to what is recorded in the astral record are more prone to seeing these scars and are able to see ghosts. Ghosts definitely exist and are a form of life. They are hungry for impressions, as they need to draw new impressions from living beings to keep alive. When people see ghosts and go into a shock response they feed them with energy.

Just as there are ghosts in the planet's energy field, so we carry ghosts in our own energy field caused by traumatic events in our personal history. They want to keep being fed energy because as long as they are fed, they are able to keep alive in our aura. By working with the techniques of shields and superimposure, you can reduce the power of these ghosts.

Certain experiences can cause extended psychological reactions and the ghosts of such traumas can be active in a person's energy field for years or even decades. To clear such a ghost, the first step is to make the decision that you will no longer be affected by this ghost from your past. The next step is to banish it every time it reappears. A very effective way to do this is to make a conscious mark of banishment in your energy field when an associated memory is evoked. This can be done with whatever gesture and mental picture you choose. It does not need to be visible or obvious to anyone else.

12. Prevent Emotional Cyclones

All of us have energetic cyclones that we release in our energy field at some time in our life when we experience mental and emotional disturbances. These psychological twisters can be large or small, depending upon the extent and power of the disturbances. In the same way a tropical cyclone picks up power as it moves across water and then blows itself out upon land, these emotional twisters draw power from our upset emotional states and can swiftly move out of our control. Most often they are then grounded by destructive expression and behavior of some kind. This often involves releasing the twister upon another person. When the energetic disturbance has used up all its available fuel and burned itself out it leaves its host energetically and emotionally exhausted and drained. It also causes devastation in the person on the receiving end which can be hard to recover from and repair.

Like a cyclone, when these these emotional twisters are active they pick up anything in the district to throw around, causing damage that can be long lasting or permanent. Often both the sender and recipient find themselves shaking after the twister has blown through their energy systems because the nervous system is overloaded by the sudden surge of power from the lower energy worlds. This can literally have a shattering effect upon the nerves and bring a person to the point of temporary nervous exhaustion and breakdown.

In an effort to head off these twisters before they gather too much power it is important to learn how to recognize the warning signs in others and particularly in ourselves. Because people often want to avoid confrontation and conflict they tend to ignore or deny the warning signs they instinctively feel and brush these issues under the carpet hoping they will not escalate and simply go away. Often this does not happen and in fact the situation gets worse.

If the issues that are arising are ignored they can gather in power and come back stronger. What we suppress today we often find waiting for us in greater power tomorrow. It is better to take on these twisters when they are small and we can control them rather than seeking to avoid them and letting them grow to the point where they are out of control and damaging to the people we are in relationship with and to ourselves. This calls for a greater conscious awareness of the warning signs and psychological triggers in ourselves and those around us.

Talking things out is a deeply effective technique as this allows emotional issues to be ventilated and clears away misinterpreted signals and possible causes of conflict and friction. This practice prevents resentments, frustrations and other negative emotions from festering and acts as a drainage of hurtful issues from the relationship field. The importance of talking things through cannot be underestimated. By engaging in a "talking things out" process a couple can usher potentially damaging and toxic contents out from their relationship field before blow-ups and damage occur.

Negative emotions can act within us like pressure building up in a pressure cooker. The pressure cooker is rendered safe because it is designed to allow a regular venting of steam, otherwise the cooker would explode, the lid would blow off and the contents would spatter all over the kitchen. By talking through our emotional issues as they occur and not allowing them to bottle up inside us, we can safely pre-vent our internal pressures from building up and exploding. The word prevent gives us a great clue here as to pre-vent is to vent something before time, thus preventing a possibly violent explosion later.

Very often one partner in a relationship is better at taking on confrontation before time than the other. To have in place an agreement whereby they can flag the fact they see early warning signs is very constructive in a relationship. Our partners and friends are usually the people we can more easily approach to talk things out and prevent our internal twisters from growing in power. This is also one of the prime services that therapists offer and why a key to successful therapy is listening intently to what the client is saying. This is very core to Energy Systems Therapy.

13. Repetitive Cycles

Like all your natural energies, addictive energies also work on cycles according to the timings of events in your life. If you are experiencing depression or difficulties today but know of no immediate cause for it, look and see what was happening in the cycle of your life four years ago. Of all the numbers, four represents the cyclical nature of things. The energies we printed into our life in the past come and find us again in the future in a cyclical manner. This is why it is so important to overprint old energies with the new frequencies we want, because these fresh energies will then be waiting for us in our future.

There are the repetitive cycles of your life to take into account and also the cycles of Creation. Being aware of the cycles of the moon can help you understand and plot your energetic and biological rhythms. The seasons of the planet clearly affect our energies, moods and dispositions in many ways. All people are affected by the natural cycles of Creation and a person who pays attention to the personal cycles of their life and the energetic cycles of Creation has a better chance of building a balanced energy field, both within themselves and also with others.

Our Energies Define Us

In the energy worlds, what you see, really is what you get. What a person will do once, they will often do again unless they take themselves through a definite program of development to make a spiritual shift and change the energetic foundations of their life. This is a crucial understanding in energy dating. Everything a person does, says and thinks is telling you what they are like, what their make-up is and what they may be like in the future.

You can never change someone. A person can only ever change themselves. You can certainly influence the changes they choose to make, but you cannot make the changes for them.

We are all alike in this. Over the passage of time we build certain ways of going on into our systems by habit and the energies associated with these habits are always close by. They come to occupy our aura and become the energies that we are familiar and even feel comfortable with. This is why to genuinely change the energies that live with us takes real time and effort. Also, as we age, the energies that live within our energy field tend to become more fixed and we need to apply ourselves more to make the changes we want.

It is possible to make our way through life inside a portable prison of our own making—the prison of our addictive energies. Enormous amounts of potential power can be locked into these addictions. By releasing some of these energies back into the pathways of our life it is amazing how much energy we can once again have to work with. We do, in this sense, retrieve energies that have been locked away by past behaviors and this in itself is a form of soul retrieval as certain therapies are now called.

In energy dating, the more energies that are locked in energetic addictions, the less are available in the now for conducting quality relationships. This is why it is so vital to move on from addictive behaviors to clear the way for new energy dating possibilities and to build refreshed and recharged relationship fields that offer greater well-being both to ourselves and our partners in passion.

Chapter Twelve
Energy Pairings

As in all human relationships, long term pairings begin energies first. When two people encounter each other for the first time they check each other out energetically and physically and if there is an energetic attraction between them, they may arrange to meet again. If the attraction continues, they spend more time with each other during which the degree of passion between them can increase. The relationship may then progress to the point where they wish to confirm it to themselves and others by becoming engaged. This commitment is often accompanied by the exchange of rings.

The giving and accepting of engagement rings makes a statement to each other and the world at large that the couple intend to unite their forces and build an energetic partnership and long term relationship field together. The engagement rings also signal other would-be suitors that the man and woman are spoken for and are not open to other intimate energetic and sexual relations. If the engagement holds, the couple will set a wedding date at which time the traditionally silver engagement rings are augmented by gold wedding rings. The wedding rings are a daily physical reminder of the vows the couple have taken to approach life as a pairing and are designed to reflect what is now the case in their energy fields. If they are energetically committed to each other, their personal energy fields become sealed off from intimate sexual and emotional exchanges with others. Physically wearing a ring, however, does not guarantee this commitment and although a person may be engaged or married in law, they may or may not be so in the energy worlds. If they are not energetically committed, then their energy field still sends out a signal of being open for emotional and sexual relationships. Just as pairing is signaled first from the energy worlds, so too is divorce.

Marriage and Divorce

Traditionally, we are brought up with the idea of a man and woman pairing for life as a fundamental platform of our society. Even though we know that in the United States today more than sixty-seven percent of marriages end in divorce, men and women are still lining up to take vows of loyalty, fidelity and partnership for life.

When we dig into world history, we find there have been many different kinds of partnerships in passion between men and women that reflected the beliefs and customs of their society and time. With the Cherokee people, a man and woman became committed energy partners when the man constructed a dwelling and invited the woman to share it. If she moved in, their partnership began. If she later put his belongings outside their dwelling, then they were divorced. She would then keep the dwelling and any children and he would move on. If he chose to divorce her, he would put his own possessions outside of the home and then follow them out. Cherokee marriage thus became known as serial monogamy, as they were faithful to one partner at a time, but could divorce and form new energy pairings easily.

As we grow up, we tend to believe that the only way to think about energy pairings is according to the conventions of the particular society in which we were raised. The truth of the matter is, however, that there have been many different forms of energetic partnerships arising in different societies around the world. Our current idea of marriage is only one of them. It is not the right way, it is simply the way that is endorsed by the society we are part of at this time. It may be exactly right for you and your partner in passion or it may not be. It is worthwhile to talk this matter through with your proposed partner carefully and thoroughly so it can be a conscious decision, rather than being the assumed thing to do because this is what society recommends.

Another interesting feature in our society is that we still have a marriage ceremony that is "until death do us part." This does not take into account that our life expectancy is much longer now than ever before. If we go back two hundred years, marriage meant approximately twenty years together on average because life expectancy was much shorter. Today it often means fifty years and more. It is interesting how many couples over fifty are now deciding to divorce because they look at being together until possibly their eighties with the partner they chose in their twenties and do not find this an attractive prospect. Also by the time a couple are in their fifties, the children are mostly grown up and have left home, so there is no reason anymore to stay together "for the sake of the children."

Perhaps it is time to look at the idea of a two-stage marriage: the first stage being twenty-five years, which often is time enough for the children to grow up and then a second marriage to confirm that both partners want to stay together for the second half of their life. If not, they could equitably divide their belongings according to a pre-arranged agreement and move on. They could also consciously decide to stay together and, in fact, many couples today are choosing to reconfirm their vows in renewal ceremonies.

Another possible option is a short term marriage for, perhaps five years, in which both partners can discover if they wish to commit for longer. They could then have a second ceremony to confirm that they choose to stay together for another five years. At the end of each five year period each partner would be offered an "out" with a pre-agreed financial settlement.

Still another option would be to have a marriage that works by annual renewal. Both partners could agree not to have children during this time unless they decide to switch their marriage contract into a longer term agreement.

These examples are given as alternative ways of thinking and are not meant to support any particular version of marriage, but to offer an encouragement to be open and flexible about different possibilities. It may be that you and your partner in passion come together energetically and decide that this is for life and it may prove to be so. However, for almost seventy percent of people who have had this intention, it turns out not to be the case. I do not believe that these people went into their partnerships expecting to divorce. Life brought changes in their relationship fields and in their personal energy fields that caused them to move in different directions.

The Tests of Time

In astrology the Ancients indicated three energies as the primary forces that power all life on Earth. These three energies are the powers of the moon, the planet and the sun. These three forces have been described in the traditions of both the East and West as three dragons, being great energetic powers from the unseen worlds of energy. The lunar dragon has often been ascribed with the colors dark red and green, the planetary dragon with royal blue and silver, while the solar dragon was often given the colors gold and bright red. It was the solar dragon that in mythology breathed tongues of living fire, as it was connected to the illumination and power of the sun.

In the worlds of energy we find that human affairs often are governed by energies that break into three divisions corresponding with the powers of the moon, planet and sun. There are also three natural types of relationships that correspond with these three energies. One of the tests as to which level of energy is at play in any relationship is the test of time, because the energies of the moon, planet and sun correspond with short term, mid-term and long term relationships. These three levels of energy offer different possibilities of energy pairing.

C. The Moon Relationship

This level of relationship is short term and works in accordance with the twenty-eight day cycle of the moon. There are many processes within our body and soul that are synchronized with this cycle. One example is the process of menstruation. Another is the life of our skin cells. Apart from the cells of the eyes, which are directly connected to the brain, all our outer skin cells are sloughed off every twenty-eight days. They are attuned to the process of the moon. Fortunately, all our skin cells are not shed at the same time, otherwise we would shed our skins in the way of a snake! Instead, our skin cells are released gradually over a twenty-eight day period. Indeed, when we dust and vacuum our house, a large part of the debris that we sweep up is that which is released from our own skin. "Where does all this dust come from?" we ask, as we set about sweeping ourselves up!

Any energetic relationship we enter into has an initial testing period of one lunar month, which consists of four periods of seven days. This is the first test of time. If a relationship does not make it past the first twenty-eight days, it often means it was based in a brief magnetic attraction, though this does not mean that it is lacking in passion!

The level of sexual and emotional passion that can happen between two people in a twenty-eight fling is very high. The sexual center is one of the most powerful energy centers in our human system; the continuance of the human race depends upon it. Two people can be attracted sexually and there can be a powerful energetic red and green flash between them which leads them to take each other out for a test drive. If they find, however, that outside of this level of attraction they do not enjoy each other's company, then they are most likely to part. The relationship can turn out to be a flash in the pan, a one-night stand or a one week wonder. If it has not withstood the first test of the moon dragon, it will not go on to meet the next test of time which is the planetary dragon.

B. The Planetary Relationship

Every seven years we have a new physical body. All our cells, except those of our brain, are replaced, although each new cell inherits the memory of what was there before. This cellular change lends credence to the "seven-year itch" as a real phenomenon, because we can look at the person we are with after seven years and say, "You are not the person I married" and it will be true because every cell in their body will have been replaced, except the cells of the brain matter in the head and spine and the ova in the female.

The seven-year itch represents another cycle of twenty-eight, only this time it is not days, but planetary seasons. This mid-term level of relationship corresponds with the cycle of the four seasons of the planet. At this level the energy partners enter into a deeper and longer lasting energetic relationship. This is potentially the transition period from being partners in passion into becoming partners in purpose.

During this time the partners in passion explore far more than their initial sexual and emotional feelings for each other and enter into the domains of what they find to be of mutual interest. This is the time in which crucial patterns are set in the relationship field for potentially years to come.

A relationship that lasts through twenty-eight seasons, or seven years, is also far more likely to produce children than the twenty-eight day test drive. At the end of this seven-year cycle, however, one or both of the partners may decide that they prefer to move on and try to establish an energy pairing with someone new. If this happens, they will not go on to meet the third test of time which is the solar dragon.

A. *The Solar Relationship*

A different order of cellular construction in our human system is the cellular life of the brain. The brain cells, including the cells in our eyes, last for a lifetime. These are the cells that are able to contain some of the highest energies of our life. The brain system includes both the brain in the head and the spine which are the prime residences of our nuclear and immortal spirit.

A solar level commitment can only be successfully accomplished if there is a great deal of exchange between the partners about their life's purpose and they are able to move into well-established and confirmed connection to the higher energy worlds. This makes it possible for partners in passion and purpose to build a long term, spiritually illumined relationship field between them which transcends the idea of soul-mates and touches upon becoming spiritual kin.

It is during this third test of time that the relationship field can most readily move from being one that is centered upon the two partners being partners in passion (moon), to partners in purpose (planet), to becoming partners in evolution (sun).

In relation to the cycle of twenty-eight it is notable that within the solar relationship at approximately the twenty-eight to thirty year mark there is the completion of four seven and a half year astrological cycles of Saturn, known together as one generation. This marks another test of time within the three energy pairings which occurs approximately between the twenty-eighth and thirtieth years. Beyond the four seven and a half year Saturn cycles, if the relationship has held for this third test of time and been able to grow in spirituality and power, even higher connective possibilities open up.

The Three Pairings

We can engage the energies of our mind and brains at any or all of these three levels. What comes to be important over time is where the center of gravity of our pre-occupations comes to be and what powers and forces we attract and grow within our mutual relationship field.

When someone is looking for an energy date at the level of the moon, they may well be looking for a one-night stand. This often belongs with early sexual experimentation and the drive to satisfy a short term sexual need.

The next level is the search for a soulmate at the level of the planet. This journey is marked in cycles of seven years. At this level, there is enough transference of soul power to cause both partners to move beyond a moon-level, short term relationship and become more committed to each other.

 The next level up is the search for a lifetime partner who will companion us through a generation of twenty-eight years and possibly all of our days. This is the highest of the three levels and it is in this level that our modern marriage ceremony is based, even though the reality of the ceremonized relationship often turns out to be different.

The truth is that no relationship runs only on one of these levels, they are all intertwined. What is crucial is where the center of gravity of the relationship comes to be over time. Two people may take each other on a test drive at moon level because they are physically attracted by the equivalent of animal magnetism. As they do so, they may discover that they power each other's souls at planetary level and enjoy each other's company over the longer term. In talking and exchanging energies together they may gradually find themselves talking more about their life's purpose and discovering their compatibility at the level of the sun. This is a relationship in which a couple finds that over time their love grows stronger and the bonding and affection between them increases. Their relationship gradually offers increasing spiritual illumination, both to themselves and the lives around them.

Two people can be powerfully attracted at the level of the moon and planet. They may come together with a tremendous passion at these levels and they may even decide to marry based upon what they feel. However, as they live together, they may discover that the core passions that liberate their inner life draw them in different directions. They may then look at each other and come to discover that the other person contains many properties they do not like at all. This is the story of many of the divorces in our time.

There are as many examples and stories as there are relationship fields that are formed between people. No two stories are exactly the same and every person feels the emotional love or pain caused by the interaction with another and the relationship field caused thereby to be special and uniquely their own.

Each new poet and songwriter feels that his or her love is new, special and worth expressing. This is true. Their feelings of joy, sorrow and love have never happened in their particular energy field before but they certainly have happened within the energy fields of over ten billion other people, as these powerful emotions have been caused in human beings ever since we evolved into consciousness and first felt the power of love.

Reach for the Stars

The cells in our bodies can be classified as being of short, medium and long term durations. These three levels of our cellular organization reflect three levels of relationship: a short term relationship based on the magnetism of the body, a longer lasting relationship based upon compatibility of the soul and a contractual relationship that seeks to liberate the spirit. The relationship that builds the most powerful energy field and has the best possibility of continuance is one that includes all three levels of body, soul and spirit.

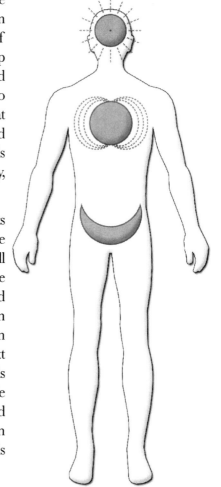

For a relationship to withstand the tests of time and energetically refine over the years, there needs to be exchange at all three levels: the moon, the planet and the sun. Once these three levels are established and working simultaneously, partners in passion, purpose and evolution can begin to reach for the stars, which is the next level of energies from the energy worlds it is possible to connect to. The whole idea of becoming a star, being touched by stardust and being star-struck is born out of the possibility of connecting to this level of Creation energy.

The alchemists of Europe left us drawings in which the moon, planet and solar energies were ascribed to different parts of the human body.

Moon energies were depicted as being processed below the waist, planetary energies within the internal organs and solar energies in the head. Star energies and other higher powers were often shown as being in the area above the head. The traditional wizard's hat upon which symbols for the moon, planet, sun and stars were portrayed also represents this idea.

Together Forever?

The words "always" and "forever" are often used in the full flush of moon-level passion. This short term energy rush is of such power that a couple may decide they will be "together forever." They mean it, but the words they are saying are filled with the short term energies of the moon. It is only when the words can be spoken from the power of the inner sun and stars that they have full meaning. The words then become contractual, as the energies are coming from the potent core of their life.

Banks of Energy

The realm of finance demonstrates many truths about the workings of the energy worlds because money itself is a powerful energy in the fields of human exchange and relationships. In the field of energy banking, moon level would represent the daily expenses needed to keep body and soul together, such as the funds required for food and transportation. Planetary level is like our longer-term maintenance expense, such as paying the mortgage for the house. Solar level is like our investments for the future. These investments cost us today, but pay us back in the long term and actually will provide the funds we need to sustain our planetary and moon level requirements over the long term.

A partnership that does not invest energy into its future by asking questions such as, "What are we doing?" "Where are we going?" "Are we happy together?" "What is the direction of our life?" makes no investment in its tomorrows. At some point it will find itself going energetically bankrupt, as the energies of passion that grace the beginning of a new relationship run out either in the first few months or in the first seven years. A relationship that is for the long term will invest in long term frequencies. Thus it is that two people can truly say, "We belong together," in which the word "belong" tells the story—it is the ability to actually "be long" in thought and intention in the energetic worlds. Long-range frequencies include long term projections, purposes, plans and discussions.

Mutually Agreed Purposes

The partnership that invests energetically in spiritual practices and processes can become immensely spiritually rich and have enough spiritual energy and power not only for themselves but also to inspire people they meet. At the core of this idea sits the theme of living as consciously as possible and making deliberate decisions with our life's energies, knowing we will not be perfect and that this place, planet Earth, offers the opportunity for making mistakes. The great lesson is to learn from our mistakes. We can be vibrantly alive in the now and be investing in our future simultaneously.

The mutual decision to pursue a spiritual purpose and engage with it together on a day by day basis produces the most consistent and illuminated results in the mutual relationship field. When you decide to live a life with a focus upon spiritual development and evolution, you become open to be able to engage with the higher levels of the energy worlds and bring enhanced spiritual illumination into your mutual journey. The **Mutually Agreed Purpose** that you come to is the MAP that you need for your journey. No two maps are exactly the same, just as no two partnerships are exactly alike.

When we decide to base our mutually agreed purposes on the values of spiritual development and natural equality, we begin to balance the power and multiply the passion in our core relationships in a deeper way. In so doing we set our feet upon the path of becoming partners in evolution. With our partners in passion we can decide we want to try for this advanced level of relationship field, build our relationship on the energies of the moon, planet, sun and even reach for what the ancient Egyptians called "the imperishable stars."

Marrying Energies

When we date someone, we not only date them, we also date the powers and forces that live in their personal energy field and everything they are connected to. We energy date everywhere they have ever been, everything they have ever done and every energy connection that is active in their aura.

When we marry someone, we marry the whole energetic package: that which is upfront attractive to us and that which is held back and not immediately displayed.

How can we detect what it is that we are marrying, bearing in mind that the closer we bring someone to us and the longer we are with them, the more of their energy and frequency we bring into ourselves? This is where being able to better detect the energy worlds and understand the laws that govern them is so invaluable.

Even when we are married, our marriage energetically changes every day, because every day we and our partner make new energy connections and the energy dynamics of our mutual relationship field shift. We cannot, therefore, rely upon the fact of being married to someone to secure our energy relationship into the future. We need to be energy dating our partner every day if the marriage is not to get stuck and stagnate in the backwaters of assumption and familiarity.

The Energy Secrets of a Successful Marriage

To succeed, any long term relationship has to have a powerful energetic base. In my years of EnergyWorlds coaching and counseling I have researched the relationship field dynamics that allow some couples to generate a high level of energetic love and stay together for the long term. In this process I have found there are certain ingredients that are almost always present.

To follow are fifteen of these core ingredients set out in an introductory fashion:

1. Be True to Yourself

When two people first fall in love, they are attracted by the unique energy field, way, style and personality of their partner in passion. It is this unique combination of signals that attracts them. The danger in living together is that sometimes both parties try to change each other into how they would like the other person to be. If they succeed, very often the attraction between them will diminish as they move further from their own unique nature and inner power and become something that neither really likes anymore.

When two people marry, traditionally the bride wears white and the groom wears black. This demonstrates that they represent two different natures of energy. If in their going forward into life they are both able to be themselves and remain black and white within the partnership, then their passion has a far greater chance of continuance than if they blur together and both become a shade of grey.

The colors black and white are the colors that are currently most often used to graphically portray the yin/yang symbol. They represent most dramatically the distinct natures of the masculine and feminine energies. Imagine if the black and white of the yin/yang symbol were changed to a uniform grey. The attraction between the masculine and feminine power would be diminished and you would not be able to distinguish between the two shapes depicted in the circle.

This diminished attraction is the result of not being true to yourself in your energy partnership or trying to make your partner into what you want them to be, rather than encouraging them to be true to their inner nature. All too often our efforts to improve another are based in how we are, rather than in what is best for them. If both partners succeed in changing each other according to their own image, the passion of black meeting white will move into becoming a grey mulch, which has a lesser possibility of passionate exchange.

Stick to what it means to be you and be true to yourself. Discuss this with your partner. If you can both be true to yourselves inside a mission that you mutually agree upon, then you have the basis for a highly passionate and constructive relationship. It is important to be true to yourself in the context of being positive and not harming others, otherwise we can take being true to ourselves as an excuse to do anything we feel like. All actions bring consequences and we are responsible for what we cause in ourselves, in others and in the world around us.

2. Have Mutually Agreed Purposes

The first energy connection that any relationship field comes to rely upon in the long term is the reason why the partners are together. If it is simply "because we are in love," then this may last up to seven years, but is unlikely to last much longer than that. A relationship that begins in sexual and emotional attraction, but does not develop at other levels, is unlikely to satisfy for long. What will keep a couple together for the long term are shared purposes and interests at many levels. As we saw in Chapter 9, The Seven Levels of Love and Sex, the relationship will work best if there is a powerful connection through all seven chakras and the five energy centers, so that the couple can share a full-spectrum passion in the higher levels of the energy worlds.

When both people share the same religion, have a shared quest for the meaning of life, enjoy each other's company, enjoy sharing ideas and providing an energizing ecology to live in and have a mutually satisfying sexual and emotional life, then their relationship has a much better chance of succeeding for the long term than if they are attracted by the other person's fame or wealth, but then find they have little else to share.

Many Christians believe that the couple that prays together stays together, as this is daily living evidence of the fact that they are committed to a power that is higher than both of them. The shared energy of prayer bonds them inside the living purpose of their life. Prayer, however, can take many forms. It need not mean praying in the traditional fashion of any organized religion. There is no more powerful prayer than the applied energy of work, and when two people come into partnership and work for a mutually agreed purpose, then they share a very powerful bond indeed.

An example of mutually agreed purpose is the conscious decision to offer an ecology for new spirits to enter the world and be responsible for their early formation. If, however, the decision to have children is made to try and keep a marriage together or if it becomes the sole reason for a union, then it is often doomed to failure, sometimes with traumatized children as a side effect.

One of the most profound examples of a mutually agreed purpose is the decision to help each other find and fulfill their individual "sacred contract" as Caroline Myss, author of *Anatomy of the Spirit*, describes it. This is the inner purpose for which a person believes that they are here on Earth. This purpose is of such depth and power that it stretches from the cradle to the grave and beyond. This powerful contract also involves knowing that the other person is going to be making their way through death's door without you, and being prepared to offer them spirit-to-spirit support all the way to the ending of your life together.

We can never fully know whom we are married to. We do not know what part of the universe their inner spirit comes from or where it will be going. This is part of the great mystery that can keep a relationship fresh as we make our way through the seven ages of life.

3. Work at the Relationship

Work is the application of energy toward a desired result. In other words, work is an energy transmission towards what you want. It is the most practical form of prayer that exists. If you want something to exist, it is a fundamental energy law that you have to work at it, meaning to consciously apply energy into it. The more conscious this process, the more the energy can be deliberately applied and the better the chance of a successful outcome. This is why couples with long-lasting marriages have always applied energy into their relationships on a regular basis, and by the application of conscious work have consequently made their relationship succeed.

It is crucial that both partners work at building, maintaining and enriching their relationship field and their efforts are confirmed and reciprocated. If one partner puts the energies of their life into the relationship while the other chooses to coast on their efforts, then this is clearly not healthy for the long term. A vital part of balancing the power in relationships is to balance the work that goes into them. This includes the apparently mundane level of household chores, such as who cleans the dishes and who takes out the trash. If we expect any relationship to take care of itself and not to have to work at it, then we are daydreaming. The laws of the energy worlds in relationships simply do not work this way. Once we understand that there are actual laws that apply to all marriages and relationships, then we can apply these laws and work at how we want our energy relationships and our lives to be. In support of this I would recommend keeping the section "The Seven Laws of Energetic Love" in Chapter 15 of this book close by as a handy reference tool.

4. Build an Energy Home

Our first energy home is the home that we build in our personal energy field—

the energy home we carry with us everywhere we go. The early Anglo-Saxons used to call their body their "bone-house" which represents this idea well. Our second energy home are the relationship fields we build together with others that know us. Our energy transfers to them and to the joint relationship field that is formed between us, even at distance, because they carry a home in their energy field for what is happening with us, just as we carry a home in our energy field for the energies of their life and what is happening with them. These relationship fields are primarily formed with our really close friends and loved ones.

When we share our lives with a partner in passion and purpose who becomes what is today known as "our significant other," also known in times gone by as "our other half" and "our better half," this naturally and inevitably is most likely to become the key relationship field in our life. This key relationship field remains open even when we are at distance from each other, so long as we maintain in regular communication, even if this can only be in the energy worlds by having a consistent time of day when we think upon the other person and, for example, contemplate their photograph, knowing that they will do the same. Most often, however, this core relationship field is formed by living with the other person.

When we live with someone as our partner in passion and purpose we build a tangible energy field within the home ecology we form with them. This energy ecology is usually held within a physical place: a house, an apartment, a houseboat, whatever the space is that we share with them. This is our third energy home and is actually the most temporary.

The house we occupy becomes a home because of the energy transmissions we generate within it. Indeed, this is the key difference between a house and a home, as we explored earlier. It is not the physical stuff lodged in a place that makes a home; it is the energies that are transmitted into it and are anchored there. One vital piece of advice about forming a strong relationship field within a home is for both partners to work at it every day and seek to be finding small ways to improve the level and quality of service and comfortability the home provides.

When a place starts to feel like it is no longer home to either party, it is because there has been some kind of shift that the energy sensing faculties are registering and letting them know about. This is why the first signs of a relationship coming to an end are often not passionate fights and arguments, but a sense of coming home to an empty house, even when the other person is there. What is being registered is that a certain something is becoming absent. That "something" is not physical; it is energetic. The energies that gave you a mutual feeling of home have been repelled and you feel that love doesn't live here any more. If you value the relationship and want it to continue, this is a call to action, because if this sense of absence continues, it will grow and can lead to the end of the relationship.

When a couple decides to live together and build a shared energetic and material environment, they make a contract to strengthen and build the relationship field between them. It is the strength and power of the energetic love in this relationship field that turns a house into a home. This love is an intangible and yet most real thing. In a house where there is sufficient energetic love, even though a couple may not be materially rich, they can be spiritually rich and their house will radiate an attractive glow.

This energetic love can then be used to sustain many different kinds of endeavor, according to the dreams and desires of the couple, and acts as a platform of emotional support that both are able to rely upon for their needs. They will feel mutually helped and supported by their mutual energy field on their journey through life. The love of a good woman and the love of a good man can fill the atmosphere of a house. When children are born into such an ecology, they are born into an atmosphere that is loaded for success.

5. Refresh Your Commitments

This is something that can be done by repeating a couple's wedding vows or by writing new statements of commitment. Mark Victor Hansen, co-creator of the *Chicken Soup for the Soul* series, has an annual ceremony with his wife in which they re-affirm their wish to be together. This is an excellent idea for helping to keep the commitment and the romance fresh. It enhances the passion in any relationship as it reconfirms the desire and the decision to live together through the changing energy currents of life.

You do not even have to wait for an annual recommitment. You can make small ceremonies every day or every week to confirm your partnership. A powerful ceremony is to arrange a specific time and place for conscious energy dating on a regular basis.

6. Keep Your Energy Dating Conscious

Although you and your partner have decided to live together, do not assume that you no longer need to set time aside for dating. As you live together and the demands upon your energies and your time increase, it is vital that you make definite arrangements for dates between you. All the advice given earlier and the techniques still to come about energy dating apply here. Set a date and time and agree that you will power down the cell phones, send the children to bed and concentrate upon each other, your mutual passion and purpose.

It is hard for a newly-married couple to conceive that there may come a time in their relationship when they will need to reserve special time for energy dating and even for sex. But it will almost certainly happen. It is a wise couple that keeps the energies between them fresh by reserving at least one night a week for full spectrum passion between them. This way they can both be regularly updated on what is happening with each other and ensure that they do their best to keep each other satisfied at all levels.

Like any real skill, learning how to maximize the passion with your partner takes a definite decision and time commitment. If you do not take the step of guaranteeing this early in your marriage, you are likely to run into trouble later. The energy relationship with your partner is the most core and stabilizing energy relationship that you will ever have, at least in a successful marriage.

7. Play Together to Stay Together

There is nothing that disperses lower energies faster than humor. The ability to play, laugh at ourselves and not take ourselves too seriously has saved many relationships. Natural laughter is a tremendous healing property as laughter releases and flushes away lower energies, such as worry and fear that get stuck in our relationship fields.

The word recreation tells us that we can re-create ourselves through the right kind of play. Reserve some energy dating time to do things together you both enjoy. Whether it is dancing, reading to each other, playing Scrabble or going out to dinner does not matter, so long as you have some playtime together.

8. Have a Relationship Priority System

We all have hundreds, if not thousands, of active connections with other people. Which of these people are the most important to you? Who do you feel closest to? Do you know and is this knowledge consciously formed in you? In generating quality relationship fields it is tremendously helpful to know consciously who you count on as being your closest energy relations.

To cause this priority system to become conscious in you, try this exercise. Take a sheet of paper and write down the first twenty-five people you can think of that you know. Don't think about it, do it at speed. Now take the numbers one to four and put a number by each person. Now go back through the list and group all the number ones together, the number twos and so on.

Number ones are those people who are closest to you, who, for example, if they were to need you, you would drop everything and dedicate your energy to help, no matter where in the world they would be. Number twos are the people that you care for a great deal but you do not put as much of the core energy of your life their way. Number threes are casual friends and number fours are acquaintances.

This energy map will tell you who your really close energy partners are. Now when it comes to keeping agreements, being prompt, fulfilling promises and pledges, the most important promises are to the number one people, and so on, all the way to number four.

We are often taught to fulfill our promises to number fours before number ones, when the reality is that it needs to be the other way around if we are to be a person of character and integrity and build long-lasting relationships. This is a vital key to a successful marriage. The promises you make to the people who are closest to you are the most important energetic promises you will ever make. If your husband, wife, boyfriend, girlfriend or other close energy partner is not on your number one list, then it is time to acknowledge it and either do repair work or move into divorce proceedings! If you did not put them on your list at all, you need to think about this, because it says you take them so much for granted that you no longer even think of them as a person. If this is the case, you will know immediately you have a major problem with familiarity and assumption.

9. Take Time out to Think About Your Partner

This may seem almost too obvious to mention, but it is one of the most important pieces of advice for a successful marriage. The couples I know that have successful long term marriages share a deep and conscious consideration for each other. Mostly what passes for thinking about the other person in relationships is reactive against their most recent behaviors. This is not thinking about the other person at all; it is being reactive against the latest happenings of life. Thinking about the other person involves actually taking a kind of internal time-out from the going-on of life between you to consider what you know of their trace, their wishes, wants, desires and needs and putting yourself out to find some way to help them forward in their life and its processes.

When you do this, inevitably you will think of some way to help their life that is not bound by the timing of a birthday or anniversary, but is an actual energetic surprise and complement to their life. You may see that they are going through a difficult time at the moment and that extra confirmation is needed, so you go out of your way to confirm the features that you support. You may see that they are in need of a practical skill and look up a training course that would be suitable for them and suggest that they take it. You may even offer to pay for it. You may see that they need a treat and so you give them a hundred dollars to spend in whatever way they want. Even if you have a joint bank account, you can still do this. You may send them on a holiday. You may see that they were a very tidy person when you met them but have become more disorganized recently due to stress. You could clear your diary and offer them a day of your time to use in whatever way they choose, at a time of their choosing.

All of these and tens of thousands more ideas are possible options when you are able to take a short time-out from the ongoing of your lives to actually think about the other person, not in the context of you and your needs, but in the context of what you know of them and what they want as a life. It means thinking in a non self-focused way, which is connective into level four of the energy worlds. When you can think at this level, there are always fresh ideas for you to discover to help you generate a higher level of energetic love in your relationship. Give freely in this way and over time it will come back to you.

10. Have Family not Familiarity

If you wish to build charismatic relationships in your life, there is no substitute for actually caring for the other person that you are in relationship with. There is always a tendency over time for familiarity to set in. The root of the word "familiarity" is "family" and it is a strange contradiction in human behavior that often we give better consideration to people we meet only rarely than to the people we live with and meet every day.

Familiarity is corrosive to value, love and mutual relationship fields. It is a product of the lower energy worlds and is always nearby, hanging out in the lands of "don't care" and "don't bother," ready to corrupt the most important relationships in your life. To maintain a high level of energetic love it is vital to regularly do unexpected little things to keep the love alive and fresh in your relationships. The unexpected small gift that shows you were thinking of the other person when you were not together is a fine example of how love is kept alive. It is not the expensiveness of the gift itself that counts. The gift is the material evidence that demonstrates you were thinking of your partner. Find small ways that confirm what you uphold and respect in how your partner goes on every day. These are important ways to push back the living fog of familiarity, which otherwise can engulf the power and the passion in any relationship. Knowing the nature of the beast really helps here. None of us are immune from familiarity and it takes active work in the field of relationships to keep pushing it back and to cause the charisma between you and your partner to sparkle.

If you are more prompt in meeting a new personal or business acquaintance than you are in meeting your partner in passion, know that you have a major problem which, if extended over time and into other domains, is going to land your relationship in serious trouble. It means you are becoming a person that is more concerned with how you appear to others than how you actually are and that you are becoming more governed by external than internal considerations. By analogy, this will produce a fruit that is nice to look at on the outside but is rotten at the core. If you have powerful values for those close to you, the fruit will be sound at the center, though the outside may have a few bruises! Other people who are of any calibre and account will respect you better when they discover you are a person of core character and integrity that puts the people that are close to the core of your life first.

One of the most corrosive close cousins of familiarity is assumption. After marriage, if either or both partners assume that they are together for life and they do not need to work at it, the relationship is almost certainly doomed. This is the "together forever" syndrome, which swiftly brings "forever" to an abrupt close. Any relationship is only kept fresh by the ongoing generation of work into it.

If both partners know that the other is free to leave at any time, as are they, this has a marvelous anti-familiarity effect. The couple stays together every day because they choose to and every day the decision to stay together is actively reconfirmed. This freedom lends itself to a relationship field that contains a high level of happiness and happiness is a vital ingredient in any successful marriage.

11. Maintain an Allergy Watch

One of the greatest dangers in any relationship is becoming allergic to the energies and ways of the other person. This is born out of familiarity and is a process that is correctly called becoming "fed up" with each other. Being fed up says that there is too much of a particular frequency coming into your system, so that you become allergic to it. This happens in relationships that become stagnant and lose their freshness, zing and sparkle.

The word "allergy" by shapeshift says "all grey" and the danger is that what was once a powerful spark between the husband and wife, born out of their unique characters and characteristics, becomes that grey mulch of sameness that was spoken of earlier in this chapter. When two people keep receiving back their own signal from their partner, they become increasingly fed up and start to look for a new kind of signal to brighten up their lives. This is when extra marital affairs can begin, to escape what feels like an imprisonment.

A key way to approach this danger is to ensure that your lives together are always moving into new energetic currencies. It is also important to give each other space. One example is in sleeping arrangements. When two people sleep in each other's energy fields, there is an equalizing of energies that takes place. To keep a zing in your relationship, you may decide to sleep together only six nights a week so that each of you is able to experience the recharging of your energy field once a week without interference from the other person. Alternatively, you may find it better to sleep apart six nights a week and together only once a week. Be open to experiment in such matters and thereby keep the energetic signals between you bright and fresh.

Remember that we most often become allergic to foods and also energies that are our favorites. The person who loves chocolate and eats it all the time is more likely to become allergic to it than the person who eats it more sparingly. Do not eat so much of the other person's frequencies that you become allergic to them. If there is any danger of this happening, take a short break from each other before it becomes chronic.

Early on in any romantic relationship the two people involved usually feel, "I can't get enough of you." This is because their new partner in passion represents an energy food that they have not had access to before. Unless they come to a mutual purpose and contract in their life, this phase does not usually last longer than seven years, when the "seven year itch" propels them both into wondering if they cannot find more exciting energetic food elsewhere.

The cure for this is to have a mutual life that is moving forward into new energy currents, because then the relationship is able to keep fresh. If both partners are changing and evolving in their life, it is not "same old me" meets "same old you," but "changing and developing me" meets "changing and developing you." If we are both moving in agreed directions, then there is always new information and energies to update each other with. At this stage an evening with your existing partner in purpose or, better yet, partner in evolution is more attractive than an evening with a potential new partner in passion. The existing relationship field is so strong and potent that you would not wish to be in relationship with anyone else instead.

12. Keep Your Partner Satisfied

While moving forward into fresh territories together it is also important to keep each other satisfied at sexual and emotional levels and offer each other warmth and security. In the chakra system this means ensuring that the lower two chakras, those that represent security and sexuality, are satisfied ongoingly. If these become deprived, they will swiftly threaten all other processes within the relationship.

Sexuality can sometimes become not a priority in a relationship because of external pressures, but it is wise to ensure that every week there is a time-out from ongoing pressures of life to demonstrate to each other by the investment of time and energy that your partner is still number one with you. Sex is only one part of this whole dynamic, but it is a very important part. In the realms of energy, if the sexual desires and drives are not satisfied, then the relationship has an underlying tension. Sex is above all a process of energetic transference between the two parties and is part of the energetic bond of a successful marriage.

13. Understand Energetic Consequences

As long as we occupy the same space and are in a declared, committed relationship, the energy consequences of the decisions we make transfer to the person we are with. Whatever one spouse brings into the mutual relationship field, both parties carry its energetic consequences. You are no longer responsible for what happens in your personal force field alone; you are also responsible for what transfers from your field into theirs. This is why in certain ancient civilizations if one member of a family was found guilty of a crime, the whole family would carry the punishment, as they all became energetically touched by it. I am not suggesting a return to such measures, but it does powerfully demonstrate how strongly these peoples believed in the sharing of energies within a family.

It is impossible to overestimate the importance of understanding the laws of energy exchange within a relationship The Passion Multiplier. offers three powerful steps to help build a powerful mutual relationship field. Time taken out to discuss these principles between you and your partner will pay enormous dividends in the future.

14. Build Your Mutual Energy Account

Think of the energetic love that you and your partner share as a kind of energetic bank account of love. When you do not fulfill what you say, act in an uncaring manner and are selfish and insensitive to their needs, you withdraw some credit from the account. This is burned up and reduces your credit balance. When you act in a caring, considerate way and take time to build a full spectrum relationship, you put energetic love into the account and invest for the future. The more you invest energetically in the relationship on a daily basis, the stronger the energetic love you will share with your partner and the more you will have to draw upon in times of challenge and difficulty. The more you can work on building the good times between you, the more memories and energies of harmony you will be able to draw upon. This can produce such powerful bonds that the relationship will grow, prosper and illuminate "until death do us part" and both of you will be able to energetically support the other into a mutually happy old age.

15. *Check and Double-Check*

Your mutually agreed purposes create the fundamental security inside your relationship. The wise partners check and double-check that their mutually agreed purposes still hold. This will be reflected in everything from their priorities to how they direct their time, their energies and their money. "The firm" that you and your partner constitute can have a monthly meeting in which you review your calendars, your finances and explore together how you are investing the energies of your lives. In addition to checking these dynamics, the meeting can also cover what both partners have been thinking about and feeling since the previous month. Obviously, there can be many mini-meetings on the way through the month, but by deliberately fixing a monthly meeting you can check that your partnership is on track and not being drawn into new directions without you being consciously aware of it.

Energy Drift

The energies that lead to the ending of an energy pairing and a parting of the ways are most often caused not by a single occurrence but by a process of energy drift over time, in which one or both partners move away from the mutually agreed purposes of the relationship. Sometimes divorce and the ending of the contract between both parties is the best resolution under these circumstances, when it turns out that the two partners are genuinely incompatible. This incompatibility, however, is often caused by unconscious and semiconscious energy drift, rather than by the deliberate conscious actions of either partner.

Energy drift often begins due to a lack of understanding of the laws of energetic love, beginning with a shortfall in education about necessary life skills and the energy dynamics of relationships and how they work. At school we are taught history, geography, algebra and many other topics that we find to be of greater or lesser use on our journey in life, but we are not taught such basics of living as the fundamental natures of the masculine and feminine forces and how these forces cause men and women to be compatible but different. When we better understand the nature of these energies, we can appreciate what helps a relationship withstand the tests of time. This gives us a greater ability to sustain our intimate relationships for the long term if this is our wish, want and desire.

Chapter Thirteen
Energy Partings

Men and women have two great fault lines that, in my experience, are at the root of most relationship problems. When you know how to recognize these two fault lines you will be in a much stronger position to build lasting relationships as the same failings keep striking through the man/woman relationship field again and again. They are to be found at the root of most divorces and are at the core of most of the global issues that plague us today.

The Two Great Fault Lines

The two fault lines are the heads and tails of the same coin. They are inter-dependant and feed off each other.

1. Man's Greatest Fault Line

The greatest fault line of the man is his egomania and pride which prevents him from being able to show weakness and causes in him an internal demand to be always right and never to be found at fault. He would rather go on being wrong than show vulnerability. A classic example of this is the man who will continue to drive in the wrong direction rather than stop and ask for help, particularly when in the presence of his wife or girlfriend. The man gets hot and short-tempered and insists that he should not be challenged.

This egomania and pride is the main fault line of the masculine power. We can see examples of it all around, whether in small such as in the example given above, all the way to full-blown megalomania in which the man would rather see the destruction of everything around him rather than admitting to the defeat of being wrong. The behavior of Adolf Hitler at the end of World War II gives us an ultimate example of this. Once Hitler knew his Reich was over and that he had lost, he gave orders for the entire destruction of Germany. In his megalomania he preferred to destroy everything rather than leave it in place to support the lives of others.

It is just this runaway egomania that causes men to lock women into subjugation. This way the man is never to be challenged and his ego can run amok without there being any possibility of disturbance to his assumed superiority and pride of self-image. A dramatic example of this is where women are forbidden to leave their homes without a male escort and are forbidden the opportunity of education. They are never to be given access to information that could cause them to challenge the male. This abuse of power has led men to instigate countless cruelties and oppressions. It is an antithesis to natural development and is a huge prevention to human evolution and progress. It acts in prevention of the principles of The Passion Multiplier and needs to stop.

This fault line in the man is linked to the nature of the masculine power and is produced by the lowest expression of the great masculine energy. In its higher expression the power of the rod, associated by the Ancients to the number 1, always wants to be the best it can be and works constructively for a greater purpose. In its higher expression this leads to the accomplishment of great works and the upholding of great qualities. In the lower expression it leads to competition and the bashing down of anything else that may compete with it. It is easy to see evidence of this behavior in world history and business. These two contrasting expressions of the male energy are personified in many tales of chivalry in which the forces of constructive behavior (good) face off against the forces of destructive behavior (evil).

Turning This Around

The antidote to the energy of ego is humility and appreciating a situation for what it actually is. For a man to be able to do this he needs to take counsel and advice from women. This is because, as we have seen, the innate design of each gender brings an alternative perception to whatever is looked at. Together a man and woman can have a much greater field of vision as, by analogy, if each gender has a 180° view of the world by harmonizing both views a 360° picture is possible. When the man is prepared to have humility, he reduces the size of his swollen ego and becomes a self-acknowledged mortal, born to live, die and depart.

An example of man's swollen ego is when, like the Roman Emperor Nero, he declares himself to be an immortal God. He may then name months of the year after himself, as did "President for Life" Saparmurat Niyazor, the leader of Turkmenistan, and believe that he will never die. Statues of "the great leader" inevitably appear all over the country as he founds a cult upon his own self-image. The leader of North Korea, Kim Jong-il, is another example of this madness at work. Thankfully, Creation is governed by forces and powers greater than men or their invented masculine gods and such men do die. The closer a man moves to the real worlds and the natural laws that govern them, the more his swelled head reduces down to size.

In ancient Rome when the triumphant general returned and was granted a celebration through the streets there would always be a slave beside him to whisper in his ear "Memento mori," "Remember that you are mortal."

Footage of Mussolini, Hitler, Stalin and Mao reviewing their troops provides a vivid portrayal of what happens when the low end of the red male genetic runs away with itself and gets out of control. It resorts to violence to enforce its views and it is this frequency which has repetitively arisen to write the history of the world. Only occasionally do we see the lowest aspects of this rampant male energy giving itself full expression as in the previous examples of infamous dictators, but do we not see these same propensities played out in the office, the sports field and the boardroom every day? This renegade power needs to be governed down both at the level of personal and global relationships. Men can do this for themselves in seeking to live by the truth of the design and purpose of life on Earth which includes an equal, balanced and harmonious relationship with women.

To balance this renegade power it is crucial that men and women come into dynamics of genuine equality.

2. Woman's Greatest Fault Line

The greatest fault line of the woman is seeing herself as only having value when in relationship with a man and/or her children. This often leads to the lowering of her standards, a sense of being compromised and not being able to stand on her own two feet.

This is clearly quite a different fault line to masculine egomania and often appears as a clinging dependency that works primarily through the emotions. "I only have value when in a relationship with a man" is a fundamental mental and emotional sickness. This emotional and mental disease has been created by patriarchal dominance, is encouraged by men and re-inforced by generations of women who have felt they only have value in relation to the masculine power and the ability to produce and rear children.

If feminine power is to fulfill its own self-arising nature then this fault line needs to be seriously addressed because a liberated feminine force will not be possible if it is always looking to the masculine power to lead it. This state of affairs also continues because women have been conditioned into thinking that "father knows best" and that women need help in thinking for themselves. World religions, enforced by male bishops, male rabbis, male mullahs and male priests, have particularly caused this effect. Right-wing Christians and fundamentalist Muslims share a belief that it is the man's job to be the law-giver of the household, whether he is right or wrong, as this is fraudulently portrayed as a commandment of their mythical masculine god.

When women see themselves as having value only when in relationship with men, they also tend to become catty with each other as they compete over who will get what they consider to be "the prize," being the perceived best man of the bunch. This is often measured by status, money and power. I have often heard women comment how they are able to be cooperative together when there are no men around and how harmonious it can be when they are engaged in a project together, but introduce a few men into that same scenario and suddenly some women start showing off, cutting each other up and vying for the men's attentions. This behavior is an expression of this great fault line because with a high internal value for their own life, the cattiness would not suddenly commence and the co-operation between women would be able to hold.

This great fault line is produced by a warped manifestation of the low end of the great feminine energy. In its higher expression the feminine energy is nurturing, encouraging and supportive, with the ability to have a long view and to conceive and give birth to new life. In its lower, warped expression it can see itself to only be of value in relation to the existence of something else. This can produce surrender of the wrong kind and even a blind obedience.

Turning This Around

A woman can only get over her dependency issues by taking up positions of leadership, thinking for herself and speaking her mind regardless of whether or not she maintains her popularity with men in general or with one man in particular. In this process it is vital that women can take up the opportunity to educate their minds and overcome the dictates of a world that has taught them to focus on being dependant. When a man can get over his ego by taking counsel with women and facilitating their freedom and success and women are proud to speak their minds the two halves of yin and yang can come together in a full, free and proud fashion rather than either power being shackled or subjugated.

If the masculine power is not able to be free and be itself but is under subjection by the feminine, then this is also unnatural and produces a degenerate result. The way forward is the way of equal power and true equality. Equality in this sense is caused by the quality of exchange between the two powers. If one party comes into a counsel chamber repressed or oppressed by the other, then there is no possibility of a quality counsel.

As long as women are afraid to walk the streets at night because of the behavior of men, we do not have a balance of men, women and power. As men have the greater physical strength, it is for them to make the ecology safe for the women. This means primarily making it safe from other men. Men also need to make space for women to be fully themselves, in a parity of relationships. This opens the way through which we can balance the power and multiply the passion in all our relationships.

Though we may not immediately be able to cause this on a world scale, we can certainly begin this process within our own home and within the sphere of our personal influence. Thus we will begin to change the fundamental balance of man/woman relationships throughout the world.

Understanding the Two Great Fault Lines

When a man and woman in relationship understand the nature of these two great fault lines and how they are the lower two expressions of the masculine and feminine force, they can watch out for them and even laugh at their manifestation when they crop up. Nicknames can really help. "Here comes Napoleon" can deflate the man, just as his ego is becoming outrageous. "Look out, it's the clinging vine" can be a reminder to the woman if she takes up too dependent a position.

Taken to the extreme these two fault lines in a household lead to the silent woman who is so desperate to be in a relationship that she will support the man in anything he does because he is "her" man. It also leads a man to being so secure in his egomania and power that he can make the most ridiculous assertions confident in the belief that no woman in "his" household would dare challenge him. A vital part of resetting the balance is that women are not afraid to speak their views and feelings and that men actually learn to listen, rather than rushing forward with their next opinion.

Every man/woman relationship is subject to these two fault lines. This is because they reflect the fundamental natures of the masculine and feminine powers in their lower expression. The nature of the man, as expressed by the rod-like symbol of the number 1, is prone to being individualistic and closed to external advice. The nature of woman, as expressed by the curving symbol of the number 2, is more inclined to be flexible and realistic. Together in equality they can move in a mutually purposeful direction, as expressed by the number 3. Only by working together in a third direction of what is best for the relationship of both can the two fault lines move from being our two greatest weaknesses into becoming our two greatest strengths.

It is also important to note here that the two great fault lines appear can appear within any expression of the great masculine and feminine force. Thus in same-sex relationships, where a man may base himself more in his feminine yin part, so-called catty behavior is just as likely to break out as amongst a group of women. Also, in a place where women are centered in their masculine yang power, they are as likely to take up positions of egomania, dominance and pride as their masculine counterparts.

There is no way to escape connection to the great yin and yang powers at whatever level we actually make connection and give expression to them. As human beings we are designed to give expression to these two great forces and are destined to do so for as long as we live on this Gemini-natured planet, whose primary law is the binary law of two powers being in apparent opposition to each other while they each hold part of the other within themselves.

Division of Forces

Divorce begins in the energetic worlds. Just as two people are drawn together energetically and then physically, so the process of divorce begins when the energies of the two lives begin to move in incompatible directions. This often begins in the realms of secrecy and is accompanied by feelings of guilt.

One partner may start to put some of their life's energies in a direction that they feel the other would not approve of. Rather than being up front and saying it, which means that the energy is shared, they may choose to suppress the information. There may even be so little communication between both parties that they drift apart in ignorance, not recognizing that the decisions they are making are leading them away from their partner.

When two people decide to live together and join forces, they agree to process each other's energies at all levels. Whatever your partner does, they transfer the energies from that experience to you. This happens at three levels: consciously, semiconsciously and unconsciously.

When one partner begins to conceal things from the other that are of importance, an energetic contradiction is caused between the partners and enters the relationship field. This is because one partner now registers a change in the balance of energies within the relationship but does not know the reason why this has happened as the necessary information has not been shared.

A common example is a husband who develops a close working relationship with a woman at the office, which involves a high degree of energetic exchange. Nothing may have happened physically between them, but the balances in his energy field are changed. He no longer has the same quantity of masculine power to exchange with his wife because he is exchanging energies with his co-worker.

Over time the wife can feel that something has gone missing from the relationship.

He says nothing has changed, but she knows that energetically it has. If he had told her about the new relationship at work and let his wife know that his marriage to her is secure, then she would have a context for this change in circumstance. It is the not knowing that is the hardest part to handle. He knows that nothing physically has happened but feels a sense of guilt and awkwardness, an unwillingness to talk about the new relationship in his life. It is just this unwillingness that should be the energetic warning sign for him. If he ignores it, he will build a small wall of denial between the truth of what is happening with him and what he is telling his partner. From little walls, big walls can easily grow. This can be the beginning of a process that leads to divorce a few years later, because the division of forces has begun.

This story highlights how, when two people come together in energetic partnership, whatever the one experiences energetically transfers to the other. Whatever one spouse does energetically passes to the other and vice-versa. This is a vital understanding about what it actually means to come into energetic partnership with someone. The energy worlds mechanics of this mostly work to help keep couples together as their personal energy fields contain energies that are similar to each other and, by the law that like things are attracted to like things, they tend to hold together.

When one partner starts to keep their thoughts and feelings to themselves, however, they prevent the full exchange of energies between them in their relationship field and set up a contradiction between the energies that are exchanged and the conscious exchange of words and ideas that belong with it. The partner who still thinks they are in the relationship as it was yesterday, starts to ask questions like "Is something the matter?" "Is everything all right?' or "You don't seem quite yourself..."

To continue with our example of the husband and his new relationship at work, when the spouses sleep together, during the exchange of energies that takes place between their energy fields at night, the wife will receive the energies of the husband's colleague at work and may have dreams about her, even though they have never met and she doesn't know consciously of her existence. The divorce process, in terms of the division of energies, has now begun. If this process continues over weeks, months or even years inevitably the two people will grow apart. Divorce happens energetically first and may later be confirmed physically.

Energetically a relationship can be over for many years before the papers finally go through the divorce courts. Once we begin to hide energetic secrets and do not share what is going on with our partner we begin to move away from them energetically and, of course, if this starts to happen with you, then it most likely has started going on with them as well.

The wife in our example may start to feel that something has gone missing in the relationship and the look from her eyes and the signal from her energy field now changes also. This look releases a power that was not there before. It may be picked up on by another man and a new relationship may begin.

If a person persists in secret behavior, whatever it is, then the energetic difference in the relationship they share with their partner becomes deeper. What then accompanies this is often a lot of secondary self-explaining behavior to cover up the fact. This secret behavior can be in any realm: financial, emotional, sexual, spiritual and religious. It does not matter so much what the realm is, it is the fact of growing apart that is important. This does not mean that two people cannot have their own lives, which is a crucial part of any successful relationship. What is vital is that their motivations and conduct are known about and agreed upon.

Divorce happens because of the dividing of forces. Once these forces have divided beyond a certain point then physical separation becomes inevitable, unless the two people decide to stay together for the children or for material reasons, whereupon it then moves from being a living partnership in passion and purpose into a marriage of obligation.

Divorcing Successfully

The following two keys to divorcing successfully, apply not only to marriages but also to any circumstance in which you have made an energetic contract with another person or group of people that is coming to an end. Depending upon how much time, energy and finance you have invested in the partnership will you experience greater or lesser symptoms of divorce trauma. This is also affected by your experience of life. If you have already experienced many energetic contracts, some of which have held and some of which have not, you will be in a much stronger position to come successfully through the trauma of divorce than a man or woman who is building the projection of their future on their first relationship and is putting all their energetic eggs in one basket, so to speak

1. *Value You*

The first cruciality in a successful divorce is having a profound value, respect and love for your own life, its purpose and possibility. If you have a self-view and identity that only evaluates your worth in the context of your partner and the relationship field you share together then divorce is going to be far more traumatic than if you feel and know that you are your own person first, self-determining and with a network of self-chosen energy partnerships and friends. It will simply be that you are bringing one of your energetic relationships to a close. It may be a partnership you thought was the most core and important and it may be that you did not want it to end, but all energy partnerships are a two-way deal and you cannot make another person stay in contract with you if they don't want to.

The longer and more intensely you have invested in the relationship the harder it is to let go, but it is vital to do so. If the relationship is coming to an end, try giving yourself a pre-determined time for grieving and then close off the energetic connection and get on with your life. Many of the technologies that are set out in the section on moving on from abusive relationships in Chapter 11 can be applied here. The energies of your relationship may not have been abusive at all, but it is just as crucial to close the energetic chapter you are leaving so that you can move on.

2. *Let Go*

A vital part of the divorce process is in actually letting go. If the personal energy fields of both partners have moved so far apart that the mutual relationship field no longer holds power and they are happier away from each other, then it is time to acknowledge this reality and to let go. If the prospect of separating brings more a sense of relief than grief, then it is a good time to take a break in which to add up whether or not you actually want to stay together. Life is short and if you decide you are impeding each other's progress and process rather than helping, it is time to look at alternatives, including refreshing your relationship.

This was brought into sharp focus for me a few years ago when a friend asked me for advice. He explained that his wife had gone away for a few days a number of times in the previous months and he realized each time, as the time drew closer for her return, he did not look forward to her coming back. He enjoyed his life more without her.

He asked me what advice I could give him and I said that the relationship was clearly in an energetic divorce process and that if he wanted to turn it around then he needed to sit with his partner and talk through how they both felt about their relationship, their mission and purpose together. He came back to me two weeks later and said that they had decided to divorce, as she also found that she did not look forward to returning home and felt better without him. Energetically their relationship was already over and talking it through together made it clear to both of them.

Relationship Field Indicators

There are many indicators that can be used to gauge whether your mutual relationship field is strengthening or weakening. Here are two powerful and easy to use indicators.

The first indicator is: do you regularly make each other laugh anymore? When humor leaves a relationship it is often an early sign that energetic enhancement is also leaving. Laughter is like an energetic lubricant that helps a relationship along and clears out old and stuck energies. When laughter is no longer possible, it often means that energetic issues have become locked in too deeply to be released.

A second key indicator to the health of the mutual relationship field is simply: do you enjoy each other's company and can you focus on your partner when sitting down to a meal together or do you always seek a distracting force, like what is on television?

In my experience, if for some reason the mutual relationship field has weakened there are many techniques and practical steps that can be taken to refresh and recharge this field if it has not become too toxic and if both partners are really prepared to try. If these practical techniques have been tried and there is still difficulty, it makes sense to go to a third party, such as a therapist or couples counselor for help.

Both partners are responsible for charging, refreshing and renewing the third power of their mutual relationship field, which is neither the product of one or the other, but the shared field between them both. If, as an example, one of the partners feel that the relationship lacks warmth, it is their responsibility to start putting extra warmth into the relationship field initially, as they were the first to spot this lack. After they start adding extra warmth it is reasonable that their partner then begins to reciprocate. This is one small facet of what it means to view relationships "field first."

Energy Matters

In any relationship there is always the transference of very fine energetic matter. This is because whenever there is a movement of energy or force it is always accompanied by fine or subtle matter. This can be a very minor exchange, such as that which takes place between casual acquaintances, or it can be very deep and powerful, as in the exchange between two people who have lived together as partners in purpose for many years.

In a sexual relationship the transfer of matter is both physical and obvious, but there is also the very fine and subtle matter that transfers between the energy fields of two people. The longer a couple is together and the more of each other's energies they share the more of each other's fine matter they carry. This is where the expression "you matter to me" comes from.

When a couple is together for many years, they build large deposits of each other's fine matter within their energetic fields and even in the cellular structure of their bodies. When a couple becomes engaged it says they commit to the growth and continuance of the energetic exchange between them and the building of a mutual relationship field. Their wedding day is the day that the couple celebrates their decision to marry their energies together and have this fact energetically confirmed by friends, family and all those that matter to them the most. Wedding rings are a physical confirmation and reminder of how their energies are now bound together by witnessed mutual agreement. Gold contains a binding energy and so it is that gold rings are traditionally used.

Ceremonies With Meaning

Many wedding ceremonies in the world are based on traditional vows and agreements. There is a growing trend, however, to have a ceremony which is unique to the individuals involved. Joanna Infeld, co-founder of Ceremonies with Meaning, produces tailored ceremonies for weddings and all major rites of passage including birth, puberty, engagement, marriage, the renewal of vows, parting and departure. Each ceremony is unique and written with the direct input and collaboration of the individuals who are at the core of the ceremony. Ceremonies with Meaning also offers a ceremony of endearment to confirm divorce in a harmonious manner and help the two partners separate out from their mutual relationship field as the core commitment of their life and move on into new relationships. For more information on Ceremonies with Meaning see the Resource section.

Dealing With Grief

If you decide to break up with your partner or they break up with you, then anticipate that there will be some grief. Grief is the sensation of energies you have stored within you, leaving you. There may be grief for the good times that were, but can be no more; grief for the falling away of all the plans, projections and hopes you shared together; grief for all the years you have been collecting energies from the other person and they from you. These energies have entered your system and have even become part of you at cellular level.

When you decide to divorce and stop this process of energetic exchange, there is a natural surge of grief because certain energetic processes that your system has come to rely upon and become habituated to, stop. Over time the energies you received from the other person gradually return to them and do not live inside you in the same energized way anymore. This understanding is at the root of that much invoked folk wisdom, "Time is the great healer" and that often offered advice "just give it time."

The symptoms of the dividing of forces not only occur within energy relationships that have moved to the point of marriage. Whether it is a breakup of an energetic pairing in the teenage years or a marriage of many years coming to an end, the feelings that accompany the parting from a mutual relationship field can be extremely acute. As the energy exchange between any couple continues and deepens, it brings them closer to each other and they come to contain greater amounts of each other's energies and fine matter. When the two personal energy fields are pulled apart, it is often accompanied by a painful, tearing sensation brought on by the fact that the relationship field itself is literally being torn apart as both parties bring their energies back to themselves. The dividing of material property at the time of divorce is a material confirmation of this energetic fact and it is the pulling asunder in the energy worlds that brings with it the real pain and grief, not the fact of the material objects being split between them. The depth and power of this grief depends entirely upon the intensity of the forces and powers that are at play between the force-fields of the two people.

Dealing With Emotional Pain

To be in relationship with someone with an expectation of it continuing and to have the relationship come to an abrupt end causes pain at many levels. The sexual center can ache for the presence of the other person in as real a way as the stomach longs for dinner. Add to this an expectation of emotional and mental exchange no longer fulfilled and the pain of breaking up can seriously disrupt any life. This pain can come at the breakup of an engagement, the end of a marriage or even after an intense relationship of only weeks or months.

Because the sexual and emotional centers work with very high power energies, the pain of a breakup can be much deeper and last longer than the pain of a broken leg. It can take a person to such extremes that they even question the value of their own life and may, possibly, contemplate suicide. The person literally feels, "I cannot live without you." The combined power of the sexual and emotional centers can take a person to such a pitch of energetic pain that suicide may seem the only way out.

This Too Will Pass

Like King Solomon in his quest to escape depression, you may want to inscribe the words "This too will pass" on a piece of paper to put in your wallet, handbag or somewhere else you will see it often to help you realize that over time, the emotional and sexual pain you feel will diminish. Time is, indeed, the great healer in the realms of emotional pain and you may become a richer, more compassionate person for the experience.

Whatever it takes, even through your tears, find ways to engage with what it is that you love to do and you will recreate the power, passion and purpose in your life. In so doing you will build new power in your personal energy field and prepare yourself for a new tomorrow and enhanced energy dating possibilities in the future.

Chapter Fourteen
Enhanced Energy Dating

Enhanced energy dating is about causing the exchange between you and your partner in passion to become as conscious and full as possible. This means becoming more conscious of what you are feeling so you can diagnose the energy sensations you are registering inside yourself as they are happening. It also means learning how to use the energy dating techniques outlined in this chapter to help enhance your dating experience.

Forty Days or Forty Years

All of the considerations, techniques and opportunities of enhanced energy dating apply equally if you have been married for years or only been dating for days. The difference is that the longer you have been together the deeper and more powerful your energy dating experiences can become.

After forty years you can still approach your partner in passion as a first date, except that you have between you a vast relationship field of shared reference, experience and energetic content to work with. The power of your energetic love can be deeper, stronger, more passionate and potent. It is true that you may not again experience the excitement of the first touch and first love, but that is part of the history you share, now augmented by ten thousand other experiences.

Whether you are meeting for the first time or the ten thousandth time, you can still prepare for your energy date, clean your energetic pathways, clear your schedule, switch off the cell phone and get ready to meet the other person as if he or she is the only person in the world for those few hours. You are never too old for a passionate relationship!

Meditate Upon Your Date

Before you meet, meditate upon the date, time and place of your meeting. This means projecting energy towards the encounter. Envision how you want to be, not how you want the other person to be, but how you want to be from the inside out. Do you want to be calm and confident? What order of charisma do you want to radiate? The closer to your core, authentic self you can be the greater the possibility for a powerful energy date and the beginning of a powerful relationship field. This is because you will be emanating out from yourself the core properties of who and what you really are. Pretense can only obscure the natural you and jam the potential relationship field. The most powerful meeting between two people is always from core to core, from real self to real self.

Before your date, prepare your internal energies so you can be in the present when you meet the energies of the other person. You can only meet them with who and what you are and with the energies that live inside you. Pretending to be something that you are not, like trying to take on the role of a particular celebrity or character in a novel, can only confuse the issue and cloud the essence of the real you. If the person you are meeting does not want the real you, it is best to find out early and move on. There is no reason to hide behind a fake identity that you think is more attractive than your inner self. There is nothing more attractive that you can offer than the authentic inner content of the real you. If the other person does not appreciate this, then you do not need them in your life. Who has time for a masquerade?

It is vital that the properties you meditate upon and project resonate with how you actually are inside, so you feel comfortable with them. Otherwise, what you will be doing is role-playing at being someone different from yourself. Meditating upon your date is for the purpose of being closer to your true or essence self, rather than preparing a personality act that can never hold in the long term and will make you awkward because it is far away from what you are really like.

Zen and the Art of Energy Dating

To be present in the now, you need to be clean and clear of other personal and business responsibilities and be close to the inner core of you. If a water pipe has burst in the house or if your dog is at home waiting to be walked and this is your responsibility, then you are not clear for energy dating.

Enhanced energy dating is possible when you are living your life in such a way that you are clear to be where you are, when you are. You cannot be in the now if your basic responsibilities have not been attended to because there will be energy leakage from your personal energy field to those things that you are contracted to do but have not yet done. The art of living in a way that allows enhanced energy dating includes the need to be thorough and tie off the energies of the past so they do not arrest your energies now. This will help you access the power of now.

In these days of cell-phones, pagers and other mobile communication devices, it is more important than ever to demonstrate to the other person the importance of your date by switching all such interrupting devices off. It tells your date that you are going to concentrate all your energy upon them during your time together and that you are closing out other energetic connections. If you are a doctor on 24-hour call, make this clear up front and say you are fully present but may have to take calls for this reason. If at all possible get away from the 24/7 mental attitude that says the priority in your life is your job—unless that really is the case—in which instance you may appear to be a candidate for marriage, but it is more likely that you are a candidate for divorce!

The Japanese tea ceremony provides us with an excellent example of the principles of enhanced energy dating actively at play. For such a ceremony both participants prepare their inner state in advance. They deliberately clear their minds of energetic and emotional clutter so they can focus their consciousness and be vitally present in the moment. The space where they are to meet is physically and energetically cleaned and cleared thoroughly by the host in preparation for the creation of a powerful mutual relationship field.

Hiring a cleaning person to come in and clean up the ecology would not have the same effect as doing it yourself because it is the applied energy of the host that actually loads the atmosphere and makes it special. As the host cleans and prepares the ecology he or she also grooms and prepares their inner being. The ceremony takes place in an ecology that has minimal distractions so the participants can focus upon the moments they are to share together. Everything is very carefully prepared to help both participants be in a heightened state of awareness and consciousness, both in their personal energy field and in their jointly created mutual relationship field in the here and now.

You may not live in Japan but you can still take advantage of the understandings and techniques their Zen masters have left for us to enjoy. Invite your partner for a special energy date. Let them know you will be preparing the ecology with extra time and energy so you can both focus on your precious time together. Use the space clearing and charging technologies set out in Chapter 6, Energize Your Space and prepare the place both physically and energetically.

As your partner may not know what to expect, ask them to slow down their speeds and also to remove their shoes at the door. Shoes link us to the street and also carry whatever dirt they have come into contact with that day. It is always best to leave your shoes at the door when you enter your house and invite your guests to do the same. If you have cold floors, have an extra pair of slippers available for guests or ask them to bring slippers with them.

After you have prepared your mutual meeting space in such a manner, do not be surprised if you find the atmosphere between you becomes especially charged!

Feed the Five Senses of the Soul

You can augment the atmosphere in your cleaned and prepared ecology with the frequencies of particular colors, sounds and aromas. The following chart lists the colors that correspond with the five energy centers of the Chinese pentagramic system and more about what they cause. You can also work with the spectrum colors of the seven chakras.

Green
- produces a high-energy creative atmosphere.
- good for talking through new ideas and projects with your partner.

Yellow
- charges the emotional connection, making it easier to produce an emotional bond.
- good for offering your partner emotional warmth, security and a sense of sanctuary.
- the finer the emotion the paler the yellow that is produced.

Blue
- produces a cool, calm atmosphere which is a good platform for talking through difficult issues.
- reduces heat and friction between you and your partner.
- pale blue, in particular, is very cooling and relaxing to the nerves.

Red
- produces a more physical charge and can lead to a passionate engagement in the lower energy centers.
- produces vigor and stamina.
- good for administration and getting things done.

White
- is excellent to prepare the atmosphere towards a mental process, such as research and study.
- good for approaching things in an unbiased, neutral way.

You can charge your space with these colors simply by thinking them, thereby filling your personal energy field and that of the room. You can also imagine the color being transmitted from your hands and deliberately walk around the space projecting it or you can change the nature of atmosphere in the room by using colored light bulbs.

You can prepare a space with particular aromas which will influence the atmosphere. It is easy to purchase essential oils that can be warmed by a small diffuser so the vapors are gradually released and enhance the atmosphere in the room.

Different oils cause different effects, such as lavender, that can help to produce a very clean atmosphere that is attractive to higher energy worlds processes , while essence of rose is very charging emotionally. The quality and purity of the essential oils you use is important. The supplier I personally recommend and use is Young Living Essential Oils (see Resource section). Essential oils and herbs are connected to different astrological energies and this research can open into a fascinating and enjoyable study.

Beeswax candles can also be used to enhance the atmosphere. They produce both a warming, yellow glow and also help clean the atmosphere unlike paraffin candles which release petroleum by-products into the air. I do not recommend paraffin products or artificially scented candles.

The music you choose to play in your specially cleaned, charged and enhanced atmosphere is a further enjoyable research. All music carries with it a vibrational frequency which is highly connective into the worlds of energy. At starter level there is the music you like or dislike, but then comes the question why is it that certain kinds of music attract you while other music does not. Also, you can discover what kinds of music your energy date likes the most and play this music for them so they feel more at home inside the ecology you have created.

This naturally leads to the research of music as the expression of different energetic frequencies which cause different energetic effects in the atmosphere. What energetic effects do you want to produce with sound and why? If you want to produce an intimate atmosphere, there are certain kinds of music that will enhance this. Much of what is called "New Age" music is designed to produce a calming, peaceful effect in a red, hot world. This music tends to work more with the frequencies of blue, yellow and green while much of popular music today, such as hip-hop and heavy metal works in the hotter end of the spectrum from red, through orange to the low end of yellow.

What is important inside this preparation process is whatever colors, sounds and aromas you choose to work with, you are becoming more conscious about what you are doing in the realms of energy and why. There is no substitute for conscious energy dating in which you are present, in the present. These techniques are all ways to help enhance this.

Having prepared to feed the senses that work by sight, smell and sound, you can prepare to feed the other two senses of taste and touch. With the sense of taste, by researching the different properties of foods, you quickly discover how different foods affect the possibility of your energy dating experience. A heavy stew or goulash produces a very different energetic state than a light fruit or vegetable salad. Hard alcoholic drinks produce a different energy dating possibility than a light wine or sparkling mineral water.

It is fascinating that the shapeshifting of the word "taste" says "state" and the foods we eat do significantly change our energy state. Some will power the lower red systems, others will power the higher systems. Thus it is that oysters, with their high zinc content, have a reputation as an aphrodisiac and many women are said to be energetically stimulated by chocolate. All of this understanding about food can be brought to bear in your preparation for your energy date.

The fifth sense that feeds our soul with physical and energy impressions is the sense of touch. This is possibly the most intimate sense of all. The longer you know your partner in passion and the more you have experienced touch together, the more you know what kind of touch relaxes them and makes them feel well. Touch is very important to us. Case studies conducted in which young babies were scarcely touched in their first weeks of life found that diminished human contact was the strongest contributing factor to what has been termed "failure to thrive" syndrome. This indicates how vital touch is in our lives. You can use physical touch with your partner to convey security and to give warmth and pleasure. There are many workshops that offer techniques of whole body massage and this is something that partners in passion may want to investigate together. Essential oils can also be integrated into this practice for greater mutual enhancement.

Essential Oils

To give a further insight into the power and potency of essential oils I include here a brief introduction and examples of oils used to enhance the relationship field written specially for *Partners in Passion* by Dr. Sabina DeVita. Dr. DeVita is the founder of the federally approved Institute of Energy Wellness Studies in Ontario, Canada who works with Young Living Essential Oils, a world leader in therapeutic Grade A quality essential oils with whom she has a longstanding association. Further details on Dr. DeVita's institute and practice can be found in the Resource Section.

Essential oils are a great adjunct to any household for a myriad of uses. When it comes to relationships they can also be used in your massage practice to evoke particular sensations and to nurture different aspects of your partner's energy systems. Essential oils have a rich history dating back to Egypt where the Egyptians first discovered the therapeutic potential of essential oils. They were used throughout history for medicines, beauty, spiritual ceremonies, emotional healing, for baths, relaxation and various fragrances were used to enhance romanticism. Essential oils are simply the subtle volatile liquid distilled from plants, be it the roots, bark or flowers; they are the lifeblood or the life-force of the plant, containing its regenerating, rejuvenating and oxygenating immune defense properties. The therapeutic quality of an essential oil is of utmost importance in order to deliver the full benefits.

Jasmine is traditionally considered a fertility herb; treasured for its beautiful, seductive fragrance it is a powerful aphrodisiac. It is uplifting, counteracts hopelessness, nervous exhaustion, anxiety, depression, indifference and listlessness. Jasmine has even been found to improve mental accuracy and concentration when diffused into the environment.

Ylang ylang flowers, meaning "flower of the flowers," were strewn on the beds of Indonesian newlyweds, as it was considered a powerful aphrodisiac. The oil fragrance traditionally balances male/female energies, enhances spiritual attunement, combats anger and low self-esteem, depression, regulates heartbeat and increases focus of thoughts, while filtering out negative energy. It also restores confidence and peace.

Patchouli oil may be used by those whose work involves a high degree of pressure and mental strain. The scent is musky and earthy. It is a relaxant, allowing the discarding of jealousies, obsessions and insecurities and it will also help a person to relax for intimate moments. It is also another sexual tonic that originates from Southeast Asia.

Cardamom oil is mentioned in one of the oldest known medical records, Ebers Papyrus (dating from sixteenth century B.C.), an ancient Egyptian list of 877 prescriptions and recipes. It is uplifting, refreshing and invigorating. Like patchouli, which is more earth than fire, it also enhances a desire for intimacy. It is suited to those who are afraid of losing their self-identity.

Ginger oil, besides the physical properties as a digestive aid and expectorant, is gentle, stimulating and endows physical energy and courage. Traditionally, women in the West African country of Senegal weave belts of ginger root to restore their mate's sexual potency. The ginger oil is an entirely different sexual tonic to, say, jasmine or ylang ylang. While these sweet, floral essences encourage us to relax, ginger is spicy, hot and invigorating.

Juniper berry oil warms the kidneys, promoting both vigor and self-assurance. The fragrance also evokes feelings of health, love and peace. Although it is not a sexual tonic, it benefits those who, due to worry and self-absorption, cut themselves off emotionally.

Lavender has long been used for its calming as well as relaxing and balancing properties, both physically and emotionally. Found to increase beta waves in the brain, suggesting heightened relaxation. It also reduces depression and improves cognitive performance. The scent is fresh with a hint of spice and can be used to help relax either you or your partner. If you are feeling tense after a long day, lavender can help ease anxiety and make room for romance.

Rose is an essential oil that is luxurious and sweet with intense floral notes. Its beautiful fragrance is intoxicating and aphrodisiac-like. It helps bring balance and harmony, allowing one to overcome insecurities. It is stimulating and elevating to the mind, creating a sense of well-being. Rose oil is said to have been used by Cleopatra to seduce Mark Antony. It has soothing properties that helps us relax after a long, stressful day. Rose also enhances the feminine aspect within us.

Dr. DeVita also recommends two blends from Young Living Essential Oils that are specially prepared to enhance the relationship field.

Sensation Blend is specially prepared to produce a romantic, refreshing and arousing field. It amplifies excitement of experiencing new heights of self-expression and awareness. Sensation Blend is also nourishing and hydrating for the skin and is beneficial for many skin problems. It contains ylang ylang, rosewood and jasmine.

Acceptance Blend is designed to stimulate the mind, compelling us to become open and accept new things, people or relationships in life, allowing us to reach a higher potential. It helps to overcome procrastination and denial. It contains neroli (used by the ancient Egyptians for healing the mind, body and spirit), sandalwood, blue tansy, rosewood, geranium and frankincense.

The Five Centers of the Soul

By consciously preparing and structuring your energy date to feed all five senses and energy centers of the soul, you will be doing your best to guarantee energetic satisfaction and enhancement to your partner and also to yourself. It means an additional investment of time and effort, but your relationship and the construction of a mutually beneficial relationship is field worth it.

If you take the extra steps and put in the extra energy you will be amazed at how this helps to multiply the passion in the field between you and your partner. However long you and your energy partner have been together, it is always wise to arrange a specific date, time and place for an energy date in which you will feed the five senses and focus upon full spectrum passion between you.

Seven Satisfactions

Full spectrum passion involves the conscious production of satisfactions for all seven chakras or wheels of energy as they relate to the seven colors of the spectrum. This is vital in the ongoing energy balance between you and your partner in your life together. You can set about deliberately providing seven satisfactions for the chakras, just as you did with the five senses. Here are some ways to do this:

Root Chakra (Red)

Let each other know you are in a secure place and you are not going to be interrupted. Switch off the phone, turn off the pager. Share some quality food together, which is both grounding and securing. Security is very important for this root or earth energy and the quality of your energy date together will depend upon how secure you feel with each other.

Sexual Chakra (Orange)

Set up a specific space that is comfortable and warm and give each other a thorough massage using therapeutic massage oils. The sexual chakra enjoys many forms of stimulation; it does not only respond to physical sex. What is described as whole body sex is thoroughly stimulating for the sexual chakra and involves touch over the whole body.

Solar Plexus Chakra (Yellow)

The solar plexus chakra is also known as the power chakra and at this level what is crucial is the shared balance of power between you. If one partner is dominant and the other is in fear, there can be very little passion and enhanced energetic transference. At this power level it is vital that you are partners sharing together. This is the level where mutual warmth and encouragement is vital and the freedom to be and express yourselves. The sharing of stories and intimacy will help in bringing the yellow glow of satisfaction at this level.

Heart Chakra (Green)

To fortify the heart center you can confirm in your partner qualities you see that you have endearment for and hold in honor, respect and love. This may be a little awkward at first if you are not used to it, but it will do wonders for the passionate exchange that is able to happen between you. Again, this does not need to be separate from the other seven satisfactions. They can interweave and intertwine together.

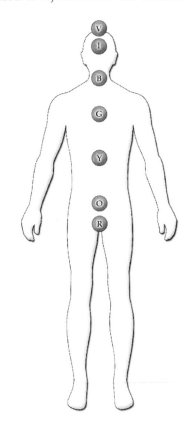

Throat Chakra (Blue)

Exchanging energies through the power of the voice is a vital satisfaction. This includes telling each about your day, sharing with each other your favorite poems and stories and even singing together. Laughing and sharing humor is another energetic intimacy at this level. When you enjoy laughter together you clear blockages between you. In helping each other find your own voice you offer each other a great service.

Third Eye Chakra (Indigo)

At this level you can exchange visionary ideas with your partner about the future and your hopes, plans and goals. You can plan trips and holidays together, discuss career plans and project the kind of life you wish to share together. Financial forecasts have a place here as part of your joint affairs.

You may also practice clairvoyant exercises together in which you try and link up your clairvoyant and telepathic faculties within your relationship field so you can send messages to each other over distance. An example of a clairvoyance exercise is to take a pack of playing cards and have each partner take turns in saying the color or suit of the card that the other partner looks at and projects towards them. You may also practice your energetic vision together, as explained in Chapter 5, Energy Dating..

Crown Chakra (Violet)

At this crowning level you may discuss your personal beliefs about matters such as the purpose of life, God and Creation. These are your most intimate, sacred views and feelings. These subjects often arise naturally when the other six levels are experiencing a natural flow and satisfaction. Your minds may turn more naturally to the power of Creation and the purpose of all life on Earth. The atmosphere between you may now become particularly potent and charged. You may find yourselves silently sitting together simply enjoying the fact of being in each other's company.

Seven Together

From time to time you may arrange a special time and place in which you deliberately work through the seven satisfactions. A weekend getaway together is ideal for such a pursuit. A place that has a Jacuzzi or a hot tub is excellent as running water is highly effective for removing static energy charges. This would also represent an excellent time for the renewing of vows and contracts between you at depth, because all seven energy centers of both partners would be included in this process, producing a full spectrum agreement between you.

It's all About Consciousness

It does not matter if you have known your partner for twenty years or if tonight is your first energy date. The first secret of being a great lover in the energy worlds is to be consciously present in the here and now.

If you set a date for Friday night, prepare for it during the week by clearing away any unfinished business that you can. By so doing, you can be more powerfully in the now. You may not be preparing for a Japanese tea ceremony, but you are preparing yourself and your life's energies to be in the present and in passion with another life and their energies.

Clean Your Energetic Pathways

In the energetic worlds every unresolved issue, uncompleted task and unfulfilled intention draws power from our energy field. This is because we are like electro-magnetic spiders, connected by threads to whatever is on our mind and attached to our emotions.

If we are pre-occupied and our energy field is therefore partially closed, it makes it much more difficult for energy to transfer. A key part of enhanced energy dating is to learn how to clear space in our energy field and in the ecology around us so the pathways of communication are clear. If we are carrying in our aura the scars, bruising and active ghosts of relationships past, it makes it hard to engage in the present.

For a couple with many years together it is vital that they are able to relegate the hurts they have caused each other in the past, so they can meet fresh and clear in the present. Often it is the accumulation of old scars, energy addictions and allergies that produce irreconcilable differences between two people who were once in love. These can develop to the point where the couple can no longer stand being in each other's company and staying together is no longer possible.

At this stage their mutual energy field has moved from being mutually supporting to mutually corrosive and even destructive. Beyond a certain point this process becomes irreversible, as the mutual damage done has been too great and the toxicity evoked between them is too intense. So it is that a once loving couple can no longer stand even being in the same room together. Their passion has become poisonous.

By using enhanced energy dating techniques regularly you have a much better chance of your relationship holding for the long term and preventing such a disastrous outcome.

Clearing Inhibitions

Many factors come into play in enhanced energy dating such as the level of inhibitions a person has. If any of the seven levels of the chakra system is blocked, there can only be a small amount of energy exchange at this level. These energetic channels can be cleared by engaging them as described in "The Seven Satisfactions." You can help your partner through their inhibitions just as they can help you through yours. This entails making a deliberate investment of time and energy in each other, which is at the root of any successful relationship.

Anything that blocks your energy flow from being fresh and active in the present means that as an energy date you become less attractive, as you have less to offer because your energies are locked up in the past. This means you become arrested in your development and in your ability to share at this level. Thus it is you can find an advanced mathematician who is emotionally at the level of a child or a person with sexual prowess who doesn't think of thinking for themselves at all.

An energy field can actually feel and smell old when we develop our sensitivity to the energy worlds. A person whose energies are locked up in old unfulfilled intentions and has a house full of clutter, energetically starts to feel and smell like a second-hand store. This means that a person young in years can be energetically old because their pathways are already closing, while someone who is physically older can still have the energy field of a much younger person. "You are only as old as you feel" is very true in the energy worlds.

Psychological scars block the flow of current energy in our lives. This is why it is so important for someone who wants to have a strong energy flow in their life to be current with their own mental, emotional and sexual affairs. If you had a painful breakup with someone, possibly twenty years ago, do all parts of you know that you have moved on or are there still parts of you stuck in the past, replaying the emotional and mental recordings of those previous experiences? It is vital to get the message through to all parts of you, even at cellular level, that your life has changed and that you have moved on. Meditating upon the path and purpose of your life can help greatly with this, as can talking things through with your partner in passion regularly. Issues not dealt with represent energetic clutter in our energy field that we carry around with us and make for less energetic passion in the present. Regular talks help to keep our pathways clear and clean.

Selecting a Place for Your Energy Date

If you are choosing the place where your energy date is to happen, think in advance and perhaps even visit the place that you are thinking of, so you ensure the ecology fits the kind of date you are preparing for. Different ecologies contain different kinds of energies. When you meet your date in the place where you live, you are able to control the ecology and set a certain energy note before they arrive. When you go to the place where they live, they set the tone and you encounter their energetic universe and whatever it contains. When you invite them out or are invited out to a neutral space, the nature of energetic ecology is often outside of your control. Here is where the person trained in sensitivity to energies is able to choose an ecology to go to, not only based in what the place is like physically but also in the nature of vibration the place actually has.

Different buildings are dedicated to different kinds of energetic process. When you go to visit a museum you walk into a very different energy vibration than if you go to a night club. Restaurants contain different energetic ecologies, partly based in décor, music, ethnicity and in the quality and quantity of food.

You may deliberately choose an energy date that is not indoors at all, but is a special space in nature where you are able to be in more direct communication with the energies of earth, water, air and fire. To hear the wind blowing through the trees while listening to a mountain stream babbling over rocks is to be in the presence of nature's music. You can smell the natural scents while feeling the touch of grass beneath you as your eyes take in the colors of the natural worlds. This is energy dating in a pure form and can produce energetic experiences of such power that both you and your partner will remember them for the rest of your days as a very special time.

Vacations

The holiday romance is often an outstanding experience in people's lives, whether it is a romance with a partner they have been with for many years or someone new they meet for the first time while away.

Again, words have much to tell us. As mentioned earlier, people literally go on holiday to vacate or cause old energies to leave them. A vacation is an attempt to shed or vacate the energetic impressions we are accustomed to and live in every day so we can take into our energy fields fresh, new currents of energy. In this context it is interesting how many of us vacation by the seaside, a place where the water is constantly working at breaking up the fixed structures of the land and where negative ions are generated in abundance.

Where there is a movement of a large body of water there is also the generation of huge quantities of negative ions that are naturally charging to the human system. These negative ions are healing to our body and soul. They are more feminine, blue and alkaline in their charge as compared with the red, acidic power that is concentrated in cities or that comes from our television sets, machinery and computers. It is not by chance that honeymooners head for Niagara Falls where there is one of the largest natural generators of negative ions on the planet.

The holiday romance is made more possible when we can go to a place that is high in negative ions, shed the hot, red-inclined energies of the city and recharge with cooler, blue-inclined negative ions. This brings us closer to the natural healing energies of our blue, feminine planet and helps us feel well in our body and soul. This also helps us relax and recharge and often produces a higher quality of exchange at all levels, including sexual.

In this vacation state our energy fields become potentially much more open for energy transference than when we are going to work on a regular weekday clothed in the energies of our worries and daily concerns. We clear our calendar and clear the decks to be in the now. This then produces a far greater openness to the possibility of romance because when we are with another in a similar state there can be a massive transference of power between us.

Honeymoons

The honeymoon is a powerful example of energy dating in which all other matters are put to one side to make space for an enhanced experience and energy exchange between newlyweds. Other people recognize this as a special time in a relationship and the honeymoon that follows marriage marks a celebrated time of intensive energy exchange. The honeymoon is often combined with a vacation in which other daily concerns are vacated out from the energy fields so the couple can focus on each other and the energies that are caused between them. It is interesting to note that the term "honeymoon" or "a honeymoon period" describes a twenty-eight day cycle and even if able to be sustained for a full month it naturally comes to a close and the issues of life need to once again be dealt with. This is where the partners in passion now need to graduate over time into becoming partners in purpose if their relationship field is to hold for the long term.

Energy Gifting

Energy gifting is buying or finding something for the other person that is on their energy frequency as a first principle, not yours.

Men will often go the traditional route and buy chocolates or flowers for their energy date because this is how they have been trained. Energy gifting, however, means reading the signals in the other person's energy field from everything you know about them and searching for that exact something that will match their nature. This calls for trying to get inside thinking and feeling like the person and then looking for something that matches their frequency.

If your date is a person of fine distinctions, then find him or her something simple and elegant. If they are strong administrators and like everything to be "just so," then possibly buy them something that will help them be more organized. If they champion the sacred feminine, then look to Celtic designs which are based on the spiral and other feminine forms. For someone with a powerful yellow life, buy them a CD of violin sonatas. The more you understand about the energy worlds and its contents, the better your chances of choosing gifts that are appropriate for your date.

When energy gifting it is crucial to put aside what you like and summon up in yourself the energetic frequency of your date before you go shopping. Doing this will take you to places that you would never normally go to during the course of your own routines. This is usually tougher for men to do than women, as men often have more trouble developing their energetic sensitivity. This attitude is partly born out of the cultural conditioning of men not to be sissies and to be "tough." It is natural, however, for a man to be both a poet and a warrior and there is nothing unmanly about deliberately developing one's electrical sensitivity.

New Faces

Both you and your date possess energetic connections and frequencies that are unknown even to you. To begin the following energy dating technique, first clean, clear and charge a room as set out in Chapter 6, Energize Your Space. Now turn the lights down low, or possibly have a candle lit. Stand about three to four feet from your partner and using your energetic vision, allow your eyes to soften. Gaze at the level of your partner's forehead around the area of the third eye. Let your eyesight travel long distance through your partner, through the walls, off the planet and into eternity.

For this exercise keep this way of looking for longer than usual so you can really relax into it. Let your eyes gently move down to your partner's face while maintaining a soft, unfocused gaze. What may start to appear after a while is a succession of energetic or electrical faces. Your partner may be a Caucasian male, but all of a sudden you may see the face of an Asiatic woman and then it may change from being a youthful face into a face of great age.

There are many different theories about what these energetic faces are and what they mean. What they mean is secondary to the living fact of what you are able to see when doing this exercise. A popular interpretation is that these are the faces of the past lives that are still printed in the energy field and become visible when working with energetic vision for a prolonged period of time. I have observed, however, that these faces change according to the particular nature of atmosphere in a room and often reflect the nature of power or force which is present in a person's aura. When someone engages in an intense research into ancient China, it is more likely that a Chinese face will appear in their energy field. These faces may be demonstrations of past lives, but it seems more likely that they represent characterizations of forces that are strong in the person's energy field at the time. This is why they are not fixed, but change from one day to the next.

I have seen many such faces on people. To me they are part of the deep mystery of life on Earth, the mystery of who and what we are. I do know that when seeing such faces it causes a depth of appreciation for the other person, for what they represent and a deepening respect for the possibility of their life. It certainly helps us to see our partner and ourselves energy worlds first, as spiritual beings within temporary mortal bodies. The fact that these energetic faces can be masculine or feminine also inspires a further powered reason for the equality of masculine and feminine opportunity. You do not know in what gender you may appear in the future!

The more we are able to open our eyes and our sensitivity to the miracle of human life, the greater the respect that naturally grows within us about the fact of our own life and that of our partner in passion.

Cleaning Your Partner's Energy Field

With practice we can see many colors, patterns and shapes in an energy field. We can sometimes even detect when our partner has a headache coming on. Headaches are often caused by lower energies that are usually a murky, orange/red color that get lodged in the field around the head. This is mostly static electricity.

The word "static" says this very well because it is not moving. It is a ball of stuck energy. A way to help remove a headache is to break up this stuck energy so the energy currents can move again. This can be done using the energy charge from the hands and eyes and is actually quite simple to do.

Many Feng Shui and geomancy practices are based in the need to clear stuck or static energies and to allow a free flow of fresh, clean energy through a particular place. As it is in a place, so it is also in a person and in the relationship field. Keeping the energies in our relationship fields fresh and current is one of the great keys to successful energy dating and building mutually enhancing relationships over the long term.

For this practical and mutually enhancing exercise, you will need to prepare a space using the energy clearing techniques given earlier in Chapter 6 Energize Your Space. Place a chair in the center of the room and ask your partner to sit comfortably with their arms and legs uncrossed. This is because when the arms and legs are crossed it impedes the flow of energies through the human system and into the atmosphere.

Stand outside the energy field of your partner and gradually approach them with your hands slightly outstretched and your sleeves rolled up. As you approach your partner with your hands outstretched, you will likely feel a slight change in the atmosphere when you are a few feet away. This often feels like a tingling or slight prickling sensation in the hands and may come with a slight temperature change. Your hands may feel cooler or warmer, depending upon what kind of charge is in the energy field of you and your partner on this particular day.

Once you have found the edge of their energy field, also known as the auric sheath or cortex of the aura, you can clean it by using your hands in a circular motion, rather like waxing the polish on a car. This cleaning process clears away static and refreshes their window on the world, which their aura actually is. When your hands start to feel hot and energetically sticky, it is best to flick or shake off this hot energy. You can shake it off into a plant because plants can absorb this kind of energy without it doing them harm.

After you have cleared and cleaned your partner's energetic field they can clear and clean yours in the same way. Before moving on to the second partner, however, it is advisable to energetically clear the space in which this aura cleaning is to happen. A modified version of space clearing using just the clapping and belling technologies shown in Chapter 6, Energize your Space should suffice. It is also advisable for both participants to wash their hands and face before they engage in this practice, so any residual static or stuck energies can be removed. A mutual aura cleaning is a marvelous healing and enhancing energy date and a fantastic service that you can offer each other.

The Mastery and the Mystery

There is so much more to human life than the physical systems that we occupy, incredible as these are. As you develop your sensitivity to the unseen worlds of energy and the forces and powers that live there, you are opening up a whole new world of possibility for yourself. This new world will be with you for the rest of your life. Your increased awareness and sensitivity will enable you to engage with all the energy dating exercises set out in this chapter and many others that are not written here. You will also be able to develop your own exercises and technologies as you build your understanding of and connection to these energy worlds.

You will never have total mastery of this universal energy. There will always be more to learn and discover. As we live in a growing, expanding, ever-changing universe there will always be new energetic experiences to explore. You can, however, develop increased mastery within the mystery that the unseen worlds of energy and power offer to you.

Chapter Fifteen
The Seven Laws of Energetic Love

There are definite seeable, knowable, touchable laws that govern all life on Earth, including yours. Approaching a state of inner peace, happiness and contentment is only possible by bringing oneself into better harmony with these laws and bringing our relationships into balance can only be accomplished by working in harmony with the energy systems, laws and ways provided to us by Creation. The further we move away from these natural laws, the less at ease we become. As we move away from the natural state of ease, dis-ease grows in our systems and in our relationships.

Getting in Tune With the Laws

Our body, soul, brain and mind work according to the same laws that determine the cycles of the moon and the movements of the planets, suns, stars and galaxies. These same universal laws govern the dynamics of energy exchange and the level of energetic love we are able to generate and experience. These laws can be seen in the workings of the universe, the planet and in our own human design.

The human race has learned that if it wants to fly it needs to make a machine that is able to work within the laws of gravity and aerodynamics. Just as there are laws that govern physical matter, so there are laws that govern the growth of spirituality and energetic love. To become spiritually wealthy and to grow a lasting relationship field rich in energetic love is only possible by working within the framework of the natural laws and energies of Creation. We cannot draw upon energies that do not exist. Our energies come from the seven levels of the planet's energy worlds and the occult signals they contain. They come to us from the actual powers and energies of the Great Creation of which we ourselves are also made.

According to how we think, feel and act do we call to ourselves the energies that make up the substance of our personal and global relationships. The more we can live our lives in harmony with the natural laws, the closer we can get to mirroring the ways of heaven here on Earth. The ancient Greeks, in establishing their laws stated that their intents were to bring the laws of men as close as possible to the ways and laws of Creation. A prime purpose of their acropolis in Athens was to attempt to divine what these laws were and then to enact them in the ongoing ways and means governing their society.

The first great shift we can make to come closer to the laws of Creation in our time and to produce a new template for world government is to balance the power between the twin expressions of the human race, feminine and masculine. This requires establishing a new template for man/woman relationships in which all oppression of one gender by the other is superimposed upon by a real energetic balance of power between the genders..

The Seven Laws of Energetic Love

The following are seven laws of energetic love through which our lives and relationship fields can be greatly enhanced. By consciously working with these laws and applying the understandings they reveal, you will be able to better balance the power and multiply the passion in your own life and relationships. This in turn will help balance the power and multiply the passion on the larger stage of the world.

These seven laws determine the degree of attraction and energy transference between any two people and how this attraction plays out between them. These seven laws of energetic love also apply to all other exchanges of power and passion, including hope, anger, revenge, fear, belief, violence, trust and any of the invisible powers that are the true driving forces of human behavior.

1. The Law of Passion Potential

The level and power of passion between people is determined by the potential for energy transference that exists between their energy fields.

The Law of Passion Potential is governing upon all the other laws that follow and has two prime factors.

a) The first level of potential energy attraction and transference is caused by the fundamental energy properties born into any life and its energy field during its time in the womb, up to and including the moment of its first appearance on Earth. These include hereditary and genetic factors, timing, astrological influences, gender, the pedigree and power of their spirit and soul, the experience of the mother while the child is forming in the womb, together with the influence of any past lives in the resulting energy field into which the child is born.

This first level is entirely outside of our conscious control. We cannot go back and change the time and place of our birth, the nature and nationality of our parents, our gender and our genetic inheritance. We can only work with what we have inherited, in which being glad to be alive and grateful for whatever opportunity that was our lot to be born into is an excellent fundamental attitude. We might not have been born at all, or possibly been born into a form of far less capability than human, like a donkey or a blade of grass.

b) The second level of potential attraction and transference is caused by the gathering and printing in our energy field of all the accumulated experiences of our life up to now. These include the effects of the energy fields and home atmospheres of our parents, the energies of our schooling, language, religious education, belief systems, attitudes, psychologies, first loves, employment, self-estimated successes and failures and the million other factors that go to form up the personalized aspect of our energy field.

The majority of this second level was outside our control in our early formative years. We did not choose whether to speak English, Chinese or Hindustani as our first language, to be Mohammedan, Christian, Jew, atheist or Jain. All this was initially formed in us by the household in which we grew up. It certainly, however, came increasingly into our control and responsibility as we grew older.

How consciously we choose to take control of our life and revisit the fundamental energy patterns and beliefs that we inherited in our home and school is really up to us. If we have been so deeply printed in our youth that we are never able to think outside the paradigms put into us by our parents and teachers, then this is the only world we will ever know. We will live our lives traveling along the mental and emotional tracks that were laid down for us in our youth. The Jesuit motto, "Give me a child until he is seven and I will give you the man" epitomizes the attempt by the guardians of conformity and the existing paradigms of thought to insert a framework into the young whereby they can never think outside of the box that is provided for them. No one is born a Catholic, a Muslim or a Jew, but it is very hard to escape being one after years of energetic programming.

The first two levels of energies—those born into us during our formation in the womb and those we form in our energy field by our living experience day by day—represent the potential for energy attraction and transference in any person. Relationships always begin energy worlds first and the potential for passion between two people is written into their energy fields long before they ever meet. How they then work with these energies in response to the experience of their meeting will determine what happens next and works in accordance with the six laws that follow. The combined effects of these first two levels of energies set the stage for what may happen in our interactions with all other energetic beings. At any moment they are the basic properties that determine what may or may not be able to transfer between ourselves and another person with whom we enter into energy relations. What is in our energy field and in the energy field of the other person we meet, at the moment of our meeting, determines the passion potential of what may pass between us in that space and time.

As passion plays such a vital part in these seven laws, it is worth repeating the definition given in Chapter 1, Men, Women and Passion. The word "passion" says to "pass-ion". It is to have something pass through us of an energetic or ionic nature. Therefore, to have a passion for someone is to transmit a stream of ions towards them that they may feel and reciprocate, or not. The passions that we feel can be of many different natures but they are all based in the worlds of power, force and energy. We humans are energetic beings that produce negatively and positively charged particles. These particles aggregating together produce waves of energy that pass through us and lodge in our energy field and in the energy fields of others. They can be of such power that they can transmit and be received over distance.

When we mix and meet with another person over time we build a mutually charged relationship field that is neither one nor the other of us, but the unique combination of both, together with any other energies and powers that may be attracted to this field from the energy worlds of the planet's astral light. The relationship field that forms may be lightly charged and of short duration or it may become highly charged and last for a long duration. It all depends on the passions generated within the relationship.

Passions can be high or low, refined or coarse. They can be pleasant to receive and give us enjoyable sensations throughout our being, or they can be very unpleasant to receive. Our passions even have colors that become visible when one has the eyes to see them and they range through the full spectrum of red to violet. The passions we transmit and receive are as real as the physical world which is also made of charged particles, albeit in a denser form.

Although the energy waves that make up our passions are intangible when compared to a physical object such as a car or house, their results last longer, as every passion that passes through us is printed in the record of our energy field and in the greater energy field of the planet's aura: the astral light. Indeed, human history is a story of multiple passions shaping the material world, rather than the other way around.

2. The Law of Simile

The more there is in simile between people's energy fields, the greater the attraction and passion that happens between them.

The second law begins to describe the realm of what actually happens in the worlds of energy transference between people and why. We move from the realms of energy potential into the principles and processes of realization. How much of that energetic potential between people is realized and why?

Sometimes we can swiftly recognize the shared passion two people have in common: two artists meet and are immediately able to speak passionately with each other about their art or two philosophers discover each shares a passion for the search for the truth and meaning of human life on Earth.

Shared experience is also a powerful bonding agent within a relationship field. Soldiers who have trained and fought together often remain friends until death. Alumni from a particular college or university often stay in touch because of the experiences that they had shared. This shared experience is an energy bridge between them along which passion flows.

The passions these different combinations of people share are of different energetic levels, natures and properties, but they are all made of waves of intangible energy passing between them. The shared passion between two people may not be obvious in the conscious realms but can be very powerful in the semiconscious and unconscious realms. An example of this is the person who has simultaneously nurtured and repressed their wish to be rebellious and experience a different style of life from that which they have been raised. This may not be detectable in their obvious outward behaviors, however, in the energy worlds ultimately "truth will out" and so there comes a day when the energy signals that have been repressed and amassed in the person's aura burst out, causing them to act out of character and surprise their family and friends. It may manifest in a surprising choice of girlfriend or boyfriend, a wild fling with an unexpected partner, or a sudden change in the direction of the person's career. There are particular times when these repressed signals burst out in concentrate, such as in the time of the mid-life crisis, which I prefer to call the mid-life opportunity, but it can happen at any time in a life's journey according to what a person has amassed and suppressed in their energy fields.

The Law of Simile says that two energy fields that are alike are deeply attracted to each other. This works at multiple levels, some of which are easy to see and some which are not. We can be attracted to someone without understanding the reason why. The passion between us can be rooted in conscious reference and experience and it can also be rooted in emotional and sexual powers that we have amassed in our energy field without conscious realization. If we reflect deeply upon what we are like and upon the trace of our life, however, including both what we have done and what we have avoided and repressed, we will likely find the reasons why. What we repress issues a very powerful, active signal in our energy field and beacons outwardly to others just as powerfully as what we have actively participated in within our life. This is often the root of the saying "opposites attract," as what a person has repressed in themselves they often find powerfully attractive in another.

What we power mentally and emotionally but repress in ourselves and do not give expression to, builds a strong signal in our energy field. This bank of energy can be so powerfully attracted to what another person has collected and powered in their aura that it compels us to act upon this energy, perhaps for the first time in our lives. Sometimes the attraction is so overpowering and instant that it calls up the idea of past lives that have been shared and are influencing upon this life now. In this context the idea of soul mates and predestined relationships often appears.

The Law of Simile specifically states that the more there is in common between two energy fields, the greater the amount of attraction and passion that can potentially take place between them rather than does take place between them. This is because the passion potential is not converted into actual energy transference by the Law of Simile alone, otherwise these first two laws would automatically determine our relationships and the field of human relationships would be a much simpler study. There are five other factors that come powerfully into play, beginning with the third law.

3. The Law of Now

The level and flow of passion between people is determined by their ability to be consciously present in the now.

There are many factors that influence our ability to be in the now. The first key to being in the now begins in the worlds of energy, in training ourselves to think and feel energy worlds first.

There are forces and powers that we can build up in our personal energy field which act as clouds of prevention to block our reception and transmission of current energies and anesthetize us to the now. Certain kinds of energy literally cloud over our energy field and prevent the clear reception of incoming signals. They also prevent our energies from radiating outwards except in minimal amounts. Examples of these blockers are worries, preoccupations, obsessions, daydreams, escapism, nostalgia for the past and projection into the future. Blending together in our personal energy field they can form a kind of living fog inside which we live our life.

People who regularly see into the energy worlds often say that when they see people walking down the street, they see them walking inside energy fields that contain weather systems based upon the person's worries, preoccupations and emotional states. In the worlds of energy you can literally be under a cloud or under the weather. It is as if each person is walking in their own energetic world, mostly cut off from the people around them who are also lost in their own thoughts and feelings. This means that the amount of energy that is actually available for passion in the now is quite minimal.

A woman and man may meet and the potential for attraction and transference may be very high due to a great similarity between their auras at that moment. However, they also immediately meet the conventions within which they were raised and the after-effects of all their previous dating experiences that are still residual in their aura. Shyness, fear of rejection and pain may prevent them from ever speaking out what they feel. The codes of conduct and psychological residues of the past may arrest them in the present, making them unable to act. We become acutely aware of feeling frozen in the moment, but awareness of this tongue-tied state does not enable us to get through it at the point. This is where alcohol is often used as a way to loosen inhibitions and help liberate the inner urges and passions from the bonds of social convention and personal inhibition.

Rather than relying upon alcohol and drugs we can train ourselves to be able to act in the present. This is best done away from pressure and is a process of training and development. This training and development begins with knowledge and understanding about the human energy systems, the energy worlds and the construction of mutual energy fields.

In addition to clouds of prevention, there are many other inhibitors potentially blocking the quality of our relationships, such as the messages that are lodged in our semiconscious mind, emotions and energy fields by the repetitive messages we receive from the mass media. It takes an unusually awake and courageous person to stand up to these vast hypnotic influences that are designed to prevent us from thinking for ourselves and living our best life now. The ability to do this largely depends upon whether or not we have the knowledge that will allow us to think for ourselves and enhance the energetic love that we can both give and receive.

Many exercises are given within this book to help clear stuck energies, both within your own energy field and in the energy field where you live. Being current in your own energy is a crucial step to being able to generate a high degree of passion in your life and is vital to your energy dating success. Being able to be current in your own energies depends largely upon your knowledge of the worlds of human energy and how to work with them. It is this knowledge that is so vital in learning how to clear the way, so that fresh currents of passion can pass through you every day.

4. The Law of Knowledge

The degree of energy transference between people is enhanced by the knowledge they share about the inner workings of the energy worlds.

Once a person knows they have inhibitions lodged in their mind, emotions and energy fields and they begin to understand the energy worlds, they know that these inhibiting factors will not simply go away on their own. These inhibitors wait in the realms of the aura until the time of the next passionate potential and then re-awaken. In going through the day by day matters of life it can seem that these inhibitions are no longer there, but once the pressure and energy levels rise and there is a power surge of passion throughout the system they are caused to re-awaken. The person then finds themselves held under the grip of their inhibitions once again and feels they are back in the same trap and that change is not possible.

This return to the house of arrestation and fear can make us feel desperate and alone and can lead to feelings of mounting frustration. It can even bring a person to suicide if they feel deeply enough that nothing can change and they are forever bound on the wheel of repetition. With real knowledge about the energy worlds and how they power all human relationships, real change comes within our grasp. We can take more effective control of our own life and begin to move in the directions we consciously decide to go.

Life inhibitors are usually not installed by the person but are often imprinted by traumatic experiences or through the vigorous conditioning of parents, teachers and friends. If a person wishes to change this kind of in-depth programming, they need to have the knowledge of how this can be done. Without knowledge, trying to change our energy field and thereby ourselves is really a game of roulette; we hope we will get the outcome we want, but we cannot be sure. Once we know, as an example, that it takes repetitive affirmations over a period of at least twenty-eight days to actually reprogram our conscious, semiconscious and unconscious mind, as set out in Chapter 11, Addictions, Vices and Abusive Relationships we can tackle the job more effectively. Very often our lack of success is simply that we have not had the right tools to work with, or we have not understood how to apply them effectively.

Real and accurate knowledge of the energy worlds, the laws that govern them and how they influence human behavior is crucial in our journey towards enhancement. By having knowledge of how energies transfer between men and women and how mutual relationship fields are formed, we can train ourselves to work in harmony with these energies. Knowledge is a vital step in being able to improve all our relationships, including our relationship with ourselves, with others and even our relationship with what we feel to be our Causing Principle or God. However, another vital step is needed, for knowledge alone is not enough. Unless knowledge brings active changes in the way and style of our behaviors, it remains sterile.

5. *The Law of Application of Knowledge*

The practical application of this knowledge determines the enhancement of the passion between them.

Having real knowledge about the working of the energy worlds and the dynamics that determine the enhancement of relationships and the resulting mutual relationship fields is one level, actually doing something about it and applying that knowledge is another. Knowledge without application is the recipe for one of the most energy depleting and debilitating sicknesses of our time: the illness of intellectualism. With both knowledge and application as working properties in our lives everything is possible, including the enhancement of all our relationships and a great increase in passion.

There are countless books, magazines and diet programs available that offer knowledge about weight loss and how to improve our physical health. Yet despite this abundance of knowledge, obesity is epidemic in our society. Knowledge is useless unless firstly it is accurate and secondly there is the desire and the will to apply it.

It is the same in seeking to improve our relationships and increase the energetic love in our lives. It is a vital step to come into new knowledge about how they work; another vital step is to then begin to apply it. Successful application calls for five key ingredients:

1. The Will to do something.
2. The Energy levels which make it possible.

3. The Love that brings us back to it again and again.
4. The Discipline to support our will.
5. The Strategies that help us to succeed.

The combination of will, energy, love, discipline and strategies gives us the acronym WELDS. Through the first four powers we are able to weld new energetic properties into our lives in such a way that they become integrated in our personal energy field and will always be part of us. In seeking to bring new energetic properties into our lives we need to be smart in how we approach this proposition. Not street smart or school smart, but energy smart. Strategy is, therefore, the fifth element that helps ensure our success and welds new energy properties into our life.

There is a vast difference in energetic power between theoretical and applied knowledge. The first lives in the realms of the mind and in the realms of intention. The second moves from the realms of the mind into manifestation, bringing a huge increase in energetic power as it does so. The theory of the splitting of the atom contained a certain energy possibility. Once the theory was applied the actual energy result was magnified a trillion-fold. To give an example closer to home, there is a vast energetic difference between reading that the human lives inside an energy field—an amazing coat of many colors—and actually seeing it. The first is interesting, theoretical knowledge, which has little impact on a life except to know that it may be possible. The second indelibly prints one's consciousness with the fact that this is so. We have the evidence of our own eyes and will never see the world quite the same way again. To hear that conscious astral travel is possible intrigues us and titillates our brains, mind and emotions with a new possibility. Actually astral travelling changes the way we view ourselves, other people and the way we view the prospect of life after death.

Throughout the pages of this book I offer many practical techniques to enhance the quality of energetic love in your life and your appreciation of the energy worlds. If you read and do nothing with them, you will have interesting theoretical knowledge. If, however, you try them for yourself, you have the power to change your life. Try some of these techniques for yourself and then with some of those people you are in relationship with, and the results will astonish you.

6. *The Law of Generation and Attraction*

According to the energies you generate, so you will attract to yourself more of those energies (and other properties associated with them,) magnified many times over.

In the Parable of the Talents (Matthew 25) this law of human energies was stated as "For unto every one that hath shall be given." This maxim is a concise statement of a fundamental energy law. The ancient alchemists said, "In order to get gold, you have to have a little gold." It was their belief that for a base metal such as lead to become gold by a process of transformation there had to be a little gold in the mix to lead the way. To the early alchemists, gold was also a code name for higher spiritual development and illumination, while base metals were symbolic of grosser human energies.

Nothing can only bring to itself more of nothing. We, therefore, have to first give out from ourselves that which we wish to receive. This is a very profound law in the realms of the relationship field. It means that if you feel that you lack encouragement in your life the way to energetically ask for it is to deliberately start offering it to others. Lack confirmation? Start offering confirmation to others. Lack energetic love? Start offering more of it to others. Gandhi expressed this profound law of generation when he said, "Become the change."

To work with this energetic law in the realms of relationships is to decide what you want to have in your mutual relationship field and to set about deliberately generating it. If you feel that your life lacks generosity, it does not work to go around demanding it from others or blaming others for not generating it. The Biblical proverb, "Ask, and it shall be given you" does not describe asking by words alone but also by conscious energetic generation. If you want people to be direct and honest with you, lead by being direct and honest with them. "Do unto others as you would have them do unto you" is another profound statement of the law of generation as it applies to relationships.

The Law of Generation and Attraction also says that if you want to know what you are like, you only have to look at your friends and at the people you attract to yourself. You are, in some way, on their energetic frequency. Your generation attracts them to you and their generation attracts you to them. "Birds of a feather flock together" is another true saying in this context. You can tell very much about yourself and the energies you work with by looking at who your friends are and what energies they generate.

The Law of Generation and Attraction reveals how the Universe responds to what you generate most powerfully in your field, rather than what you simply ask for. To ask by word for something produces a beginning level of energy transmission in your energy systems and in your field, but when you add feeling and action to this generation, your petition is far more powerful and likely to be answered. Stated concisely this law says "As you generate, so you will attract."

When a person is able to apply the knowledge they have about the workings of the energy worlds and thereby deliberately generate powerful signals within their energy field, they are on the road to becoming a conscious energy worker rather than being subject to the various energetic weather systems that inevitably buffet us every day of our lives.

The law of generation and attraction works by individual, by couple and by group. It is why people will act differently when they are with their peers than when they are alone, unless they have built the force field and charisma of being a strong character from the inside out. A charismatic leader is someone who has built a powerful force field in their personal energy field and is able to transmit or radiate out from this force field to influence others. If you come into a relationship field with someone whose generation is much more powerful than yours, your behavior patterns, thoughts and feelings are likely to change, possibly substantially, as you come within their sphere of influence.

This sixth power, the law of generation works in close combination with the seventh law that focuses upon a uniquely human feature: the power of choice.

7. The Law of Choice

When you make new choices and change the patterns and powers in your energy field, you attract new forces, energies and people into your life.

It is our choices that above all determine what we will become. Our choices are the real destiny makers of our life. In the world of relationships we may think that we choose to date a particular man or woman, but the truth is that our potential for energy dating with others is predetermined by the thousands of smaller choices we make day by day that go to building our energy portrait. The decisions we make about the way we use our body, mind and soul; the foods we choose to eat; the movies we choose to see; the books we choose to read; what we choose to think about; the music we choose to listen to; the places we choose to go; the friends we choose to hang out with; the mission we choose to champion—all of these decisions and more go to create the living portrait of our human energy field and make us the person we are, moment by aggregating moment.

It is this living portrait that is attractive to another person's energy field and brings them into our energetic orbit. It is only after they are within our orbit that we begin to think consciously about whether or not we will go out with them. Ninety-percent of the work has already been done by the cumulative effect of the choices we have made in our lives and how they cause us to be in the present moment. Just as ninety-percent of the work has already been done by the cumulative effect of the choices they have made in their lives and how they cause them to be in the present moment. When the two fields collide and the ninety percent charge of one field meets the ninety percent charge of the other, sparks can ignite in a flurry of passion, not much may happen, or any other variation in-between.

Like the seventh wave breaking on the seashore, so this seventh law offers us the greatest opportunity for our enhancement possibility. This is the law within which we have the greatest control and through which we can access the other six laws most directly. By the power of choice (Law 7) we can choose what we will generate (Law 6), what knowledge we will apply (Laws 5 and 4), whether or not we will try to be more consciously in the present (Law 3) and what we will be in simile with (Law 2). By the aggregating power of our choices we even change our energy potential moment by moment (Law 1).

By the power of choice we can over-print the fundamentals imprinted within our energy field in the particular circumstance in which we grew up. We can break out of the box of the paradigms that we were raised in and win a second chance at life. By the choices we make we can generate new energy signals and attract new kinds of experience, people and relationships into our lives. If the first law sets the initial potential of our lives, the seventh law provides the keyway into being personally creative within that potential and offers us the chance to create our own blueprint for living. After our initial integration with the founding energies of our birth, our personal creative journey develops by the power of choice. In seeking to enhance the quality of our relationship fields and grow more energetic love in our life, the transformation begins where it always has: by making the conscious choice and decision to try.

The Seven Laws of Energetic Love

1. THE LAW OF PASSION POTENTIAL
The level and power of passion between people is determined by the potential for energy transference that exists between their energy fields.

2. THE LAW OF SIMILE
The more there is in simile between people's energy fields, the greater the attraction and passion that happens between them.

3. THE LAW OF NOW
The level and flow of passion between people is determined by their ability to be consciously present in the now.

4. THE LAW OF KNOWLEDGE
The degree of energy transference between people is enhanced by the knowledge they share about the inner workings of the energy worlds.

5. THE LAW OF APPLICATION OF KNOWLEDGE
The practical application of this knowledge determines the enhancement of the passion between them.

6. THE LAW OF GENERATION AND ATTRACTION
According to the energies you generate, so you will attract to yourself more of those energies (and other properties associated with them), magnified many times over.

7. THE LAW OF CHOICE
When you make new choices and change the patterns and powers in your energy field, you attract new forces, energies and people into your life.

RESOURCES

Young Living Essential Oils –Suppliers of essential oils.
www.youngliving.com
Young Living Essential Oils, the leading provider of essential oils, offers more than 300 essential oil singles and blends. Every essential oil Young Living distills or sources has the optimal naturally-occurring blend of constituents to maximize the desired effect.

Prinknash Abbey – Suppliers of incense and charcoal tablets.
www.prinknashabbey.org.uk
The Benedictine Monks of Prinknash Abbey have been blending outstanding incense since 1906. Decades of care in the blending of these superior incenses have ensured their excellence. Prinknash is also a supplier of the best quality charcoal tablets.

Ceremonies with Meaning
www.ceremonieswithmeaning.com
Meaningful ceremonies specially designed for all occasions in consultation with the client.

Institute of Energy Wellness Studies
www.energywellnessstudies.com
Offers professional, certified educational programs in the field of Energy medicine and wellness.

Therapy with a Twist
www.therapywithatwist.com
Counseling and psychotherapy for youth, adults, couples and families. Wendy Ludlow, LCSW, RPT-S offers counseling services in a non-judgmental, lighthearted atmosphere.

Joanna Infeld
www.joannainfeld.com
EnergyWorlds Practitioner, author, coach and co-founder of Ceremonies With Meaning. Joanna is available for personal coaching, seminars, workshops and keynote speaker engagements

Templates For Change Coaching Academy
www.tfc-CoachingAcademy.com
Offers coaching for meaning and purpose, mediating conflict and leadership.

Kora Press
www.korapress.com
For a complete catalogue of Kora Press publications.

Visit
WWW.DPFRANCIS.COM

For information on:

- Partners in Passion seminars and workshops.
- Becoming a certified EnergyWorlds Practitioner.
- Private consultations for couples and individuals.
- The latest schedule of David's appearances, upcoming teleseminars, new publications and other related news.
- Inviting David as a guest speaker for your next event.
- Booking David as a media guest.
- Subscribing to David's free EnergyWorlds Newsletter.
- Guided tours of ancient and esoteric sites around the world with David through EnergyWorld Tours.

Ways to Connect with David:

- Facebook - David Price Francis fan page
- EnergyWorlds Facebook group
- EnergyWorlds Meetup group (New York)
- EnergyWorlds twitter
- David's EnergyWorlds blog:
  http://energyworlds.blogspot.com

A free gift from david

24 WAYS TO SUPER-CHARGE YOUR CHARISMA

To instantly receive your free 23-page report
"24 Ways to Super-Charge Your Charisma"
based on the energy principles in Partners in Passion
visit www.partnersinpassion.com.

Coming soon...

Available now
To order visit
www.dpfrancis.com

"Throughout history," began Dr. Woo,
"there has only ever been The Way."
The Tales of Dr. Woo presents life lessons and spiritual insights as recorded
in the time of the legendary Yellow Emperor by a former student from
the ancient Chinese mystery school of Dr. Woo. Using subtle humor,
parables and his powerful grasp on the deeper significance of human
existence, the wise and venerable Dr. Woo masterfully coaches his
students into the way of truth to help them live lives of greater meaning
and purpose. These unique tales resonate with penetrating insights
and timeless wisdoms on the human condition while offering gems
of revelation into subjects as diverse as man/woman relationships,
finance, psychology, the domains of human and planetary energies and
the purpose of life. This blend of world views and philosophic wisdom
offers us moments for deeper self-reflection and demonstrates that
the opportunity to work on our personal development and spiritual
growth is as nearby as a stroll through a garden or a morning cup of tea.
These stories are sure to delight, entertain and provoke questions and
contemplations in the wonderer within us all.

CPSIA information can be obtained at www.ICGtesting.com
Printed in the USA
BVOW001650050513

319926BV00001B/8/P